Economic Slowdown in India

The devastating effect of Covid-19 on the Indian economy is by now well-known. The growth rate of the economy slumped to a negative figure in the year 2020–21. What is less talked about, however, is the fact that growth slowdown in India had started several years before the pandemic struck. The two questions that naturally arise are "what explains the long economic slowdown?" and "what can be done about it?" This book is an in-depth analysis of the economic slowdown in India in recent years and the reasons behind the persistent slowdown in the growth rate of the Indian economy in the 2010s, especially in the latter half of the decade. While discussing both macro- and microeconomic policies, the volume examines how the perspective on economic policy has evolved over time in consonance with experience by investigating major instances of such slowdowns in the past. Three global slowdowns (namely the Great Depression of 1929, the stagflation induced by the oil crisis of the 1970s and the Global Financial Crisis of 2007) and the industrial deceleration in India in the late 1960s and early 1970s are discussed.

The author also probes into the problems of inequality, poverty, inflation in the Indian economy pre- and post-pandemic and policies targeted towards development, manufacturing and distribution of vaccines. The book further discusses possible economic impacts of the Ukraine War and the long-term problem of global warming.

Concise and thoroughly researched, this book will be of interest to beginners, scholars, research students and teachers interested in economics, policy-making and development studies.

Asis Kumar Banerjee, Ph.D. (Johns Hopkins), is a former vice-chancellor and a former professor of economics, University of Calcutta. He has held visiting positions at Presidency College, Calcutta; the Indian Statistical Institute, New Delhi; and the University of California, Riverside, California. His research interests include development economics, welfare economics, game theory and the measurement of inequality and poverty. His previous publications include the book *Measuring Development: An Inequality Dominance Approach* (2020).

Economic Slowdown in India
An Introductory Analysis

Asis Kumar Banerjee

Routledge
Taylor & Francis Group
LONDON AND NEW YORK

First published 2023
by Routledge
4 Park Square, Milton Park, Abingdon, Oxon OX14 4RN

and by Routledge
605 Third Avenue, New York, NY 10158

Routledge is an imprint of the Taylor & Francis Group, an informa business

British Library Cataloguing-in-Publication Data
A catalogue record for this book is available from the British Library

ISBN: 978-1-032-39124-3 (hbk)
ISBN: 978-1-032-39602-6 (pbk)
ISBN: 978-1-003-35051-4 (ebk)

DOI: 10.4324/9781003350514

Typeset in Sabon
by Apex CoVantage, LLC

To
Archan

Contents

Tables

Abbreviations

AEs	advanced economies
CII	Co.nfederation of Indian Industry
CNG	compressed natural gas
COVAX	Covid-19 Vaccines Global Access Facility
CPI	consumer price index
CPI	(AL) consumer price index (agricultural labourers)
CPI	(IW) consumer price index (industrial workers)
CRI	Central Research Institute
DBT	Direct Benefit Transfer
EMDEs	emerging markets and developing economies
EU	European Union
Fed	Federal Reserve System
FRBM	Fiscal Responsibility and Budget Management
GCF	gross capital formation
GFCF	gross fixed capital formation
GDP	gross domestic product
GNP	gross national product
GOI	Government of India
G-SAP	government securities acquisition programme
GST	goods and services tax
GVA	gross value added
HDI	Human Development Index
IBRD	International Bank for Reconstruction and Development
ICMR	Indian Council of Medical Research
ILO	International Labour Organization
IMF	International Monetary Fund
IOL	Indian Oil Limited
IPR	intellectual property rights
IVC	Integrated Vaccine Complex
LPG	liquefied petroleum gas
MMT	modern monetary theory
NIV	National Institute of Virology
NNI	net national income

NNP	net national product
NSO	National Statistical Office
NSSO	National Sample Survey Office
OECD	Organization for Economic Cooperation and Development
ONGC	Oil and Natural Gas Corporation
OPEC	Organization of Petroleum Exporting Countries
PSE	public sector enterprise
PSU	public sector undertaking
QE	quantitative easing
RBI	Reserve Bank of India
SLR	statutory liquidity ratio
TRIPS	Trade-Related Aspects of Intellectual Property Rights
VAT	value-added tax
WHO	World Health Organization
WTI	Western Texas Intermediate
WTO	World Trade Organization

Preface

This book is an introduction to economic policies with particular reference to the contemporary Indian economy. The initial motivation for writing the book came from the economic devastation in the country left by the Covid-19 pandemic in its trail and from the need to ask what economic policy planners could do to improve matters. As I proceeded with the project, however, my focus shifted a little. It came to my notice that while the pandemic itself was certainly a bolt from the blue, the root of our failure to minimise its economic impact went back to the failure to adopt appropriate economic policies in the pre-pandemic years. As a matter of fact, at the time of writing this preface, the Indian economy is going through what is arguably the longest period of growth slowdown that it has experienced in recent decades. Moreover, the persistent slowdown seems to be a distinguishing feature of the Indian economy since this has not been the experience of too many other countries of the world. The two questions that naturally arise in this context are (i) "what explains the long slowdown?" and (ii) "what, if anything, can be done about it?" These are the questions that the book is about. The basic message that I have sought to convey in the book is that careful policy planning can bring the Indian economy out of this predicament.

A word about the style of writing of the book and about the intended audience may be in order. The book focuses on the specific issue of growth slowdown in India and tries to delve deep into the matter, deliberately abstracting from all other issues. In this sense it is a monograph. However, it is not addressed exclusively to the experts. On the contrary, I have tried to make the exposition lucid and self-contained so that the discussion is widely accessible. In fact, no prior knowledge of economic theory on the part of the reader is presumed. All arguments are built from first principles. That is what the word "introductory" in the subtitle of the book is intended to emphasise. The book is perhaps best described as a supplementary reading for students, researchers and teachers of economics in India as well as a reference book for the general reader with an interest in economic policies.

During the process of preparing the final version of the book, I have benefitted greatly from the detailed comments of the anonymous peer reviewers of an earlier version. For discussion on various parts of the book (not always in their present forms), I am also indebted to Amiya Bagchi, Asim Dasgupta, Pradip Maiti, Sugata Marjit, Mihir Rakshit, Susmita Rakshit, Ramprasad Sengupta and Soumyen Sikdar. None of them, however, has seen the manuscript of the book in its final form. I retain the sole responsibility for any error(s) that the book may contain.

Finally, I wish to thank Shoma Choudhury, commissioning editor, Routledge, for providing vital guidance throughout the process of writing the book, and Angelin Joy, editorial assistant in the same organisation, for help in bringing the manuscript to the stage of submission.

Asis Kumar Banerjee
Kolkata, July 2022

1 Introduction

1.1 The basic questions

This book is a brief and non-technical introduction to some of the important issues relating to the contemporary Indian economy. Its immediate motivation lies in the havoc left by the Covid-19 pandemic in its trail. The consequences of the pandemic have not been limited to the health sector. Its economic impact has also been nothing less than devastating. We shall be failing in our duties, however, if we put the blame for the lamentable economic scenario of the country entirely on the pandemic and let the matter rest there. The pandemic, after all, hit the whole world. Yet, in the year 2020–21, the performance of the Indian economy was particularly poor in comparison to that of most of the other countries of the world. We are thus led to ask why we fared so badly in economic terms.

As we set out to investigate this question, however, more unanswered questions arise. It turns out that while the pandemic itself was a bolt from the blue, the root of our failure to minimise its *economic* impact goes back to the years *before* the appearance of the pandemic on the scene. In fact, it turns out that over the past several years the Indian economy has been going through what is arguably the longest period of economic slowdown that it has experienced in recent decades. Moreover, this, too, seems to be a distinguishing feature of India's recent growth experience vis-à-vis that of most of her South Asian neighbours.

The two questions that stare us in the face are (i) "what explains the long slowdown?" and (ii) "what, if anything, can be done to bring it to an end?" These are the questions that the book is about. Needless to say, the two questions are interrelated.

Since both of these questions are economic in nature, it goes without saying that in order to seek the answers we have to employ economic terms and concepts. It is emphasised, however, that no prior knowledge of economic theory is presumed. All arguments are built from first principles, and all economic terms are defined as we go along.

The plan of this introductory chapter is as follows. Since the immediate motivation of this book derives from the Covid-19 pandemic, we start with

DOI: 10.4324/9781003350514-1

the question how the present pandemic has impacted the economic performance of the advanced as well as the developing countries of the world in general and that of the Indian economy in particular. However, the very first question that arises in this connection is how the economic performance of a country in a given year is to be measured. The *summary* measure that is most widely used for the purpose is the annual rate of growth of real gross domestic product (GDP) (or the *growth rate*, for short) in the year. Section 1.2 is devoted to an explanation of what this means. Section 1.3 uses this criterion to describe the global as well as the India-specific economic effects of the pandemic and shows that the effect of the pandemic on the Indian economy has been much more disastrous than that on the other economies of South Asia. Section 1.4 draws attention to the fact that the slowdown in the growth rate of GDP started long before the Covid-19 pandemic arrived on the scene. Section 1.5 provides a preview of the rest of the book. Section 1.6 concludes the chapter.

1.2 Summary measure of economic performance: the growth rate

As stated earlier, we shall consider the annual growth rate of real GDP in a country to be the summary measure of economic performance of the country in the relevant year. GDP is the total value of all commodities (i.e. all goods and services) produced in a country in a given year.[1] The annual growth rate of GDP in a given year is simply the percentage rate of change in the given year's GDP over that of the preceding year. Thus, the growth rate of an economy in a year is positive, negative or zero accordingly as, respectively, between this year and the preceding one, GDP has increased, decreased or remained the same.

In order to decide whether the state of the economy (as per this summary measure) in a year is really better than what it was in the preceding year, however, it is important to filter out the effect of *inflation* or *deflation*. Consider the hypothetical case in which the physical amounts of *all* commodities produced in the country remain the same between two consecutive years but *all* prices double. Then GDP as defined earlier (which may now be called *nominal* GDP) would double too. However, this would hardly be a case of any *real* growth in the economy. Economists, therefore, are concerned with the growth rate of *real* GDP.

For the purpose of calculating real GDP for a given year, we use a *base year*. For instance, if the year 2010–11 is used as the base year, by real GDP in India for the year 2020–21, we would mean the value of commodities produced in 2020–21 *in terms of the prices prevailing in 2010–11*. In other words, the physical quantity of output of each commodity in 2020–21 is multiplied by the price of the commodity in 2010–11. The value of commodities in 2020–21 calculated in this way would be the real GDP in 2020–21 *with 2010–11 as the base year*.[2] Needless to say, if some other year is used as the base year in place of 2010–11, the real GDP in 2020–21 may well turn out to be different.

For a *given* base year (say, 2010–11), however, it would be meaningful to compare the *real* GDPs of two different years. The percentage rate by which real GDP of the year 2020–21 exceeds the real GDP of the preceding year 2019–20 is the annual growth rate of real GDP (or the *growth rate*, for short) in 2020–21.

Currently, the base year that is used officially in India for the purpose of real GDP calculation is 2011–12. Previously, the base year was 2004–05.[3] Growth rates of real GDP in India from the year 2013–14 with the new base year of 2011–12 are available in official reports.

In India, economic data such as GDP are reported on *fiscal year* basis. Thus, GDP for 2020–21 is the value of commodities produced in India over the time period from 1 April 2020 to 31 March 2021. A few of the other countries in Asia such as Bangladesh and Pakistan follow the same practice. In many other countries, however, the reporting is on the *calendar year* basis. Strictly speaking, this is a problem when we compare the growth rates of different countries with different conventions in this regard. In practice, this problem is overlooked. Essentially, for purposes of such inter-country comparison, a fiscal year is identified with the calendar year in which the major part of it falls. Thus, the growth rate of real GDP in India in 2020–21 is routinely compared with that in China in the calendar year 2020.

GDP estimation in India is done by the National Statistical Office (NSO), which is under the Ministry of Statistics and Programme Implementation (MOSPI), Government of India.

In this book, economic *slowdown* (or *deceleration*) will mean a fall in the annual growth rate of the economy. *Acceleration* will mean a rise in the annual growth rate.[4,5]

1.3 The impact of Covid on growth rates of countries

How has Covid affected the Indian economy? The summary measure of economic performance gives a summary answer: the annual growth rate of real GDP in India in the year in which the pandemic hit the country, 2020–21, was *negative*: –6.6 per cent. In other words, instead of growing, the Indian economy actually *contracted* by 6.6 per cent in that year. The strength of the economic impact of the pandemic can be gauged from the fact that the last time that the Indian economy contracted was more than 40 years ago (in 1979–80). The rate of contraction (5.2 per cent) in that year was, however, less than that in 2020–21. India's growth performance in 2020–21 was, in fact, the worst ever since independence. Beyond doubt, Covid was the main culprit. However, as stated earlier, few other countries of the world fared as badly in that year as did India, although the pandemic hardly spared any country. Table 1.1 displays the growth rates in 2020–21 in seven of the eight countries of South Asia.

Table 1.1 Annual real GDP growth rates (per cent) in South Asian countries, 2020–21

Country	*Growth rate (%)*
Bangladesh	3.4
Bhutan	-10.1
India	-6.6
Maldives	-33.5
Nepal	-2.4
Pakistan	-0.9
Sri Lanka	-3.6

Source: www.data.worldbank.org andWorld Bank (2022)

It may be noted that there are some differences in the ways that countries report their growth rates. For Maldives and Sri Lanka, the figures in Table 1.1 are the growth rates for the calendar year 2020. Data for the other countries relate to the fiscal year 2020–21. However, the definition of a fiscal year also varies. For India, the fiscal year 2020–21 was the period from 1 April 2020 to 31 March 2021. For Bangladesh, Bhutan and Pakistan, it was from 1 July 2020 to 30 June 2021. For Nepal, it was from mid-July 2020 to mid-July 2021.

Despite these differences in the ways in which growth data are reported by different countries, the broad picture of the comparative performances of the South Asian countries in the year 2020 when Covid hit the world should be clear from Table 1.1. With the exception of Maldives and Bhutan, no other South Asian country's growth performance has been worse than that of India. In fact, Bangladesh posted a *positive* growth rate. (The figure for Afghanistan was not available at the time of writing these lines.)

Comparisons over wider geographical regions do not change the picture very much. China registered a positive growth rate of 2.2 per cent. In Brazil and South Africa, the growth figures were, respectively, –3.9 per cent and –6.4 per cent. While the advanced economies (AEs) too had negative growth rates, in most of them the rates of *contraction* were less than that of India. In the USA. and Japan, for instance, the growth rates were –3.4 per cent and –4.6 per cent, respectively (see World Bank, 2022). The UK, with a growth rate of –9.3 per cent, was one of the very few countries in the world to have put up an even poorer economic performance than India in this year. In one exercise, it was reported that if the 2020 (or 2020–21) growth rates of 194 countries of the world are arranged in *decreasing* order, the growth rate of India would be at the 142nd place. For a country that, in the first decade of the twenty-first century, was one of the fastest-growing economies in the world, this was certainly bad news.

For further details about the impact of Covid-19 on the Indian and the world economies, see, for instance, Bhattacharyya et al. (2022), Dutta et al. (2022) and Kumar (2020).

1.4 Growth performance of the Indian economy before the pandemic: the long slowdown

Covid-19 certainly caused the gravest economic crisis that India and the world as a whole have faced in a long time. The focus of this book, however, is on a related but a more *persistent* problem faced by the Indian economy in recent years. In the second decade of the twenty-first century, India faced a *long* period of slowdown (i.e. a deceleration in the growth rate of GDP). The main purpose of the book is to try to unravel the causes behind this problem and to see what would be the appropriate policy responses if the economy of the country is to come out of this lengthy phase of economic deceleration.

Since this is the main orientation of the book, the facts and figures relating to India's growth performance in recent years need to be set out in some detail. We shall do this in a separate chapter (Chapter 3). At this point, we only mention the two most salient points of this factual description. *First*, it turns out that while the *average* annual growth rate of the economy in the first decade of this century is calculated to be 7 per cent, that of the second decade is 6 per cent, a decline of 1 full percentage point. *Second*, even as per official statistics, annual GDP growth rate in India fell continuously between the years 2016–17 and the last pre-Covid year 2019–20. Moreover, many academic economists believe that the official figures for the years immediately preceding 2016–17 (which show an upward trend in the growth rate) are controversial and that if the annual growth rates are correctly calculated, it would be seen that the deceleration of the growth rate began at least in 2013–14, if not even earlier. Such a long period of continuous economic slowdown (even if the length is calculated on the basis of the official figures) is unprecedented in recent economic history of the country. More poignantly, this, too, is a distinguishing feature of the Indian experience. No other major South Asian country has displayed such a persistent economic slowdown over these years. As stated before, this book focuses attention on this *specific* issue. Readers looking for a more comprehensive discussion of the contemporary Indian economy as a whole, may see, for instance, Goyal (2019).

1.5 Preview of the rest of the book

This section provides a preview of the rest of the book. Since we do not presume that the reader has prior familiarity with the way economic policies can be used to fight economic slowdowns, in Chapter 2, titled "Major Economic Slowdowns of the Past and the Evolution of Economic Policies", we provide an overview. We start by distinguishing between *macroeconomic* policies (i.e. policies that affect the economy as a whole) and *microeconomic* ones (i.e. policies targeted towards specific sectors of the economy). The modus operandi of the main types of macroeconomic policies is discussed in some detail. The main focus is on the case of a *demand-constrained* economy (i.e. an economy in which the main cause of economic slowdown lies in the fact that there is insufficient demand in the market) since this is the dominant economic problem of the day in India. However, the case of a supply-constrained economy will also be commented upon. Microeconomic policies too are important weapons in fighting slowdowns. These, too, will be discussed in this chapter.

The chapter also traces how the perspective on economic policy has evolved over time. For our purposes in this book, it is important to have some idea of this evolution since at different times the dominant economic paradigms of the day have taken quite different positions on the questions regarding the type of economic policies that would be most suitable for tackling the burning economic problems of the moment and, indeed, even on whether economic policies can play any useful role at all. The chapter gives a brief guided tour of this history. For this purpose, we look at major events of economic slowdown in the past, starting from the time of the Great Depression of 1929 (when, for the first time, the need for economic policy actions on the part of the government was clearly understood by economists), through the heydays of supply-side economics and neo-liberal economic philosophy in the 1970s (when the pendulum swung to the other extreme and any kind of economic policy intervention was looked upon with suspicion) and ending with the decades following the Global Financial Crisis of 2007 (when the pendulum swung back again and the need for economic policy actions resurfaced in public discourses). Apart from the instances of *global* slowdowns mentioned earlier, the industrial deceleration that took place in India in the late 1960s and the early 1970s will also be discussed.

In Chapter 3, titled "Recent Trends in Economic Growth: India and the World", we look at the overall time pattern of the growth rates of the global economy and of the economy of India in the first two decades of the present century and bring out *two* facts that will play important parts in our arguments in the subsequent chapters of the book. *One* of these is that, while the average growth rate of the *global* economy in the first of these two decades was roughly the same as that in the second, in the Indian economy the average rate was unmistakably lower in the second decade. The *other* fact noted in the chapter is that the contrast with the global picture was not confined merely to the comparative *average* decadal growth rates. It is shown that India has been experiencing *persistent* economic slowdown at least since 2017–18, if not since 2013–14. The drop in the growth rate to a negative figure in 2020–21 was merely the culmination of a fairly long process.

Chapter 4, titled "What Caused the Slowdown?", tries to pinpoint the *reasons* behind the slowdown of the Indian economy in the 2010s. It shows that the malady was the product of two different factors: (i) inequality in the distribution of income and wealth in the country and (ii) the depressed economic state of some of the countries that are important trading partners of India

Chapter 5, titled "Arresting the Slowdown: The Policy Issues", begins the discussion of our policy recommendations. We show that the details of the policy package must depend on which of two alternative *inflation* scenarios would unfold in the future. Up to the end of the year 2020–21, the rate of inflation in the country was under control. More recently, however, there have been ups and downs. After May 2021, the pace of inflation first accelerated and then slowed down. We can only keep our fingers crossed as to which of these trends will prevail in the coming months and years.[6] One possibility is that the rate of inflation remains under control. In this case, the focus should be on *demand*-management by means of *macroeconomic* policies On the other hand, if the inflation rate accelerates, we have to examine the exact *pattern* of inflation. In India, lately, so far as consumer goods prices are concerned, whenever there has been an acceleration in the rate of inflation, the pressure has been seen to come from the prices of two specific groups of commodities, namely food items and petroleum products. In such cases, *microeconomic* policy measures targeted towards controlling the inflation in these prices must be combined with the macroeconomic policies. The details of the policy mix are discussed for both of these possible scenarios. The basic message of the chapter is that economic policy must be dovetailed to the exigency of the situation. There is no "one size fits all" policy remedy for all eventualities.

In Chapter 6, titled "Economic Policies and Pandemics: The Case of Covid-19", we remind ourselves that while the Indian economy had been slowing down for a fairly long period even before the Covid-19 pandemic, it is the pandemic that brought this lingering problem to the point of a full-blown crisis. Although, in India, the worst phase of the pandemic seems to be over now (in June 2022), epidemiologists predict more frequent recurrences of pandemics of zoonotic disease in the future. It is, therefore, important to ask how such pandemics can be brought under control. Apparently, the question lies in the domain of medical experts rather than in that of economists. On a closer look, however, it is seen to have important economic aspects as well. It is these issues that constitute the subject matter of this chapter. Since the pandemic is a global problem, common sense tells us it would have been in the best interests of all if mankind could stand up in unison to face it. We discuss the factors that have hindered the adoption of such a united stand. In particular, it is shown that a major stumbling block on the way to achieving global vaccination (or, at least, an equitable distribution of the available global supply of vaccines) is the oligopolistic power of the major producers in the world market for Covid vaccines. As a result, what we see in reality is *vaccine nationalism*: each country unto itself. We make some policy recommendations for the Indian economy, taking this reality as given. It is shown that, despite the complexities of planning economic policies directed at vaccines for such hitherto-unknown diseases as Covid-19, a number of simple, yet useful, policy recommendations can be made on the basis of the lessons of experience. Some specific policy mistakes that have been made in India and the need to avoid them in future are also highlighted.

Chapter 7, titled "Where Will the Money Come From?", takes up a most obvious question that the preceding two chapters swept under the rug. In most cases, our recommended policies would involve increases in government expenditure. How would the additional expenditure be financed? Where will the money come from? Taxing the rich would be the most obvious way to go. However, academic exercises on the *optimal* rates of wealth and income taxes suggest taxing the wealthy at rates that are by far higher than those that are currently in force. Given the present supply-side orientation of government policies in India, it is difficult to imagine that such a radical proposal would be implemented in the near future.

We are also unenthusiastic about some of the other possible methods of deficit financing. For instance, advocates of the so-called modern monetary theory (MMT) are of the opinion that actually there is no limit on any type of government expenditure because the government (or the central bank on its behalf) can always *print currency* which can then be used for giving cash dole-outs to the poor or for financing public expenditure programmes. Equivalently, it can engage in *public borrowing* in *any* amount for those purposes on the basis of the fact that it can always print currency to repay the debt. While it is known that continued use of this type of policy would result in inflation *in the long run*, the advocates of the proposal contend that, in the present demand-deficient state of the Indian economy, inflation due to excess demand is a remote possibility. We shall differ with this view. We shall show that two important features of the Indian economy (namely a *persistent deceleration* in the growth rate of the economy in recent times and a high degree of *concentration of economic power*) jointly imply that *exclusive* reliance on MMT-type policies is likely to result in inflation *not only when full employment is reached but also before that*. Moreover, under the present *international financial arrangements*, the *developing countries* do not enjoy *monetary sovereignty*. In these countries, currency printing carries the *additional* risk of generating inflationary pressures by increasing the prices of *imported inputs*.

We also advise caution in using *disinvestment* in public sector enterprises (PSEs) for the purpose. We show that in the given circumstances the best course of action would be to *combine* debt-financing of government expenditure with measures aimed at reducing inequality in the distribution of economic power. On the matter of inequality, economic reforms *of the right type* can play a vital role. In particular, attention should be paid both to the issue of the concentration of *market power within the domestic economy* and to that of *lack of monetary sovereignty* of the developing economies. So far as the latter problem is concerned, what would be called for is a *reform of the international financial system* in order to bring it more in line with the system suggested by Keynes after the Second World War. Needless to say, however, modifications of the "Keynes Plan" would be necessary in order to address the problems of the contemporary world.

Chapter 8, titled "Afterword: Headwinds and Prognosis", is the concluding chapter of the book. It starts by summarising the major points made in the preceding chapters. It then asks whether growth slowdown is likely to be a lingering problem for the Indian economy in the near future and shows that the available forecasts do give rise to such an apprehension. Next, it is noted that, in general, our policy recommendations in this book lay stress on demand-boosting measures, although the need to supplement them with sector-specific supply-side policies to contain inflationary pressures, if and when such pressures arise, is also emphasised. The chapter asks how relevant this general orientation of our recommended policies for India is likely to remain in the future and finds that aggregate demand does seem likely to remain a central concern. Two supply-side issues, however, are also discussed in this chapter. One of these is the possible economic impact of the Ukraine War. The other is the longer-run problem of global warming. It is shown that mankind's failure to take effective steps to prevent the occurrence of an environmental catastrophe caused by global warming is largely due to what is called the Prisoner's Dilemma in the theory of games. The ideal solution would be a framework of international cooperation. That seems to be a far cry at the moment. However, the force of circumstances is likely to nudge the world economy to move towards an equitable framework of international economic policies in the future. The chapter closes with the observation that while the book is about economic slowdown in India, its main purpose is to show that there exists a framework of economic policies that would pull the economy of the country out of the slowdown scenario. The intended message is that continued slowdown is *not* the unavoidable future scenario of the Indian economy, contrary to what its performance in the recent past and the presently available forecasts about the possibilities of growth in the near future may lead one to apprehend.

1.6 Conclusion

We end this introductory chapter by noting, at the risk of emphasising the obvious, that our concentration in this book on the growth slowdown in India is not to deny the existence of many other important aspects of the performance of the Indian economy and society. A broad measure of socio-economic performance would include a whole gamut of other attributes such as education, health, the environment, gender equality, women's empowerment, food security, security of the child and the aged and so on. Various indices have been suggested for the purpose of capturing these diverse aspects of development. The Human Development Index (HDI), the Gender Gap Index, the World Hunger Index are just a few examples of such indices. Moreover, it is important to try to arrive at a comprehensive measure of development by *integrating* the various indices and to study India's performance with respect to such a broad criterion. Such a gargantuan programme, however, will be beyond the scope of this book which is an attempt to analyse the causes behind the growth slowdown of the recent years and to suggest policy actions. As we shall see, however, even with this limited objective, we shall have our hands full.

Notes

1 We first multiply the physical amount of each commodity's output by its price. Then, we take the sum of these values over all commodities. There are, however, some subtleties here. For instance, we must guard against *double counting*. One produced commodity (say, steel) may be used as an input in the production of another (say, automobiles). If we take the sum of the value of output of steel and that of output of automobiles, we shall get an *overestimate* of the total production of these two industries because a part of the steel output has gone into the production of automobiles. To avoid this type of mistake, for each producer, we take the measure of output to be the *value added* (i.e. the value of output *minus* the value of raw materials or intermediate inputs). There is also the issue of deciding whether the price of a commodity here should mean the *market* price or the *basic* price charged by the producer (i.e. market price *minus* indirect taxes such as *value added tax* (VAT) or *goods and services tax* (GST)). GDP is calculated at market prices. There is also a name for what we get if, instead of market prices, we use the basic prices. It is called *gross value added* (GVA). In economic theory, GVA is also called *GDP at factor cost*. For the sake of completeness, we mention here a few related concepts used by economists. GDP of a country has a *geographical* connotation. It is the total value of goods and services produced *within the borders of the country*. There is, again, a name for the total value of goods and services produced by the citizens of a country, *whatever their location in the world might be*. It is called gross national product (GNP). Thus, GNP will count the productive activities of the citizens located outside the boundary of the country but GDP will not. On the other hand, GDP will count the value of goods and services produced by *foreign citizens* currently located within the boundary of the country but GNP will not. There is also a category called the *Net National Product* (NNP). NNP = GNP minus depreciation of capital stock. The idea is that in the process of production the capital stock of a country depreciates, and if we do not take this into account, we shall not get the true picture of the level of net output of the country. Like GDP, GNP and NNP can also be calculated by using either market prices or basic prices. It is NNP at basic prices that is called net national income (or national income, for short). For reasons of availability of data regarding depreciation of capital, however, GDP is more readily calculated than GNP, NNP, etc. In this book, it would suffice to take GDP as a rough and ready indicator of what we can informally call the "output or income of a country."

2 Real GDP is also called *GDP at constant prices*. This is because in calculating it we use the same prices as those prevailing in the base year. Correspondingly, *nominal* GDP is also called GDP at current prices.

3 In real GDP calculations, it is standard practice to *change* the base year once in every few years. This is done mainly in order to take account of *new* commodities that appear on the scene from time to time. If there is a commodity that is *now* produced in India but was not there in a certain year in the past, then using that past year as the base year in calculating the present year's real GDP is obviously not possible because real GDP requires that we multiply this year's output of the commodity by its *price in the base year*. Sometimes, however, the base year is changed for other reasons also. For instance, even though the list of commodities produced in the economy remains more or less the same, it may be that the

producers make *qualitative* changes in their products so that, strictly speaking, the commodities are not quite the same in the two years.

4 Apart from the *annual* growth rates, *quarterly* growth rates of real GDP are also estimated and published regularly by many countries including India. Quarterly growth rate figures, however, are to be interpreted carefully. As per the practice followed in India, these growth rates are calculated on *year-on-year* basis. This means that the quarterly growth rate in the first quarter, Q1, of 2021–22 is the percentage rate by which the real GDP in this quarter exceeds the real GDP in Q1 of the previous *year* 2020–21. Note that it is *not* the percentage rate by which real GDP in Q1 2021–22 exceeds that of the immediately preceding *quarter*, that is the fourth quarter (Q4, i.e. the period from 1 January to 31 March) of the fiscal year 2020–21. When this practice was introduced in India, the justification that was offered was that India has a large agricultural sector and, therefore, its quarterly output figures are subject to large *seasonal* fluctuations. Comparing the GDP in a given quarter with GDP in the immediately preceding quarter, therefore, may give an exaggerated picture of economic fluctuations. However, some economists question whether this argument is as relevant today as it was, say, 25 years ago. The contribution of agriculture to GDP in India has declined drastically over time. It is now less than 20 per cent. We do not enter into this debate here. What is clear, however, is that because of the way in which it is defined in India, official data on *quarterly* growth rates do not tell us much about growth of GDP between consecutive quarters. That is why our discussion in this book will be largely centred on *annual* (rather than quarterly) growth rates.

5 There is a related term, *recession*, that is also in use. By convention, however, this term has come to acquire a specific technical meaning. An economy is said to be in recession if there is a fall in the year-on-year *quarterly* growth rates (as defined in Footnote 4) *for at least two consecutive quarters*. Since the discussion in this book will be mainly couched in terms of *annual* growth rates, the word *recession* will be avoided.

6 The *rate of inflation* is the rate at which the prices level rises. It has been seen from experience that keeping the price level absolutely fixed (i.e. achieving a *zero* rate of inflation) is not a realistic policy objective. What one can hope for is a low and *non-accelerating* rate of inflation, that is a situation where the price level is permitted to rise at a *rate* that is (i) as low as possible and (ii) stable.

References

Bhattacharyya, R., Ghosh Dsatidar, A. and Sikdar, S. (eds.) (2022): *The COVID-19 Pandemic, India and the World: Economic and Social Policy Perspectives*, Routledge, New Delhi.

Dutta, M., Husain, Z. and Sinha, A.K. (eds.) (2022): *The Impact of Covid 19 on India: A Multidisciplinary Approach*, Springer, New Delhi.

Goyal, A. (ed.) (2019): *A Concise Handbook of the Indian Economy in the 21st Century*, Oxford University Press, New Delhi.

Kumar, A. (2020): *Indian Economy's Greatest Crisis: Impact of Coronavirus and the Road Ahead*, Penguin, New Delhi.

World Bank (2022): *Global Economic Perspectives*, World Bank, Washington, DC. www.data.worldbank.org last accessed on 7 June 2022

2 Major economic slowdowns of the past and the evolution of economic policies

2.1 Plan of the chapter

As indicated in the previous chapter, a principal question that this book seeks to address is what economic policies would be appropriate for the economy of India at the present juncture. Since we do not assume that the reader would have prior familiarity with the policies that economists speak about and the terminologies associated with them, an overview of these policies is provided in this chapter. We distinguish between *macroeconomic* policies (i.e. policies that affect the economy as a whole) and *microeconomic* ones (i.e. policies targeted towards specific sectors of the economy). Since the present state of the Indian economy is an instance of economy-wide slowdown, the lion's share of our attention will be claimed by macroeconomic policies. From a common sense point of view, whenever the actual levels of output and employment in an economy are low, the reason must be that either there is not enough demand for commodities produced in the economy (i.e. the economy is *demand-constrained*) or the producers, for some reason, are unable to produce the commodities in sufficient quantities although there is adequate demand in the market (i.e. the economy is *supply-constrained*). Section 2.2 focuses on macroeconomic policies in a demand-constrained economy. In Section 2.3, we shall comment on the case of a supply-constrained economy.

Since this book is about economic slowdowns, it would be pertinent to look at the major instances of such slowdowns in the past. Our discussion of economic policies will be interwoven with a brief history of past slowdowns. There is a good reason for adopting this way of presenting the policy discourse. As we shall see, the very idea of using policies to solve economic problems was born out of the necessity of addressing the problem of slowdowns and economic depressions.

Accordingly, Section 2.4 will be devoted to a review of three major *global* economic slowdowns of the past, namely the Great Depression of the 1930s, the stagflation-induced growth slowdown of the 1970s and the Global Financial Crisis of 2007. Of these three, the Great Depression will receive most of our attention and will be discussed in some detail. This discussion

DOI: 10.4324/9781003350514-2

will have important lessons for us when we take up (in later chapters) the matter of designing macroeconomic policies for the Indian economy.

While the slowdowns referred to in the previous paragraph were *global* events, there have also been instances of slowdowns in the *Indian* economy caused largely by factors internal to the country. In Section 2.5, we shall briefly discuss the industrial deceleration in India in the late 1960s and early 1970s.

Section 2.6 discusses *microeconomic* policies, again differentiating between the cases of the demand-constrained and the supply-constrained economies. Section 2.7 concludes the chapter.

2.2 Macroeconomic policies in a demand-constrained economy

2.2.1 Components of aggregate demand

Obviously, the objective of economic policy in a demand-constrained economy would be to stimulate demand. Economists talk about *four* components of *aggregate demand* in an economy. One part of the total demand comes from *consumption* by the people. A second part is *investment* since producers need to use a part of the current year's output if they wish to increase their productive capacity. A third part is *government expenditure*. The government has to purchase goods and services from the market in order to run the administration and to implement various other programmes. Care, however, must be taken here to consider *net* government expenditure (i.e. the government's expenditure minus its revenue from taxes). The fourth part is the demand that comes from *foreign* sources, that is the part of output that is *exported*. However, the country may also *import* goods and services from abroad. Imports add to the *available* amounts of goods and services. Hence, the fourth component of aggregate demand is taken to be *net exports* (i.e. exports minus imports).

At times of inadequate demand in the market, therefore, it is necessary to find ways to stimulate one or more of these four types of demand in the economy. The best known among the policies that have been suggested for this purpose are the macroeconomic policies recommended by the legendary British economist John Maynard Keynes whose most well-known work was published in 1936 (see Keynes, 1936). These are, in fact, called *Keynesian* policies. Typically, a Keynesian policy aims at increasing demand by putting additional purchasing power at the hands of the people of the economy.

2.2.2 Fiscal policy

The leading example of a Keynesian policy is *fiscal policy*. Fiscal policy action may take the form of a cut in taxes or an increase in government expenditure. Examples of such policies include income subsidies (especially to the poor) and additional government expenditure on various types of public projects. However, such measures may result in a deficit in the government budget. The deficit has to be financed somehow. One option is to print new currency notes and use these to finance the purchases of the goods and services required for the implementation of the public projects or to pay out doles and income subsidies. Another is to borrow the required amount of money from the public or from external sources. Fiscal policy, thus, is typically used in conjunction with *monetary policy.*

2.2.3 *Monetary policy*

Monetary policy, however, can also be used independently of fiscal policy. For instance, rather than increasing expenditure or cutting taxes, the government can simply ask the central bank to take steps for increasing the amount of *lending* of money in the economy. The idea, again, is that this will place more money in the hands of the people – in this case, in the hands of the *borrowers.* What steps can the central bank take for this purpose? While the central bank does not have direct control over *all* types of lending in an economy, it does have the ability to influence lending by financial *institutions* such as the commercial banks. In any modern economy, this is an important part of the total amount of lending in an economy.

2.2.4 *Changing the statutory liquidity ratio*

There are several ways in which the central bank can induce the commercial banks to increase lending. One of these is to increase the *amount* of loanable funds at the banks' hands. The banks collect deposits from the public and lends money to the borrowers. Obviously, they do not lend out their entire deposits because the depositors may want to make withdrawals from their deposits. Experience, however, tells them that *all* depositors do not withdraw *all* of their deposits at the same time. (This is especially true of fixed deposits.) The banks, therefore, keep only a part of the total amount money in the deposits with themselves in order to meet the day-to-day withdrawal demands of the depositors and lend out the rest of the money to borrowers (at interest rates that are higher than the rates at which the banks pay interest to its depositors). In order to ensure that the banks keep enough money with themselves (so that the depositors' interests are safeguarded), the central bank specifies a proportion of deposits that all banks are to keep in liquid forms, that is in cash or in other things which can be converted into cash on short notice, for instance, short-term government securities (which are called Treasury Bills). Banks cannot lend out this part of their deposits to borrowers. This proportion is called the statutory liquidity ratio (SLR). In fact, a bank has to keep a part of its statutory reserves as deposits with the central bank. The rest of the statutory reserves it can keep with itself. One obvious way of increasing the loanable funds at the hands of the banks, therefore, is to *reduce* the SLR.

2.2.5 Changing the repo rate

However, even if the lendable funds at the hands of banks increase, it may not be the case that *actual* bank lending increases. There may not be enough *demand* for loans. A somewhat surer way of increasing the volume of bank lending in the economy is to reduce the interest rates at which banks lend to borrowers. To be sure, in normal circumstances, if interest rates are reduced, the lenders (i.e. the banks) will be less (rather than more) willing to lend. Remember, however, that we are talking about a demand-constrained economy. For such economies, the policy planners' task is to increase demand. An appropriate monetary policy would be to reduce interest rates. If the loan is for business purposes, lower interest rates will mean increased profitability. This may increase investment which, as we have said before, is a part of aggregate demand. Similarly, if the loan is for the purchase of durable goods, this will increase the demand for these types of consumer goods in the market.

But how can the central bank influence interest rates? In our country, there was a time when the Reserve Bank of India (RBI), which is our central bank, had the authority to directly set the rates of interest at which banks could lend and borrow. In the post-liberalisation era, however, this system has been discarded. Banks can now decide on the interest rates that they wish to charge the borrowers. Even now, however, there are ways in which the RBI can decrease or increase interest rates. At times of cash shortages, the banks often turn to the RBI for help. (For instance, they often face problems in coping with the SLR requirement.) At such times, the banks borrow from the RBI (usually for very short periods) against the collateral of government securities. The rate of interest that RBI charges for these loans is called the *repo rate*. "Repo" is the short form of the phrase "repurchase option." What happens here is that since the period of the loans given to the banks by RBI is very short (for instance, just one day), the banks sometimes fail to repay the loans on time. The securities pledged to RBI as collaterals are then forfeited. However, the difference from the normal borrowing-and-lending operations in the open market is that the RBI gives the banks the *option* to *repurchase* the forfeited securities within a specified time period if within that period the banks become solvent enough to do so. That is why such loans are called *loans with repurchase option* or *repo loans*. Repo rate is the rate of interest charged by the RBI on repo loans.

One of the principal ways in which the RBI influences the interest rates prevailing in the economy is to change the repo rate. Obviously, if the RBI reduces the repo rate, the banks have to make smaller repayments to the RBI. Moreover, the banks also often borrow from the RBI for reasons other than those related to the SLR. The rates of interest charged by the RBI on these loans are pegged by the RBI to the repo rate. When the repo rate falls, these rates fall too. Moreover, the rates of interest that the banks charge on *their* loans to the borrowers tend to fall. This tendency is further strengthened by the RBI's constant prods to the banks to pass on the benefits of the repo rate cuts to the banks' borrowers. It may, in fact, give the threat to withdraw the repo rate cut if the banks do not pay heed to such requests. The overall result is that a cut in the repo rate usually induces a fall in the rates of interest on the banks' loans to their borrowers. Finally, while bank lending is only a part of the total amount of lending in an economy, cuts in the interest rates on bank loans usually induce cuts in the interest rates charged by *other* lenders such as non-banking financial institutions or even the indigenous moneylenders (since, otherwise, these other lenders would lose customers to the banks). While the correlation is not perfect, it is significant. Thus, the overall result of a cut in the repo rate is a fall in the interest rates on all types of loans in the economy. The demand for loans tends to increase. Whether the loans are for the purpose of investment or for the purchase of consumer durables, aggregate demand in the economy will tend to increase. In fact, the repo rate is the main monetary policy instrument in India. For this reason, it is also called the *policy rate of interest.*

2.2.6 *Changing the reverse repo rate*

Sometimes the banks find themselves in possession of excess liquidity. This often happens at times of recession in the economy since producers are then unenthusiastic about new investments and, therefore, about taking loans from banks. In such circumstances, the RBI may want to help the banks by letting them park a part of their excess funds in the form of deposits in RBI at a reasonable rate of interest. Effectively, in such circumstances, it is the RBI that borrows from the banks. The rate of interest on these deposits is called the *reverse repo rate*. However, just as the interest rate paid by the banks to their depositors is *lower* than the rate that they charge on their loans to their borrowers, the reverse repo rate is always lower than the repo rate. In fact, if the reverse repo rate was higher, the banks would be tempted to keep all their money in deposits with the RBI (and borrow from it whenever necessary) rather than carrying on normal banking activities.

The reverse repo rate is also a policy instrument of the RBI. A cut in the reverse repo is a signal to the banks. It tells them that the RBI wishes to discourage the banks from keeping deposits at the RBI. It now wants them to increase lending to producers.

2.2.7 *Quantitative easing*

Sometimes, however, it so happens that the repo and the reverse repo rates have already been cut to very low levels so that further cuts are not feasible, and yet the economy continues to be in depression or deceleration.[1] In such situations, a central bank can use yet another weapon in its arsenal. It can take measures of the type that are known in the USA as *quantitative easing* (QE).[2] Roughly, the interest rate can be interpreted as the "price" charged by lenders on a specified amount (say, Rs. 100) of loan. The idea is that even when the "price" cannot be lowered any further because it is already near zero, a central bank can take steps that would increase the *quantity* of lending at the same "price." Typically, under these circumstances, the central bank purchases *long-term* bonds and similar financial assets in the open market. In the USA both government and corporate bonds (and even company shares) are purchased under the programme. If the current holders of these bonds have to hold on to them till maturity, the money remains blocked. Since the central bank purchases the bonds *before the dates of their maturity*, the money so received can be spent in the current period. If, as is often the case, the bonds were held by a bank or a non-banking financial institution, the money that is released can now be used for lending to businessmen. If the holder was a company, it can now be used for purposes of investment.

We have said that the term *quantitative easing* refers to the fact that this type of policy action is primarily aimed at making a greater *quantity* of funds available to lenders without seeking to decrease interest rates in the market. In fact, however, it so happens that it also has an effect on the interest rates on private loans that prevail in the open market (though not on the repo rate fixed by the central bank). This is because the central bank's purchases of bonds in the open market under the QE programme will increase the demand for private bonds in the market. If the central bank itself purchases private bonds, there will be a direct effect. Even if the central bank's purchases are limited to government bonds, there will be an indirect effect because more money is being pumped into the economy. This will push up the prices of private bonds in the market. Interest rates will fall because there is an *inverse* relationship between bond prices and interest rates.

The following is a simple hypothetical example. Consider, for simplicity, a situation where the only type of (private) bond is a 10-year bond with a face value of Rs. 100. Suppose that, in year 1, the going rate of (simple) interest in the open market for bonds is 5 per cent. Suppose, further, that the going price of a bond is, again, Rs. 100. At the beginning of year 1, a businessman wishing to take a loan of Rs. 100 for 10 years sells one such bond. The person who gives the loan buys the bond at the price of Rs. 100. As long as the bond price in the market remains Rs. 100, 5 per cent is not only the rate of interest but also the annual *yield rate* on the bond (i.e. the rate of return enjoyed by the lender). The annual yield rate is the simply amount of annual interest payment (Rs. 5) as percentage of the bond price (Rs. 100). Now suppose that in the next year (year 2), the central bank's QE operations push up the demand for bonds in the market and the bond price rises to Rs. 125. The yield rate in year 2 on the bond that was issued in year 1 will be [(Rs. 5/Rs. 125) × 100] per cent or 4 per cent. This is because if the person who purchased the bond in year 1 continues to hold on to it in year 2, he will be locking in the sum of Rs. 125 but will get the same amount of Rs. 5 as interest because that was contractually fixed in year 1 for the entire 10-year period of life of the bond. Consider now a businessman (not necessarily the same as the one we started with) who, in year 2, wants a loan of Rs. 100 for 10 years and issues a bond. It is easily seen that the rate of interest on this freshly issued bond does not need to be more than 4 per cent. A purchaser of a bond can, of course, go to the open market and buy a bond that was issued in year 1 (from somebody who holds this type of bond in year 2). He would then get an interest rate of 5 per cent, but the catch is that he would now have to pay Rs. 125 for the bond so that the yield rate he would get would be 4 per cent.

On the other hand, the rate of interest on the freshly issued bond of year 2 cannot be less than 4 per cent either. If the rate offered is less than that, the yield rate on the freshly issued bond would be less than 4 per cent so that no bond-purchaser will touch it because, as we have just seen, he can always ensure for himself an yield rate of 4 per cent on his locked-in money by going to the open market for bonds.

Thus, in year 2, the going rate of interest in the market (i.e. the rate of interest at which money can be borrowed in year 2) must be exactly 4 per cent in our example. Thus, the central bank's bond purchases in the open market under the QE programme have led to a fall in the interest rate in the market for private bonds, although the central bank has not reduced the repo rate. This is expected to stimulate investment (and, therefore, aggregate demand) in the economy.

In India, QE is called the *government securities acquisition programme* (G-SAP). This is more informative (than the term "quantitative easing") about what it entails because it is only *government securities* that the RBI purchases under the programme – not from the government but from the open market, i.e. from those who currently hold these securities. Now, while in theory any individual or organisation can hold such securities, in practice it is the financial institutions that are the major holders. Thus, when the RBI purchases these securities, the financial institutions get the money before the maturity dates. This directly increases the amount of lendable funds at the disposal of these institutions. Note that while a cut in the repo rate benefits only the banks since it is banks that keep deposits in the RBI, G-SAP pours money into all types of financial institutions including non-banking financial companies.

2.2.8 Stimulating external demand: devaluation

While fiscal and monetary policies typically aim at stimulating demand coming from *domestic* sources, the government can also seek to increase *external* demand. As we have said before, the net exports (i.e. the value of exports minus the value of imports) are also a component of aggregate demand in an economy. The government can try to make exports cheaper (so that foreign demand for the domestically produced commodities increases) and imports dearer (so that domestic consumers and producers use less of the commodities produced abroad). For instance, the government may give subsidies to (or reduce taxes on) those producers who export their products so that their costs of production (and, therefore, the prices charged by them) decrease. The exported goods become cheaper in foreign markets. This may increase foreign demand. The producers will also have an incentive to produce and export their goods in greater quantities. All these go to boost the value of exports. On the other hand, the value of imports may be controlled by imposing import tariffs (so that the prices of the imported goods in the domestic market rise and people purchase less of them) or by imposing import quotas. The imports of some inessential commodities can also be totally banned. These tax-subsidy policies, however, are *microeconomic* in nature: they are directed at those specific goods and services that the country exports and imports.

But there is also an important type of trade policy that has *economy-wide* effects. (In that sense, like the monetary and fiscal policies discussed before, it is *macroeconomic* in nature.) This is the policy of *devaluation*. Devaluation works under the *fixed exchange rate* system. Suppose that there is a fixed exchange rate between the Indian rupee and the US dollar, for instance, $1 = Rs. 70. An Indian good that is exported at a price of Rs. 140 per unit will sell for $2 per unit in the foreign markets. Now, if the government changes the exchange rate and declares that, henceforth, $1 will be the equivalent of Rs. 140, the foreign price of the Indian good will immediately fall to just $1 even though its domestic price remains unchanged at Rs. 140. Note that this makes the dollar dearer and the rupee *cheaper* in relation to one another. That is why this is called a *devaluation* of the domestic currency (or just "devaluation," for short). The fall in the dollar price of the Indian export good will increase the demand for it in the foreign market. Note, however, that while the foreign price of the exported good is falling, the quantity demanded is increasing. Strictly speaking, what will happen to the *value* (which is price multiplied by quantity) of exports is uncertain. If foreign demand is sufficiently *sensitive* to price (i.e. if it is *elastic*), the effect of the increase in quantity will prevail over that of the fall in price, so that the value of exports will increase. (*Elasticity of demand* for a commodity is defined as the percentage increase in demand for the commodity when there is a 1 per cent fall in its price.)

The opposite will happen to imports. Imports will become costlier in the *domestic* currency even if there is no change in their *dollar* prices. This will *decrease* the demand for the imported goods in the domestic market. If the domestic demand for imports is sufficiently elastic, the effect of the fall in the quantity will dominate the effect of the increase in price. The value of imports will fall. Overall, there will be a rise in net exports and, thus, a rise in aggregate demand in the economy. Under certain simplifying assumptions it is possible to establish a simple condition (involving the elasticities of demand) under which devaluation will increase net exports. The condition is that the sum of the elasticities of (foreign) demand for exports and the elasticities of (domestic) demand for the imports is greater than 1. This is the famous *Marshall-Lerner condition* named after the economists Alfred Marshall and Abba P. Lerner.

In today's world, however, the fixed exchange rate system is a thing of the past. The exchange rate is nothing but the price of foreign currencies in terms of the domestic currency, and like other prices, these are allowed to be determined in the open market. Under the present system (supervised by the International Monetary Fund (IMF)) no member-country of the IMF is allowed to devalue its currency excepting in cases of emergency. Central banks, however, are allowed to prevent wild fluctuations in exchange rates by buying or selling the foreign currencies in appropriate quantities in the market. What quantities are "appropriate" is, however, a question that is often difficult to answer. Central banks sometimes buy up large quantities of foreign exchange so that the prices of the foreign currencies go up, that is the *domestic* currency *depreciates*. The effects on net exports and on aggregate demand in the economy are the same as those of devaluation. (By convention, the term "devaluation" is used to mean a fall in the price of the domestic currency enforced by a government order. The term "depreciation" is reserved to mean the same thing if it happens in the open market on its own, i.e. without government intervention.) In recent times, the Western nations have often accused China of surreptitiously achieving effective devaluation of its currency in this way in order to shore up its exports.

2.3 Macroeconomic policies in a supply-constrained economy

So far, we have discussed macroeconomic policies that can be used to fight economic stagnation in a demand-constrained economy. Output and employment (or their growth rates), however, can fall due to problems on the supply side as well. The economy becomes supply-constrained if, for some reason, there is a drop in output because of some supply-side reason while there is adequate demand in the market. A natural calamity may give rise to such a problem. More frequently, such problems arise as a consequence of some economic or political event in the international arena.

Now, fighting economic slowdown in a *supply-constrained* economy is much more difficult than fighting it in a demand-constrained one. Supply-side problems usually cannot be solved at short notice. It takes time to rebuild the production mechanism of the country or to reorient it in appropriate ways. Meanwhile, because of the supply shortage, demand exceeds supply. The problem of *inflation* arises. The coexistence of stagnation of output and inflation of the price level has come to be called *stagflation*. It is easily seen that standard Keynesian policies or currency devaluation cannot get us out of this peculiar problem. These policies would, in fact, exacerbate the problem of excess demand and inflation while keeping output (and, therefore, employment) unchanged. Removing constraints on supply would now be the main policy objective. The way to achieve this objective would be to help the producers to cut their costs of production and to increase their revenue. This type of measures will increase profitability and stimulate production and employment. That will also take care of inflation by reducing the supply shortage. Steps should also be taken to increase the rate of saving (rather than that of consumption) in the economy. This will serve the dual purpose of helping capital accumulation (which would expand the productive capacities of the producers, thus helping them to increase output in the *future*) and of reducing *current* consumption and, therefore, *current* aggregate demand (thus reducing the severity of the problem of inflation due to excess demand) in the economy.

2.4 Major global slowdowns of the past

2.4.1 *The Great Depression of 1929 and the genesis of macroeconomic policies*

2.4.1.1 *The US economy in the 1930s*

We have so far described in general terms how macroeconomic policies work. A brief look at the historical evolution of macroeconomic policies would also be educative for our purposes since it contains important lessons that will prove to be of vital importance for us when, later in this book, we shall come to the question of the choice of appropriate economic policies for the Indian economy.

Historically, the first time that the need for policy actions at times of economic crises was brought to public attention by the force of circumstances was during the Great Depression in the USA from 1929 to the early years of the 1930s. There was a sharp decline in the growth rate. The rate was negative (i.e. the economy contracted) in the years 1930–33. There was widespread unemployment and glut (i.e. excess supply) in the markets for both manufactured and agricultural commodities. The same was true in the market for oil. World crude oil prices, in fact, showed a consistent falling trend for about half a century since 1920. Moreover, the discovery of oil in Texas led to a glut in the oil market just around this time. Clearly, the US economy of the time was demand-constrained rather than supply-constrained. The steep fall in outputs was reflected in a crisis in the financial sector also. The story of the crash of the stock market on Wall Street in New York in 1929 and of the widespread economic and human tragedies that it caused is well-known. For a more detailed discussion of these points see, for instance, Galbraith (1961).

For the first four years after 1929, no policy action was taken to combat the economic crisis. The idea of *fiscal policy* was, in fact, largely unheard of in those days. The private sector was the whole economy. While *taxes* were in place, nobody gave a thought to the idea of government expenditure (aside from the minimal amounts needed for running day-to-day administration) as a means of supplementing private expenditure.

2.4.1.1.1 MONETARY POLICY

Monetary policy in the USA is the prerogative of the Federal Reserve System (or the Fed, for short). Fed is essentially the central bank of the USA. However, there are some important differences between the central banking practices in the USA and those in most of the other countries of the world. The Fed has a federal structure. The country is divided into 12 geographical regions. Each of the regions has its own Federal Reserve Bank. A Federal Reserve Bank enjoys considerable regional autonomy and is essentially run by the banks in the region. (Unlike in some other countries, *all* banks in the USA are in the *private* sector.) At the top, there is a Federal Reserve Board headquartered in Washington, D.C. There are representatives of the regional Federal Reserve Banks on the Federal Reserve Board. The system as a whole is called the Fed. While currency notes are printed by the government and carry the signature of the Treasury Secretary of the Government of the USA, the *quantities* in which the notes of different denominations are to be printed is decided by the Fed. Thus, a major feature of the Fed is the *independence* that it enjoys with respect to the government. Essentially, the Fed represents the economic interests of the *private* sector of the US economy. In contrast, in most of the other countries (including India), while the central bank does enjoy autonomy in certain matters, in all important respects, it is essentially guided by the wishes of the government.

For quite some time after the US economy went into depression, the Fed did *not* adopt the type of monetary policies that common sense would demand (and that we have discussed in the preceding section). Today, this seems surprising. In fact, it may seem that the Fed could have taken appropriate actions, if it so desired, much *before* fiscal actions were taken. This is because nowadays in all countries monetary policy decisions can be implemented much more speedily than their fiscal counterparts. Changes in fiscal policies usually need legislative approval. Monetary policy changes do not. They can, therefore, be put in place at very short notice. It seems puzzling, therefore, that at a time when *expansionary* monetary policy was urgently called for, what happened, in fact, was that there was a *rise* in the interest rates. Some of the critics, in fact, have gone so far as to say that it was the Fed's policies that *caused* the Great Depression. While that may be an exaggeration, there seems little doubt that the Fed's failures had much to do with the *duration* of the crisis.

However, the reason for the Fed's perverse policy is not far to seek. It was ingrained in the so-called Gold Standard system. The Gold Standard was an international arrangement, established by agreement among the advanced countries of the West, under which the central bank in each of these countries agreed to keep the value of gold in terms of its own currency at a certain *fixed* level and to hold gold equal in value to a certain percentage of the total value of currency in circulation. In the USA, by a law enacted in 1913, the value of gold was fixed at $20.67 per ounce of pure gold and the Fed was always required to hold gold in an amount whose value (at that fixed price) would be 40 per cent of the total value of the Federal Reserve Notes (popularly called dollars or dollar bills) in circulation. Thus, how much currency the Fed can issue would be limited by how much physical gold it can afford to hold. Since gold was a scarce commodity, it was hoped that this would keep a check on the reckless issue of currency by the central bank, thereby keeping *inflationary* pressures in the economy under control. This was one of the rationales behind the Gold Standard system. It was thought that money supply was too important a matter to be left to the whims of human beings. It is the *system* that should decide how much money is to be supplied to the economy.

How did the Fed ensure that the price of gold in the USA would remain fixed at $20.67 per ounce? All it had to do was agree to sell and buy gold at that price in the open market. This has nothing to do with either gold or central banking. It is easy to see that if anyone (say, X) agrees to *sell and buy any amount* of a commodity at a fixed price (say, Rs. 100 per unit), then Rs. 100 will also be the price that will actually rule in the open market. This is because, on the one hand, if any *other* seller (say, Y) charges a *higher* price, he or she will not get any buyer since the commodity can be *bought* from X at Rs. 100. On the other hand, Y need not sell it to anybody at a *lower* price since it can be *sold* to X for Rs. 100.

Now, what the advocates of the Gold Standard had not foreseen was that while this system might be able to keep inflation under control, it would be of no use in combatting *deflations*. The Great Depression of 1929 witnessed not only falling levels of output and employment but also a falling price level. (If the price level was *rising*, it would have been a case of *stagflation*.) *All* prices (including the price of gold) displayed strong downward tendencies. The Fed, however, was legally required to hold the price of gold at $20.67. It had to purchase gold in the market in large quantities at that price (so that the resulting demand would hold up the price). To raise the money required for the purpose, it unloaded some of its bond holdings and sold them in the open market. This led to an increase in the supply of bonds and a decrease in bond prices. As we have seen before, bond prices and interest rates are inversely related. The result was an *increase* in the rates of interest.

Thus, it is possible to argue that the Fed's failure to adopt expansionary policies during these years was imposed on it by the Gold Standard within which it had to work. The real solution to the problem was to come out of the Gold Standard system. That was what the USA did in 1933 when Franklin Roosevelt became the president of the country. This gave the Fed the freedom to pursue expansionary monetary policies. Money supply in the economy increased. For the first few years and even after that, the Fed continued to make policy mistakes in some cases. (For instance, as many as three times in 1935 and 1936, it *increased* the statutory reserve requirements of banks.) Broadly, however, its policies now found the right direction. In particular, after 1936, interest rates started falling continuously and aided the recovery of the economy.

Historians differ over their views on the reasons why the decision to leave the Gold Standard was not taken *earlier*. Friedman and Schwartz (1963), a classic work, explains it as leadership failure at the top echelons of the Fed. Several other hypotheses have also been put forward. A detailed discussion of these alternative explanations would be irrelevant for our purposes here.

2.4.1.1.2 FISCAL POLICY: THE NEW DEAL

The regime of President Roosevelt, however, is today remembered for a quite different reason. Roosevelt adopted a whole series of *fiscal* actions. Fiscal (as distinguished from monetary) policy was quite a novelty then. The mix of fiscal policy actions taken by Roosevelt's administration came to be known as the New Deal. The New Deal was a package of policy measures. The common objective of all these measures was to increase the purchasing power of the people and to supplement private investment with public investment. Particular emphasis was laid on minimising the suffering of the unemployed workers. A number of government agencies were created for the purpose of providing aid on an emergency basis and temporary employment in public projects such as construction of roads and bridges. The Tennessee Value Authority (TVA) was set up and entrusted with the construction and maintenance of a number of dams on the Tennessee River. (TVA was the model that was later followed in India when the Damodar Valley Corporation was set up.) Youth work in the national forests was also encouraged. Minimum wage laws were enacted. It was emphasised that private producers too had to fix the rates of wages paid to their workers at a reasonably high level. These were not to be "subsistence wages." Rather, they should enable the workers to "earn a decent living." Maximum work hours were also specified for some industries. The social security legislations of 1935 and 1939 must also be mentioned in this connection. These provided for insurance against disabilities, unemployment compensation, pension for widows and the elderly, etc.

Drawing on the experience of the historic stock market crash of 1929 and the series of bank failures that marked the beginning of the great economic crisis, the government also undertook several administrative reforms in the financial sector. Since it was discovered that a number of fraudulent practices had contributed to the crisis, effective corrective actions were taken. The Securities and Exchange Commission was created in order to protect the investors from some shady stock market practices. The Federal Deposit Insurance Corporation that came into being around this time provided government insurance for depositors in those banks that were members of the Fed.

Broadly, the New Deal corresponded almost exactly to the type of Keynesian *fiscal* policies that we have discussed before. It should be noted, however, that the New Deal was inaugurated in 1933, that is *before* the publication of Keynes' famous book of 1936 that we have mentioned before.

The combination of the New Deal and the expansionary monetary policy of the Fed "worked." The worst years of the Great Depression were those from 1929 to 1933. The annual growth rate of the economy was negative in *all* of these years. In 1934, however, it turned positive and remained so for a long time. Moreover, the pro-poor New Deal sharply reduced economic inequalities and ushered a period of social cohesion that paved the way for sustained economic growth in the long run.

2.4.1.1.3 WHO GETS THE CREDIT FOR THE RECOVERY: MONETARY OR FISCAL POLICY?

One question that has been debated by economists is whether it is the *fiscal* policies under the New Deal or the *monetary* policies (in the later years of the 1930s) that should be given the credit for the recovery of the US economy from the crisis of 1929. One view is that it was the increase in money supply from 1933 onwards that enabled the government to push through the fiscal measures of the New Deal. Moreover, according to this view, since an increase in money supply makes for cheaper money and credit, it had a positive effect on *private* investment and consumption. This, by itself, would have led to the recovery anyway even if the *governmental* interventions of the New Deal were not there. Thus, as per this view, the New Deal was supposed to be of secondary importance. This line of thinking was more fully developed by Brown (1956) who argued that not only in 1933 but also throughout the 1930s fiscal policy by itself would have been insufficient to get the US economy out of the slump. Supporters of this view have also claimed that statistical estimates of the *partial* effects of fiscal policies (i.e. the estimates of what these effects would be, had there been no increase in money supply) show that this effect is rather small in magnitude.

However, it has now been shown (for instance, by Perry and Vernengo (2014) that the statistical estimates referred to by the fiscal-policy-sceptics had many limitations. The estimates depended too much on exactly which time period was studied. If the entire period from 1929 to 1945 is studied and appropriate statistical methods are followed, the effects of fiscal policies turn out to be quite significant. Moreover, intuitively, it is hardly surprising that the effect of fiscal policy *alone* would be smaller than that of fiscal policy *accompanied by* an increase in money supply. After all, the government must find the money to finance its public expenditure projects. If money and credit are cheaper, it is easier for the government to find the required resources. Besides, the increase in money supply that took place did not have much to do with the Fed's deliberate action. What happened was that this was a time of great political instability in Europe. There was a flow of *gold* from Europe to the USA as risk-averse European businessmen and other investors moved their resources. The gold inflow implied an increase in money supply. Thus, while money supply did increase, it was not a matter of "monetary policy" of the Fed. In fact, as we noted earlier, in some instances, the Fed adopted contractionary policies. In the early 1930s, it was the relentless gold inflow that led to an increase in money supply *despite* the Fed's policy mistakes. Later, however, monetary and fiscal policy did work in tandem.

The reader may wonder why we entered into such a detailed discussion of the economic policies adopted in another country during a crisis that wrecked it about a century ago. One of our *two* reasons for doing so has already been indicated earlier. From the point of view of the history of economic thought the most important contribution of the discussions centred on policy choices in the USA in the decade of the 1930s was that, for the first time, it showed that the government and the central bank can play active roles in determining the levels of output and employment in the economy and that this role can be socially beneficial. Eventually such policies were found to be useful not only in deep depressions but also in slowdowns of a less dramatic nature. Moreover, it was soon realised that, if necessary, economic policy can be made to work in the *reverse* gear also. If an economy is under excessive *inflationary* pressures (i.e. if demand is far in *excess* of supply), the government can take steps to *reduce* demand and *increase* supply. The notion of *anti-cyclical economic policy* (or *stabilisation policy*) was born. In other words, what we have discussed earlier is nothing less than the story of the birth of economic policy as a concept.

The *other* reason why we are interested in this piece of American economic history has to do with a *lesson* that can be drawn from it. The lesson here is that in a fight against a demand-side recession monetary and fiscal policies should join hands. Fiscal actions are *necessary* precisely because the root of the problem is in the inadequacy of *private* demand for consumption and investment in such times. The government must come forward and take steps to boost private consumption (especially, by increasing the purchasing power of the people in the low- and middle-income classes who constitute the overwhelming majority of the population) and also to supplement private investment by implementing public investment projects. *Monetary policy* can reduce interest rates and increase lendable funds at the hands of the lending institutions, thereby providing greater investment *opportunities*. Whether private investors would come forward to *utilise* these opportunities, however, would depend on whether there is enough demand in the market for the produced commodities. As the proverb says, you can drag your horse near the water but you cannot make it drink the water unless it is thirsty. Monetary policy by itself, therefore, is unlikely to work. On the other hand, it can play a vital role by providing *fiscal* policy the space to work in. The government can find the resources for implementing the fiscal actions only when an accommodating monetary policy is in place. This symbiotic relation between monetary and fiscal policies is the main take-home lesson here for us.

2.4.1.2 UK in the 1930s

For a complete picture of the global economic crisis of the 1930s, we would also need to look at what happened in other countries. A detailed country-by-country description is, however, unnecessary for our purposes in this book. We shall only mention the case of the UK here. It is interesting to note that while the policies, both monetary and fiscal, used in the USA were basically *Keynesian* ones in the sense that they primarily aimed at increasing the demand for consumption and investment *within* the economy, the policy orientation in Keynes's own country, the UK, was quite different. In the UK, there was a problem of economic slowdown even before 1929. The problem was coming mainly from the side of international trade. Many economists now believe that the UK had fixed its *exchange rate* wrongly in the 1920s. The pound sterling was *overvalued*, i.e. the price of 1 pound in terms of, say, the US dollar had been set at too high a level. This had made British exports too expensive in the foreign markets. The growth rate of the value of exports tended to decline. Therefore, so did the growth rate of aggregate demand in the economy. The result was economic deceleration due to demand deficiency. On the one hand, the rate of unemployment started rising. On the other hand, since the government's tax revenue nosedived, severe austerity measures were proposed in order to minimise the resulting deficit in the government budget. There was widespread public discontent and major industrial strikes. This was already the situation before 1929. The Great Depression of 1929 in the USA only made matters worse. Although the Wall Street stock market crash did not have a direct and immediate impact in other countries, the effects of the economic crisis in the US economy as a whole soon engulfed the world economy. The real GDP growth rate in the UK was *negative* in both 1930 and 1931. The rate of unemployment rose even further. As in all other countries, *domestic* demand fell too. However, the most severe problem continued to come from the side of *external* demand. Because of the global crisis, every country now had to cut down on imports. Therefore, every country's exports also fell for the simple reason that every country's export is some country's import. The value of the UK's exports, not just the *growth rate* of this value, fell. The reason that the problem attained serious proportions for the UK was that the UK's economy was extremely dependent on foreign trade. It direly needed the foreign markets where it could sell its products. Increasing exports was, therefore, the most pressing need of the hour.

As we have explained before, what a country wants to do under such circumstances is to devalue its currency. In the early 1930s, however, this type of policy was unavailable to the British policy-makers (although the IMF was yet to be born). The reason was, again, the Gold Standard. As we have seen, under this system, the price of gold in each country in terms of the domestic currency was permanently fixed. Now, it is easy to see that this means that the exchange rates between the currencies of the different countries were also automatically fixed. For instance, if the price of one ounce of gold is 20 dollars in the USA and it is 10 pounds in the UK, this implies that 20 US dollars = 10 British pounds, that is the exchange rate between the US dollar and the British pound would be: 1 dollar = half a pound. The government would be unable to tamper with this exchange rate. Under the Gold Standard, therefore, currency devaluation on the part of any country was ruled out.

Under the circumstances, exit from the Gold Standard was the only option for the UK The Gold Standard, after all, was merely an international *agreement* voluntarily arrived at through negotiations. No country could be forced to abide by this system if it did not want to. In 1931 UK left the Gold Standard unilaterally (i.e. without consulting any other country) and devalued the pound sterling. This was the main policy adopted in the UK for the purpose of battling the economic depression. Note that while this was not a *Keynesian* policy in the usual sense, it was a *macroeconomic* policy nevertheless since it had economy-wide effects. Moreover, it was also a *demand-oriented* policy: while a Keynesian policy would typically target *domestic* demand, currency devaluation targeted *foreign* demand.

Devaluation brought immediate benefits. Net exports increased, giving a fillip to aggregate demand. From 1932 onwards, the growth rate of real GDP was positive again. The exit from the Gold Standard also opened up space for expansionary monetary policy, just as it did in the USA after 1933. The cheap money policy led to a loan-financed housing boom and stimulated domestic demand. Remarkably, however, unlike in the USA, the government did *not* embark upon any large programme of public-debt-financed expansion of government expenditure. Instead, it took advantage of the better economic situation to achieve "fiscal consolidation," that is to reduce the budget deficit and to withdraw the unpopular austerity measures of the late 1920s. It was only towards the end of the 1930s (when the armament programmes began and military expenditure increased as the Second World War loomed large on the horizon), that fiscal policy instruments were used in the UK. By that time, however, the economic crisis of 1930 and 1931 had been left far behind.

As we have seen, although the Gold Standard is now a thing of the past, the scope of devaluation policy is quite limited in today's world. It is now realised that by devaluing its currency a country A gains *only at the cost* of its trading partner B. This is easiest to see if there are just these two countries in the world. By definition, A's net exports increase if and only if those of B decrease. Hence, whenever, A devalues its currency, B will also have the incentive to devalue *its*. It is easily seen that if each country changes the value of its currency by the *same* percentage, then the *exchange rate* between the two countries' currencies will remain *unchanged*. Realising this, each country will now try to outdo each other by devaluing in larger and larger proportions. It is obvious that there can be no winner in this game of *competitive devaluation* and the only result will be extreme volatility of exchange rates. The same, more or less, will also be the case if three or more countries are considered. It is for this reason that the IMF does not usually permit its member countries to devalue its currency. Most economists are of the opinion that, had this also been the case in the 1930s, the only option left to British policy planners of the time would be to use *Keynesian* macroeconomic policies in much the same way as was done in the USA.

2.4.1.3 The heydays of macroeconomic policies

The success of Keynesian macroeconomic policies in ending the economic crisis of the 1930s and ushering a long period of sustained growth in USA and in other western countries after the Second World War led to the popularity of these policies among both academic economists and governmental policy planners during these years. These were the heydays of Keynesian economics in general and macroeconomic policies in particular.

2.4.2 The oil crisis of the 1970s: the rise of supply-side economics and neo-liberalism

The golden age of Keynesian policies came to an end in the early 1970s. In 1973, there was a *supply-side* shock originating in the sudden steep increase in the price of oil enforced by OPEC, a cartel of oil-producing countries. Since oil was a crucial input in the production process, the costs of production went up dramatically almost overnight in all sectors and in all countries of the world. The growth rate of output stagnated, and, simultaneously, there was economy-wide inflation. In other words, the problem now was *stagflation*. The USA was hit the hardest because it was the most important importer of oil. The growth rate of aggregate *supply* in the US economy nosedived, although there was no dearth of demand.

Starting with the oil crisis of 1973 until the global financial crisis of 2007, stagflation was a recurring problem in most of the Western economies, especially, the USA. It was this that led to the unpopularity of Keynesian economics among economists and policy planners. As we saw in the previous section, Keynesian policies would fail to address the issue. Trying to increase demand would be of no use now since there was no problem of demand deficiency to start with. On the contrary, this will make the problem of inflation even worse. On the other hand, if demand is sought to be *decreased* by using Keynesian policies in the reverse direction (for instance, by *decreasing* government expenditure), then there will be further fall in output because the effect of increase in the cost of production will now be reinforced by that of falling demand. Stagflation does not have a Keynesian solution.

It was this problem that gave rise to what was called *supply-side economics*. It was argued that since the problem was on the side of supply, the solution must also be sought there. It was argued that the only useful role that the government can play would consist of encouraging production by *cutting* the rates of taxes on producers, scrapping minimum-wage laws, etc. Rates of income tax on high-income *individuals* should also be brought down because it is they who do most of the saving and it is saving, not consumption, that helps capital formation and expands productive capacity. (For these arguments, see, for instance, Bartlett (2010) and Canto et al. (1983.)

From here, it was only a short step to what has now come to be called *neo-liberal economics*. It was a natural extension of supply-side economics. The general idea behind this type of economic philosophy is that in the long run it is rate of growth of *output* that determines the growth rate of an economy and the best way of increasing output is to leave the producers to their own devices. Ideally, there should be no taxes at all and, therefore, no government expenditure either. In fact, ideally, there should be no government! As President Ronald Reagan of the USA famously said, "Government is not the solution to our problem; government is the problem." (Reagan, 1980) Since around 1980 until the global financial crisis of 2007, neo-liberal economics was the foundation of economic policy planning in most of the (non-socialist) countries of the world. The policies that did find favour were those that promoted liberalisation, privatisation and globalisation. Liberalisation meant getting rid of all kinds of government control on the economy including licensing policies. Privatisation required opening up all sectors of the economy for the entry of private sector producers and dismantling or selling-off of public sector production units. Globalisation referred to the promotion of free international trade and removal (or, at least, minimisation) of both import controls (for instance, tariffs and import quotas) and export subsidies.

2.4.3 *Revival of interest in economic policies: the global financial crisis of 2007*

The years following the global financial crisis of 2007. however, saw a backtracking. The financial meltdown was caused by the so-called Sub-prime Crisis in the US housing market in the autumn of 2007. The details of the origin and of the subsequent unfolding of that crisis are not of importance for our purposes here. What is important is its devastating impact on the US economy as a whole in the year 2008 and on the rest of the world economy in the immediately succeeding years. In fact, as per one estimate, the annual growth rate of real GDP of all the countries of the world taken together was –2.2 per cent in the calendar year 2009 (see World Bank, 2011). Never before, since the data on global growth rates started being reported by the international agencies, had the global economy suffered a negative growth rate (i.e. it had *actually* contracted). For a year or so, there was, again, a situation reminiscent of the Great Depression of 1929. There was, however, quick recovery. The credit for that goes to the fact that, learning from experience, governments, especially those of the advanced countries, went all-out for Keynesian economic policies similar to those followed under the New Deal in the USA of the 1930s. They undertook a massive programme of economic expansion by increasing public expenditure, cutting taxes and reducing interest rates. Results were quick to come. In the very next year, growth rates recouped all the world over. In 2010, the global growth rate was 4.1 per cent. Many commentators were pleasantly surprised at such a quick recovery from such a deep crisis.

Around this time, however, the governments in AEs started tightening their purse-strings again in an attempt to contain budget deficits. The demand problem re-appeared. In 2011 the global growth rate fell again (to 2.7 per cent) and remained in the vicinity of that figure till 2019. In fact, the 2007 crisis had laid bare some fundamental weaknesses of the neo-liberal economic philosophy. The effects of these shortcomings have lingered in one form or another. As a result, ever since then, most of the countries of the world have been experiencing demand-deficiency problems in one form or another. At the moment, Keynesian policies seem set to retain their relevance for quite some time in the global economic arena.

2.4.4 The Covid-induced crisis of 2020–21

The latest economic crisis is, of course, the one caused by the Covid-19 pandemic in and around the year 2020–21. Enough has been said in Chapter 1 about the effects of the pandemic on growth rates. At this point, therefore, we shall be brief. Needless to say, the main cause behind the economic slowdown was the lockdowns that had to be imposed in order to contain the spread of the disease. The lockdowns played havoc with both production and trading and resulted in sharp increases in unemployment, poverty and inequality. Clearly, the causes of this particular economic slowdown arose from the supply side. Presently (in 2022), however, lockdowns have been lifted in most of the countries of the world with some notable exceptions (such as parts of China). What remains is the necessity to remain alert about future outbreaks of pandemics. Apart from the obvious health-related issues, there are important economic issues here relating to the development, production and distribution of vaccines. These will be discussed in Chapter 6.

2.5 Industrial deceleration in India during the late 1960s and the early 1970s

While the cases of economic slowdown discussed in Section 2.4 were *global* phenomena affecting most of the countries of the world, there have also been cases where the Indian economy has faced growth slowdowns at times when there was no economic crisis of a global scale. The slowdown that occurred in India during the early 1960s and the early 1970s is a case in point. While India's GDP grew at the rate of 7.45 per cent in 1964–65, the growth rate crashed to the negative figure of –2.64 per cent in the very next year, 1965–66. It remained negative (−0.06 per cent) in 1966–67 too and became negative (–0.55 per cent) again in 1972–73. In the intervening years it was positive but low. The slowdown of the GDP growth rate was largely due to slowdown in the rate of *industrial* growth. For this reason, this particular slowdown has come to be called *industrial deceleration*.

There was considerable disagreement among economists over the question what caused the deceleration. Raj (1976) was of the opinion that *agricultural* growth in the first half of the 1960s had been slow and it was this that caused problems for the industries both from the supply side (by reducing the supply of raw materials produced in the agricultural sector) and from the demand side (by depressing rural incomes, thereby depressing the rural sector's demand for industrial goods). The demand problem was also stressed by Bagchi (1982) and the contributors to the edited volume Nayyar (1994) who pointed out that increasing inequality of income distribution in the country led to stagnant demand for consumer goods and, therefore, led to a fall in demand for capital goods also because capital goods are inputs in the production of consumer goods. Srinivasan and Narayana (1977) were of the view that lack of *public investment* was a major factor here since it prevented the public sector units to increase production fast enough. Since at that time India had a large public sector, this meant that there was a large negative effect on the growth rate of total output of the country, i.e. on the growth rate of GDP. On the other hand, Bhagwati and Desai (1970) put the blame on what they considered to be wrong *industrial policies* which kept many industries reserved exclusively for the public sector units and prevented private producers from entering these fields even though the government itself was finding it difficult to keep up the rate of investment in the public sector. Moreover, even in those lines where private producers were allowed entry, there was a complex bureaucratic system of control which interfered with industrial efficiency. Still other authors have pointed towards the slow pace of technical progress in the industrial sector. For a more comprehensive review of the alternative explanations of the industrial deceleration of these times, see Ahluwalia (1985, 1991).

To quickly summarise our discussion of the events of major economic slowdowns of the past, we may say that, among the *global* slowdowns that we have reviewed, the Great Depression of 1929 and the following years was essentially a demand-side phenomenon. It called for monetary, fiscal and trade policies aimed at increasing aggregate demand in the economy. The slowdown caused by the oil crisis of 1973 arose from supply-side issues. Keynesian demand-management policies were unable to control it. These policies, therefore, fell out of favour. What took their place was supply-side economics and the neo-liberal economic philosophy. The Global Financial Crisis of 2007, however, saw a revival of interest in Keynesian policies. The crisis had its genesis in the housing market in the USA. But when it engulfed the whole US economy and, gradually, the world economy as a whole, the major issue was the demand deficiency arising out of the lack of purchasing power in the hands of the people. On the other hand, the slowdown in India in the late 1960s was caused by a mixture of demand- and supply-side issues afflicting the industrial sector of the economy.

2.6 Microeconomic policies

2.6.1 *Microeconomic policies in a demand-constrained economy*

The reason why we have discussed macroeconomic policies and their evolution in detail is that the long slowdown of the Indian economy in the second decade of the present century (which, as explained in Chapter 1, is the main concern of this book) affected the Indian economy *as a whole* rather than only some specific sectors of the economy. However, there often arise situations where *microeconomic* policies play important roles in fighting slowdowns. Typically, these are policies designed to affect the production of *specific* commodities. For instance, sometimes it so happens that while all sectors of the economy are stagnating, certain sectors are in particularly bad shape and the government wishes to adopt policy measures to help them out over and above the economy-wide (i.e. macroeconomic) measures. Similarly, in *stagflations*, it is sometimes seen that there is inflation in all sectors (while outputs are stagnating) but the prices of some particular commodities are rising at a much faster rate than those of others. Policies that would stimulate the output of these commodities and would make them available to the consumers at lower prices would be warranted in such circumstances.

The most widely used among microeconomic policies are tax and subsidy policies directed at specific commodities. We are talking here about *indirect* (rather than direct) taxes. Leading examples of direct taxes are personal and corporate income taxes[3] and wealth tax while those of indirect taxes are excise duties and sales taxes.[4,5] Notionally, the distinction between a direct and an indirect tax is, roughly, that the burden of a direct tax cannot be *shifted* while that of an indirect tax can be (and usually is). If a person (or a legal entity such as a company) is liable to pay income tax, the burden is entirely on the tax payer. It cannot be transferred to somebody else (or to some other company). A sales tax, however, is *collected* by the government from a seller but that does not mean the seller is paying the tax out of his or her own pocket. Typically, it is added to the price of the commodity and it is the consumer who ultimately bears the burden.[6]

Policies affecting the rates of income and wealth taxes are *macroeconomic* policies since these would affect all persons and companies that are liable to pay these taxes, irrespective of which sectors of the economy they are engaged in. Policies that affect the rates of indirect taxes, however, are typically *microeconomic* policies since these taxes are imposed on specific commodities (goods or services).

Under the federal structure of the Indian constitution it has been a practice of long standing that direct taxes are imposed and collected mainly by the central government,[7] while both the central and the state governments impose and collect indirect taxes. Direct taxes are imposed on *individual* taxpayers (i.e. persons or companies) and the rates of these taxes do not depend on which state of India a taxpayer is located in. From the administrative point of view, therefore, it seems natural that it is the central government that should have the right to fix the rates of these taxes as well as the responsibility for collecting them. Sales taxes, however, are imposed on specific *goods*. It is possible to impose *different* rates of sales tax on the sale of the *same* good in the different states. Moreover, from the point of view of the states this may be desirable. Not all goods are produced in all states. If a good is produced in State A but not in State B, the government of State B would gain little from a sales tax on the good. Moreover, even if all goods are produced in all states, different state governments may wish to tax the goods at different rates, depending on the nature and the magnitude of the problems faced by the *local* producers of the different goods and also on the resource needs of the different state governments. There are, thus, good reasons for leaving sales taxes to the state governments.

In India, for a long time, sales tax was imposed on the basis of the *value* of a *good* sold by a seller. (There was a separate tax on the *services* sold. It was called *service tax*. This was also an indirect tax.) At one stage, however, it was realised that this system involved *double taxation* of some parts of the total output of a good, just as in calculating GDP, there will be double (or multiple) counting if we simply add the values of the outputs of all the producers in the country. (The reader may wish to look back at Note 1 of Chapter 1.) For instance, steel is an input in the production of automobiles. Now, if sellers of steel as well as those of automobiles have to pay sales taxes calculated on the basis of the values of their respective sales, then there is double taxation on the value of steel used in the production of automobiles because it was already taxed when sales tax was collected from the seller of steel who supplied it to the automobile seller. To solve the problem, we can follow the same procedure as we did in GDP calculations: for each seller, calculate the amount of tax to be paid on the basis of his or her *value added* rather than on that of the total value of sales. It was thus that the idea of value-added tax (VAT) was born. In India, VAT replaced the old-fashioned sales tax with effect from 1 April 2005. By that time the change had already taken place in most of the other countries of the world.

In common with the sales taxes of older times, however, VAT had one problem. It was frequently the case that the *rate* of VAT on a good differed widely between the different states of India. From the point of economic theory this was an undesirable situation. It was as if the economy of the country was fragmented into a number of disparate parts instead of being a single integrated one. This hindered the free movement of goods across the length and breadth of the country. Calculations showed that the actual GDP of India was considerably less than what it could have been if there was free movement of goods. At one stage, therefore, a system of goods and services tax (GST) was proposed. The most important feature of the new proposal was that any particular good would be taxed at the same rate all across the country. VAT would be abolished. A corollary of this feature was that the responsibility of collecting these taxes would no longer need to lie with the different state governments. As was the case with direct taxes, GST also would be collected by the central government but the major part of the proceeds would be shared with the states. The taxes on different *services* would continue to be imposed and administered by the central government as before. This would integrate the whole system of indirect taxation in India into a unified one.

The GST proposal was hotly debated for a long time. Many a state government was opposed to the idea of giving up the right to fix the rates of indirect taxes on goods in accordance with the needs and conveniences of the particular state. It was seen that, for *some* goods, replacing VAT by GST would result in revenue losses for *some* states. The system that was ultimately put in place was a compromise and a hotchpotch. A number of goods were left outside the purview of GST. On some of these, there would be central excise duties while on some others there would be state excise. Moreover, on all of these excluded goods, states can continue to levy VAT. All *other* goods as well as all *services* would be under GST (which would be administered by the central government). GST was made effective in India from 1 July 2017. Thus, the current system of indirect taxation in India is a combination of the central and state excise, VAT and the GST systems.

Decreasing the rates of indirect taxes can obviously be effective microeconomic policies in combatting *inflation*, Since these taxes are shifted to the consumer, the (net) prices received by the producers are unaffected by such changes in tax rates. However, the (gross) prices paid by the consumers would decrease. If there is an inflationary situation to start with, the rate of inflation of the consumer prices will fall. In this sub-section, however, we are discussing the problem of output constraints caused by insufficient demand. Are such policies of help on this context? The answer, again, is in the affirmative. The fall in the prices that the purchasers have to pay will induce them to increase the *quantities* purchased. If the commodity in question is a consumer good or service, this will stimulate *consumer demand*. If it is an investment good such as a machine that produces other goods, *investment demand* will increase. Since, as discussed before, both consumption and investment are components of *aggregate demand* in an economy, such policies are potent weapons in the fight against a demand-deficiency problem.[8]

So far we have discussed microeconomic policies aimed at increasing *domestic demand* in an economy. It is obvious, however, that under certain circumstances similar policies can play an effective role in stimulating *net exports* which, as discussed before, is also a component of aggregate demand. Taxes on goods *imported* from abroad are called *customs duties*. (They are also called *tariffs*.) Obviously, these are indirect taxes since these are added to the original (i.e. the foreign) prices of the goods when they are sold in the Indian market. In other words, the importers shift the burden of the tax to the Indian purchasers. Customs duties are administered by the central government since it is immaterial at which geographical point the imports enter the country. Now, an increase in customs duty on an imported good will increase the domestic price of the good. This will decrease the *quantity* of the good that is demanded in India. *If* the value (i.e. price multiplied by quantity) of imports of the commodity also decreases, then net exports (i.e. the value of exports *minus* that of imports) will increase and so will aggregate demand. However, since price rises and quantity falls, in general it is not clear what will happen the value of imports. We have already come across this type of ambiguity in course of our discussion of the effects of devaluation. As we saw there, the net effect will depend on the *elasticity of demand* for the good in the Indian market. Since this elasticity is simply the percentage change in quantity demanded divided by the percentage change (in the opposite direction) in price, it is not difficult to see that elasticity of demand is greater than 1 if and only if, for every 1 per cent *rise* in price, there is a greater than 1 per cent *fall* in demand. Thus, the condition under which a rise in customs duty will "work" (i.e. will increase net exports) is that the elasticity of demand for the imported good in question is greater than 1. If it is less than 1, the policy will fail to work. In fact, it will then have a perverse effect by increasing the value of imports, thereby decreasing net exports. If it is exactly 1, net exports will be left unchanged.

There is an exactly similar policy on the side of *exports*. *Subsidy* can be given to producers who export their outputs instead of selling them in the domestic markets. This would reduce costs of production and enable the producers to reduce prices. This would increase demand for the products in the *foreign* markets and, therefore, the *quantity* of exports. The policy is, again, *microeconomic* since it is targeted specifically towards the producers of *export* goods and since, typically, a country exports only *some* (and not all) of the commodities that it produces. However, whether the *value* of exports would increase would, again, depend upon elasticity of demand. Now it is the elasticity of demand in the *foreign* markets that becomes important. Value of exports and, therefore, *net* exports (because the value of imports is not affected by this policy) will increase if and only if this elasticity is greater than 1. Note also that, unlike in the case of giving subsidies to the producers of goods that are domestically consumed, from the point of the domestic economy this solves a *demand-side* (rather than a supply side) problem. The problem, to start with, was that there was insufficient demand for these products *in the foreign markets*.

2.6.2 Microeconomic policies in a supply-constrained economy

We have seen before that a supply-constrained economy is prone to *stagflation* and that it is difficult to design *macroeconomic* policies that would solve this problem. If there really is *economy-wide* stagflation, the same remark applies to microeconomic policies. For instance, if production is sought to be encouraged by subsidising producers, this may increase output in the relevant sectors but since there is *economy-wide* stagnation to begin with, *all* producers (rather than producers of some particular commodities) would need to be subsidised and this would involve a substantial increase in *government expenditure* which, it may be recalled, is a part of aggregate demand in the economy. Since there was no demand deficiency to start with, and since demand would now increase further, the net effect on the rate of *inflation* is *ambiguous because* there is increase in aggregate demand as well as in aggregate supply. Similar remarks apply to other microeconomic policies: it is difficult to find policies of this type that would *unambiguously* solve the twin problems of output stagnation and soaring inflation.

However, as noted before, it is sometimes the case that while there is inflation in all sectors (and outputs are stagnating), the prices of some particular commodities rise at a much faster rate than those of others or there is a more severe problem of output stagnation in some sectors of the economy than in others. In such cases it is possible to stimulate the production of the relevant commodities by subsidising their production without increasing total government expenditure by very large amounts. Policies focused exclusively on indirect taxes are, however, seldom seen to have unambiguously beneficial effects on the economy in such cases.[9]

2.7 Conclusion

Strictly speaking, this chapter has been little more than a litany of different types of economic policies and an explanation of the terminology associated with them. The discussion, however, has been interwoven with an overview of the evolution of the perspective on economic policies in general against the background of the major events of economic slowdown in the past. Our focus has been on macroeconomic policies. It is seen that both theoretical arguments and historical experience show that for the purpose of combatting the problem of economy-wide imbalances between demand and supply in an economy in today's world the best bet would be to combine the three main types of macroeconomic policies (namely monetary, fiscal and trade policies) rather than focusing exclusively on any one of them. It is also seen, however, that in some cases macroeconomic policies have to be combined with microeconomic ones. All this sets the stage for our main task laid out in Chapter 1, namely to investigate the nature, causes and possible remedies of the long slowdown that has afflicted the Indian economy over the past several years. In the next chapter, we set out on this journey.

Notes

1 By "depression," we mean a state of the economy where the GDP is at a low level. This, however, leaves open the question of how low GDP has to be in order for the economy to be called a depressed one. "Deceleration" is a better-defined

term. Recall, from our discussion in Chapter 1, that an economy is said to be decelerating (or slowing down) if the annual growth rate of GDP is falling over time.

2 The term *quantitative easing* was coined by the German economist Richard Werner in 1995. He suggested this type of policy in the context of Japan.

3 In the eyes of law, a public limited company is a legal entity by itself, distinct from the owners (i.e. the shareholders) of the company. Therefore, not only individuals but also the companies have to pay income tax. Income tax on the companies is called the *corporate income tax*. Usually, the rates of personal and corporate income taxes differ. Note also that a company pays dividend to its shareholders from its *after-tax* income. A shareholder's dividend income becomes his or her personal income. In theory, the shareholder has to pay personal income tax on this part of his or her total income. It is another matter that, in practice, in order to encourage investment in the economy, most governments either exempt dividend income totally from personal income taxation or tax them at very low rates. This is supposed to encourage people to buy company shares and, thus, to enable the companies to raise the money required for investment.

4 In economic theory, a sales tax calculated on the basis of *value* of sales is called an ad valorem tax. A distinction is made between ad valorem and *unit* taxes. A unit tax is a sales tax calculated on the basis of the physical *units* of the good. For instance, it may be required that a car dealer will have to pay a sales tax of, say, Rs. 50,000 for every car that is sold, whatever the price of the car (or the total value of the cars sold) may be.

5 Excise duties and sales taxes are similar in nature. One subtle distinction is that an excise duty is a tax on the *production* of a good while a sales tax, as the name implies, is a tax on *sales*. The burdens of both of these two types of taxes can be shifted on to the consumers. In India, there are *central* excise duties on a list of specified goods. Notable among these are petrol, diesel and tobacco products. There are *state* excise duties on alcoholic liquor for human consumption, narcotics, etc. *Sales taxes*, however, are (or *were* up to 2005) imposed by the state governments only. There are also some cases of overlaps. For instance, on petrol and diesel, there is central excise duty as well as a (state) sales tax.

6 The distinction is a *rough* one. Strictly speaking, changes in rates of a direct tax can also affect the consumer. For instance, a rise in the rate of *corporate income tax* may, in some situations, lead to a fall in the level of output produced by a company and a rise in its price (at least in the future, if not immediately). In this case, it is possible to argue that the consumer bears a part of the burden of the tax, i.e. that the company in question has shifted a part of the tax burden on to the consumer. However, in these cases, usually it is only a *part* of the tax burden that can be shifted in this way. Therefore, the rough distinction made in the text between direct and indirect taxes on the basis of shiftability of the tax burden will suffice for our purposes in this book.

7 We have used the word "mainly" in view of the fact that there is one exception. The right to impose and collect *agricultural income tax* (which is a direct tax) has been left to the state governments. There is a long history here. It has always been difficult for *any* government, state or central, to keep track of the amount of output of an individual farmer and of the prices at which a farmer sells the output in the market or, more usually, to middlemen. For this reason, for a long time, in all countries including India, in lieu of agricultural income tax, there was the system of *land revenue*. The amount of land owned by an individual was more easily observable than the amount of income earned from the land and was considered to be a more convenient basis of taxation. Through the centuries, it was the *local* rulers who was given the responsibility of collecting

land revenue from the land-owners and of transmitting the revenue to the central government. In India, after Independence, the elected state governments took the place of the local rulers. Moreover, the state governments needed resources for defraying their expenses. Although the central government was required to *share* the revenue that it earned from income and wealth taxes with the state governments, it was considered desirable that the states should also have some sources of revenue earmarked exclusively for them. The sales taxes served this purpose to an extent. Following up on the historically developed system of land revenue collection, land revenue was also added to this list of state taxes. At that time, the idea was that gradually the system of land revenue would be replaced by agricultural income taxation. It was thus that it came to be that agricultural income tax was left to the states. Actually, however, while land revenue has been abolished in most states of India by now, little progress has been made towards agricultural income taxation. The state governments used to earn very meagre amounts anyway by way of land revenue. Hence, its abolition has made little difference for the states. The operational difficulties of putting into place an agricultural income tax (noted earlier), however, have remained. On the other hand, *services* are also commodities. (Recall that "commodities" mean goods *and* services.) Thus, a tax on service is an indirect tax. But in India the right to impose and collect a *service tax* has been left at the hands of the central government.

8 Producers can also be encouraged to increase output by increasing the rates of *subsidies*. Such policies, however, presume that the reason for low outputs is, to start with, some problem on the supply side (rather than demand deficiency in the market).

9 It is true that changes in the rates of these taxes do not significantly affect the producers because the burden of the tax is shifted. It may, therefore, seem that a decrease in the rates of these taxes would reduce the severity of the problem of inflation in the prices paid by the consumers while leaving output unaffected. However, while that may be the *immediate* impact of the change, the fall in prices will induce an increase in demand and, since outputs are unchanged, will, after a time lag, add to the pre-existing inflationary pressures in the economy, especially if demand is elastic.

References

Ahluwalia, I.J. (1985): *Industrial Growth in India: Stagnation in the Mid-Sixties*, Oxford University Press, New Delhi.

Ahluwalia, I.J. (1991): *Productivity and Growth in Indian Manufacturing*, Oxford University Press, New Delhi.

Bagchi, A.K. (1982): *The Political Economy of Underdevelopment*, Cambridge University Press, Cambridge.

Bartlett, B. (2010): *The New American Economy*, Macmillan, New York.

Bhagwati, J. and Desai, P. (1970): *India: Planning for Industrialisation*, Oxford University Press, New Delhi.

Brown, E.C. (1956): 'Fiscal policy in the thirties: A reappraisal', *American Economic Review*, 46(5), 857–879.

Canto, V.A., Jones, D.H. and Laffer, A.B. (1983): *Foundations of Supply-Side Economics: Theory and Evidence*, Academic Press, New York.

Friedman, M. and Schwartz, A.J. (1963): *A Monetary History of the United States, 1867 – 1960*, Princeton University Press, Princeton, NJ.

Galbraith, J.K. (1961): *The Great Crash, 1929*, Pelican, New York.

Keynes, J.M. (1936): *General Theory of Employment, Interest and Money*, Macmillan, London.

Nayyar, D. (ed.) (1994): *Industrial Growth and Stagnation: The Debate in India*, Oxford University Press, New York.

Perry, N. and Vernengo, M. (2014): 'What ended the great depression? Re-evaluating the role of fiscal policy', *Cambridge Journal of Economics*, 38(2), 349–367.

Raj, K.N. (1976): 'Growth and stagnation in India's industrial development', *Economic and Political Weekly*, 11(5–7), 223–236.

Reagan, R. (1980): *First inaugural address*, 1981. www.reaganfoundation.org last accessed on 5 August 2022.

Srinivasan, T.N. and Narayana, N.S.S. (1977): 'Economic performance since the third plan and its implications for policy', *Economic and Political Weekly*, 12(6–8), 225–239.

World Bank (2011): *Global Economic Prospects*, World Bank, Washington, DC.

3 Recent trends in economic growth

India and the world

3.1 Growth in the first two decades of the twenty-first century: the global picture

In this chapter, we turn our attention from the previous century to the present. We take a look at the growth performance of the Indian and the world economies since the year 2001. From the Indian perspective, it is necessary to do so since the experience of these years contains important lessons for formulation of policies for the Covid-ravaged economy of the country. In this section, we examine the time path of the growth rate of the *global* economy over the first two decades of the twenty-first century. The corresponding exercise for the Indian case will be taken up in the next section.

Table 3.1 shows the annual growth rates of global GDP as well as those of the GDP of India for the years 2001–20.

In Indian official statistics, the growth rates are actually reported for *fiscal* years (April–March), while in most of the other countries of the world it is reported on the *calendar* year (January–December) basis. For simplicity, the World Bank data source used here displays the growth rate of the Indian economy also in terms of the relevant calendar year. Thus, in the first row of Table 3.1, while the global growth rate of 2.00 per cent is for the calendar year 2001, the Indian growth rate of 4.8 per cent is to be understood to relate to the fiscal year 2001–02. Similar remarks apply to all the other rows in the table.

Two features of the series of global growth rates presented in the second column of Table 3.1 are worth noting. The *first* (and the more obvious) of these is that, over the period covered in the table, the growth rate of the world economy as a whole has gone through ups and downs. This, of course, is hardly surprising. *Cyclical fluctuation* is a standard feature of many economic variables. The global growth rate is no exception.

The *second* feature of the trend in the global growth rate is that, while there have been fluctuations in this rate, *on the average* the growth rate is seen to have remained *almost* the same between the first and the second decades of the century, although there *was* a slight fall in the average rate in the second decade.

DOI: 10.4324/9781003350514-3

Table 3.1 Annual real GDP growth rates, 2001–20: India and the world

Year	*The global economy*	*India*
2001	2.0	4.8
2002	2.3	3.8
2003	3.2	7.9
2004	4.5	7.9
2005	4.0	7.9
2006	4.5	8.1
2007	4.5	7.7
2008	2.1	3.1
2009	−1.3	7.9
2010	4.5	8.5
2011	3.3	5.2
2012	2.7	5.5
2013	2.8	6.4
2014	3.1	7.4
2015	3.1	8.0
2016	2.8	8.3
2017	3.4	6.8
2018	3.3	6.5
2019	2.6	3.7
2020	−3.3	−6.6

Source: www.data.worldbank.org and World Bank (2022). All growth rates are rounded off to one place of decimal.

Some remarks on how to calculate the average of the annual growth rates of an economy over a number of years seem to be in order. In particular, contrary to what one may at first be tempted to assume, this average is *not* the arithmetic mean of the growth rates of the different years. We discuss the matter briefly in a short Appendix to this chapter. Readers uninterested in the computational matter involved here, however, may wish to skip the Appendix and take it on faith that the average growth rate figures referred to at various points in this chapter have been calculated by using appropriate methods.

Before quoting the actual figures for the average growth rates, however, we need to discuss a problem that arises in course of comparing growth rates of an economy in different years when there are *sudden and sharp* falls in the growth rate. The second column of Table 3.1 contains two negative growth rates: those for the years 2009 and 2020. Between 2019 and 2020, there was a big fall of the growth rate from 2.6 per cent to −3.3 per cent, a decline of 5.9 percentage points. Needless to say, the pathetic growth performance in the year 2020 was due to the ravage caused to the global economy by the Covid-19 pandemic. The negative figure for 2009, on the other hand, is explained by the global financial crisis that originated in the USA in 2007 and, within the next two years, engulfed the world as a whole. As a result, between 2008 and 2009, the growth rate fell from 2.1 per cent to −1.3 per cent, a fall of 3.4 percentage points.

For future reference, we note here a peculiar thing that is often seen in such cases of sudden steep falls in the growth rate. That major economic crises will result in sharp falls in the growth rate is not surprising. What is more curious is that if, in the *following* year, there *is* any recovery at all, it often *seems* to be a very impressive one. For instance, in Table 3.1 the global growth rate for 2010 is seen to be 4.5. This was an upward jump of 5.8 percentage points from the value of –1.3 per cent of the preceding year. Similarly, from the "Covid year" 2020 to the year 2021, there was an upward jump of 9 percentage points from –3.3 per cent to 5.7 per cent.

Needless to say, a big upward jump in growth rate is something to be elated about. Economists and statisticians, however, warn us that if there was a big *fall* in the growth rate in the *preceding* year, then this sudden rise in the growth rate may be more an illusion than a reality. In this context they talk about what is they call the *low base effect*. To see what is involved here, first recall that it is GDP that is the summary measure of economic well-being of the economy. The growth rate in a year is calculated by comparing the GDP of the year with that of the previous year. Consider, for instance, four consecutive years, 1, 2, 3 and 4. Suppose that, in years 1 and 2, real GDP was Rs. 99 and Rs. 100, respectively, but that in year 3 it falls to Rs. 90 because of some crisis. The annual growth rate in year 2 is [(100 – 99)/99] or 1.01 per cent (approximately). In the crisis year 3, the growth rate nosedives to [(90 – 100)/100] or –10 per cent. Suppose, now, that in year 4 the economy makes a *small* recovery and GDP increases from 90 to 91. The growth rate in year 4 then would be [(91 – 90)/90] = 1.11 per cent (approximately). Now look at the series of growth rates for the three years 2, 3 and 4: 1.01, –10 and 1.11 per cent. From the crisis year 3 to the post-crisis year 4, there has been a very impressive upward jump in the growth rate from –10 per cent to 1.11 per cent, an increase of as much as 11.11 percentage points. The *upward* jump is *greater* in magnitude than the *downward* fall of 11.01 percentage points (from 1.01 per cent to –10 per cent) that preceded it. Moreover, the current growth rate of 1.11 per cent exceeds the growth rate of the pre-crisis year 2 (which was 1.01 per cent). Thus, so far as the growth rate is concerned, it would seem that the economy is now doing better than it did not only in the crisis year 3 but also in the *pre-crisis* year 2. However, if we consider the state of economic well-being of the country, it turns out that the economy is far from making a recovery. It has not yet achieved the GDP level of Rs. 100 of the pre-crisis year, let alone surpassing that level of GDP. In fact, year 4's GDP, Rs. 91, is way behind even the GDP of year 1 (Rs. 99) from where the story started!

In the example of the previous paragraph, what created the illusion of an impressive recovery in year 4 is the fact that in the preceding year (which was the crisis year) GDP had registered a steep fall. Since the growth rate of a year is calculated as the change in GDP in that year expressed as a percentage of the GDP of the previous year, there has been a big change of growth rates between the years 3 and 4. As the reader can easily check, when a given number is expressed as a percentage of another number, the *lower* is the other number, the higher will be the percentage. The high percentage is the effect of the low *base*. This is the low base effect.

Economists recommend that when our objective is to decipher the *basic pattern underlying the year-to-year changes in the annual growth rate* (whether of the world economy or of a particular country), we should *ignore* not only the growth rate of a *crisis* year (for the simple reason that it is an *exceptional* year and gives an *overly pessimistic* picture of the underlying trend in the growth rate) but also that of the year that *immediately* follows the crisis (because the low base effect would make this an *overly optimistic* or exaggerated figure). In the language of economists and statisticians, both the growth rate of a crisis year and that of the year that immediately follows are *outliers*. They are out of sync with the rest of the data. When the purpose at hand is to get an idea of the long-run trend in the growth rate, it is best to leave outliers out of the picture. We shall have occasion to refer to the low base effect in the later chapters of the book also.

It is now seen that if we ignore the years 2009 and 2010, the average growth rate of the global economy in the first decade of the century (i.e. the average rate of the years 2001 to 2008) was 3.0 per cent approximately. It turns out that if we leave the year 2020 out of the picture, the average rate in the second decade (i.e. the average rate for the years from 2011 to 2019) is seen to be the same: about 3.0 per cent. The global economy grew at approximately the same average rate in the first two decades of the present century.

3.2 The Indian scenario

With the global perspective in the background, we now need to take a look at the time pattern of the growth rate of India over the same period. The global trends are important since global growth influences the growth rate of each individual country through the channels of international trade. Yet, the global pattern refers merely to the *average* of the growth rates of all the countries of the world. There is a good deal of *variation* in the growth rates of the countries around the average. For purposes of policy formulation, each country must pay attention to the lessons learnt from its own *specific* experience and to its own most urgent economic problems.

The growth rates of the Indian economy in the years from 2001 to 2020 are shown in the third column of Table 3.1. As in the case of the global growth rate, here too we see fluctuations in the rate. However, here we see a clear *slowdown* of the growth process in the *second* decade. While the average growth rate of the first decade is calculated to be about 7.0 per cent, that of the second decade is about 6.0 per cent, a decline one full percentage point. It should be noted, however, that in calculating the average growth rate of the second decade, we have left the year 2020 out of consideration on the ground that this year was an outlier.

The time path of the growth rate in India also has another characteristic. It relates to the length of time for which the problem of deceleration in the growth rate of India has *persisted* in the years *immediately preceding the pandemic*. This particular feature of the Indian growth scenario is the central concern of this book. We explain the point in a little detail.

We have already noted that India's growth performance in the first decade of the century was better than that in the second. For the purpose at hand, however, it is also important to look at the phases of *cyclical fluctuations* of the growth rate. The fiscal years from 2003–04 to 2007–08 constituted a particularly glorious period of high growth rates. The average growth rate of these five years was 7.9 per cent. The global financial crisis of 2007–08 brought it down abruptly to 3.1 per cent in 2008–09.

In the following two years, 2009–10 and 2010–11, however, there was remarkable recovery. The growth rate of 7.9 per cent in 2009–10 was quite impressive, since it was one of the highest among the growth rates of the different countries of the world in that year and since the *global* growth rate for the calendar year 2009 was *negative*. In the next year, 2010–11, the growth rate soared even higher to 8.5 per cent. This led to a sense of exuberance among our policy planners. The success was attributed to the successive rounds of economic reforms undertaken over the preceding 20 years or so. It was touted not only as a vindication of the merits of the policies of liberalisation and globalisation initiated in 1991 but also as "proof" of the "fact" that the mixed economy type of policies followed in the earlier decades were wrong.

The dream run, however, came to an end in 2011–12 when the growth rate fell sharply to 5.2 per cent. It is difficult to compare the official data about the growth rates in the years *before* 2011–12 with those that followed because of a shift in the base year used in the calculations. The base year that is used now is 2011–12. Previously, it was 2004–05. In terms of the new base year prices, the annual real GDP growth rates in the eight years from 2012–13 to the last pre-Covid year 2019–20 were as follows: 5.5, 6.4, 7.4, 8.0, 8.3, 6.8, 6.5 and 3.7 per cent. On the basis of these figures, it would seem that in the first four of these eight years there was an upward trend in the growth rate while in the last four the trend was downward.

Many economists, however, are of the opinion, even the upward trend in the first four of these eight years was a result of the base year change. For example, it has been shown that if the 2013–14 growth rate had been calculated with the older base year of 2004–05, the figure would have turned out to be about 4.7 per cent rather than the official figure of 6.4 per cent. Former Chief Economic Adviser to the Ministry of Finance, Arvind Subramanian, has estimated that while, as per official data published by the Government of India, the average growth rate of the GDP between 2011–12 and 2016–7 was close to 7 per cent, calculations based on the old base year of 2004–05 give the figure of about 4.5 per cent. In other words, the official new time series data led to an overestimate of the growth rate for these years by as much as an additive factor of 2.5 percentage points (see Subramanian, 2019). It may also be noted that, as early as in 2015 when the official figures for growth rates of GDP with 2011–12 as the base year was put out, the then Governor of RBI had voiced scepticism about the estimates (see Sheel, 2020, p. 117).

To be sure, periodic revisions of the base year is standard statistical practice in GDP calculations. This is done in order to take cognisance of the fact that with the progress of time many new types of goods and services are produced and consumed in an economy. (For instance, a smartphone was a rare thing in India in 2004–05, but by 2011–12 it was more commonly used.) The comparison between the production levels of a commodity in two different years would be meaningful only if the commodity was produced and used in both of the years. The same is true about the aggregate value of output in an economy which is sought to be measured by GDP. Continuous emergence of new goods and services necessitates shifting of the base year from to time.

While this argument for base year change is quite valid, it is difficult to believe that estimates of GDP growth in a given economy between two given years would change dramatically when the base year changes. At least this has never happened in our country ever before, *although the practice of changing the base year every five or six years has been followed for a long time*. There is, thus, a strong suspicion that, contrary to what the officially announced growth rate figures appear to suggest, the slowdown of the Indian economy in the year 2011–12 noted earlier actually continued into the immediately following years.

Note also that even if we take the *official* new time series of growth rates at face value, it is obvious that the economy started decelerating in 2016–17. In the last pre-Covid year 2019–20, the growth rate reached the low level of 3.7 per cent. If the finding in Subramanian (2019) regarding *overestimation* (by an additive factor of 2.5 percentage points) in the growth rates of the three or four years before 2017–18 is true of the later years also, then a correct estimate of the 2019–20 growth rate would be about 1.2 per cent! India's growth rate has never been as low as that in the preceding 40 years.

Add to all this the fact that in 2020–21 the growth rate of Indian economy was 6.6 per cent. The conclusion seems inevitable that while there have been fluctuations of the annual growth rate in both the first and the second decades of the current century, India has experienced *persistent* economic deceleration in the years immediately preceding the fateful year 2020–21 and there are grounds for suspecting that this has been the case practically throughout the major part of the second decade of this century.

The persistent nature of the deceleration has baffled many observers, especially in view of the fact that this has *not* been the experience of some of our *neighbouring* countries. Table 3.2 shows the growth rates of Bangladesh and Pakistan in the years from 2011–12 to 2020–21 and also displays the Indian growth rates for ready reference. As is seen from the table, between

Table 3.2 Annual real GDP growth rates in Bangladesh, Pakistan and India, 2011–12 to 2020–21

Country	*Fiscal year*									
	11–12	12–13	13–14	14–15	15–16	16–17	17–18	18–19	19–20	20–21
Bangladesh	6.5	6.5	6.0	6.1	6.6	7.1	6.6	7.3	7.9	3.4
Pakistan	2.7	3.5	4.4	4.7	4.7	5.5	4.4	6.2	3.1	-0.9
India	5.2	5.5	6.4	7.4	8.0	8.3	6.8	6.5	3.7	-6.6

Source: www.data.worldbank.org and World Bank (2022)

the years 2017–18 and 2018–19, while the growth rate decreased in India, it increased in Pakistan. Between the next couple of years, while the growth rate fell in both India and Pakistan, it increased in Bangladesh. Between 2019–20 and 2020–21, the growth rate fell in all the three countries. Note, however, that Bangladesh posted a positive growth rate in 2020–21.

It should also be noted that the figures in Table 3.2 are based on official data for all the three countries and do not take into consideration the possibility of overestimation, discussed earlier, in the officially reported growth rates of these years in India.

If we look beyond our immediate neighbours, we can find many other countries whose records of growth performance in the years immediately preceding the pandemic contrast with the monotonic deceleration experienced in India. We refrain from multiplying instances.

3.3 Summary

In this chapter, we have looked at the overall time pattern of the growth rates of the global economy and of the economy of India in the first two decades of the present century and have noted *two* facts that will play important parts in our arguments in the subsequent chapters of the book. *One* of these is that, while the average growth rate of the *global* economy in the first of these two decades was roughly the same as that in the second, in the Indian economy the average rate was unmistakably lower in the second decade. It should be remembered that here we are talking about the *basic trends* of the growth paths in these two decades. Accordingly, we have followed the practice of ignoring the *outlier* years. An outlier year may be a year of a sudden crisis or, in view of the *low base effect*, a year that immediately follows such a crisis. We emphasise, however, that this is *not* to lose sight of the fact that when a crisis hits an economy, the sudden steep fall in the growth rate has tremendous economic consequences for the people and that these will demand the *immediate* attention of the policy planners. On the contrary, what the low base effect reminds us is that the actual growth rate figures for the immediate post-crisis year may give the false impression that the crisis is over and may lead to the false policy conclusion that crisis management measures are no longer necessary.

The *other* fact noted in the chapter is that the contrast with the global picture was not confined merely to the comparative *average* decadal growth rates. There was a *monotonic* decline in the annual growth rate in the years that immediately preceded the pandemic, if not in practically all the years of the second decade (as is alleged by some critics). This was a *distinguishing* characteristic of the economic scenario of India in these years in the sense that this was not the situation in all other countries of the world, not even in some of her closest neighbours.

Appendix to Chapter 3: calculating the average of the growth rates of an economy for a number of years

Consider three consecutive years, 0, 1 and 2. Let the GDPs of an economy in the three years be Y_0, Y_1 and Y_2, respectively. Suppose that the growth rates in years 1 and 2 are r_1 per cent and r_2 per cent, respectively, that is $[(Y_1-Y_0)/Y_0] \times 100 = r_1$ and $[(Y_2-Y_1)/Y_1] \times 100 = r_2$.
Thus,

$$Y_1 = Y_0(1 + r_1/100) \tag{1}$$

$$\text{and } Y_2 = Y_1(1 + r_2/100) \tag{2}$$

The expression $(1 + r_1/100)$ is called the *growth factor* of year 1. Similarly, $(1 + r_2/100)$ is the growth factor of year 2.

Substituting the expression for Y_1 from Eqn. (1) into Eqn. (2), we get

$$Y_2 = Y_0(1 + r_1/100)(1 + r_2/100) \tag{3}$$

Now, what is the *average* growth rate of the economy over the two years 1 and 2? From a common sense point of view, the average (r, say) of the two annual growth rates r_1 and r_2 should be such that if we apply this rate to *each* of the two years 1 and 2, then the GDP of the economy in year 2 should reach the level that is actually achieved by the economy by growing at the rate r_1 in year 1 and at the rate r_2 in year 2. The GDP that is actually achieved is given by the right-hand side of Eqn. (3). The GDP that would have been achieved by growing at the rate r in each of the two years, 1 and 2, is easily seen to be

$$Y_0(1 + r/100)(1 + r/100) = Y_0(1 + r/100)^2 \tag{4}$$

Thus, if r is to be the average growth rate, then the right-hand sides of Eqns. (3) and (4) must be equal. We must have: $(1 + r/100)^2 = (1 + r_1/100)(1 + r_2/100)$.
Thus,

$$(1 + r/100) = \sqrt{[(1 + r_1/100)(1 + r_2/100)]} \tag{5}$$

In words, if we are averaging the annual growth rates of two years, and if the average growth rate is to be r per cent, then the corresponding growth factor $(1 + r/100)$ must be the *square root* of the product of the two growth factors corresponding to the actual growth rates r_1 and r_2.

It is now easily seen that if there are four years, 0, 1, 2 and 3, to start with and if we wish to calculate the average of the annual growth rates of r_1, r_2 and r_3 per cent in the three years 1, 2 and 3, respectively, then, by the same logic as before, we must have:

$$(1 + r/100)^3 = (1 + r_1/100)(1 + r_2/100)(1 + r_2/100)(1 + r_3/100) \qquad (6)$$

In this case, the growth factor $(1 + r/100)$ must be the *cube root* of the product of the three growth factors corresponding to the actual growth rates of the three years.

In the general case, suppose that there are $(n + 1)$ years: the initial year 0 followed by n years 1, 2, 3, . . . ,n. Suppose that $r_1, r_2, r_3, \ldots, r_n$ are the growth rates of economy in the n years 1, 2, 3, . . . ,n, respectively. Then the average growth rate (in percentage terms) is that number r for which the growth factor $(1 + r/100)$ is the n-th *root* of the product of the growth factors of the n different years.

The n-th *root* of the product of a set of n positive numbers is called the *geometric mean* of the numbers. We have now obtained our formula for calculating the average growth rate. The average must be calculated in such a way that the growth factor equals the geometric mean of the different years' growth factors.

To consider a simple example, go back to the simplest case of three years, 0, 1 and 2. Let Y_0 = Rs. 200, Y_1 = Rs. 400 and Y_3 = Rs. 1,200. The growth rate in year 1 is r_1 per cent where $r_1 = [(400 - 200)/200\} \times 100] = 100$. Similarly, the growth rate in year 2 is r_2 per cent where $r_2 = [\{1200 - 400\}/400\} \times 100] = 200$. If r is to be the average growth rate of the two years 1 and 2, our formula requires that $1 + r/100 = \sqrt{[(1 + 100/100)(1 + 200/100)]} = \sqrt{[(1 + 1)(1 + 2)]} = \sqrt{(2 \times 3)} = \sqrt{6} = 2.45$ (approximately). Hence, $r = 100(2.45 - 1) = 145$. Thus, the average growth rate is approximately 145 per cent.

It can now be checked that if this is taken to be growth rate of the economy in *each* of the two years 1 and 2, then, starting from Rs. 200 in year 0, the GDP of the economy would, indeed, reach about Rs. 1,200 in year 2 because then $Y_1 = Y_0(1 + r/100) = 200(1 + 145/100) = 200(1 + 1.45) = 200 \times 2.45 = 490$ so that $Y_2 = Y_1(1 + r/100) = 490(1 + 145/100) = 490 \times 2.45 = 1{,}200$ approximately. (The slight divergence from 1200 is due to the rounding error involved taking $\sqrt{6}$ to be 2.45. Actually, it is not exactly 2.45 but only approximately so.)

Note that the average annual growth rate is *not* the arithmetic mean of the growth rates of the different years (which is the sum of the annual growth rates divided by the number of years). In our example the arithmetic mean would be [(100 + 200)/2] per cent or 150 per cent. However, if we take 150 per cent to be average growth rate of the economy over the two years 1 and 2, then, starting again from the level of Rs. 200 in year 0, GDP of the economy will reach Rs. 200 $(1 + 150/100) = 200(1 + 1.5) = 200 \times 2.5 = 500$ in year 1 and, therefore, in year 2, GDP will reach Rs. $500(1 + 150/100) = 500 \times 2.5 = 1{,}250$

which will be higher than the actual GDP of Rs. 1,200 in year 2. Thus, under this procedure we would get an *overestimate* of the GDP of year 2.

Note also that the average growth rate is *not* the geometric mean of the annual growth rates either. In our example this geometric mean would be $\sqrt{(r_1 r_2)} = \sqrt{(100 \times 200)} = \sqrt{20,000} = 100\sqrt{2} = 100 \times 1.41$ (approximately) = 141. However, if we take 141 per cent to be the average growth rate, then it can be checked that in year 2 the economy would reach a GDP of Rs. $200\,(1 + 141/100)^2$ or about Rs. 1,161 which is, again, off the mark. We now get an *underestimate* of year 2's GDP.

The arithmetic and the geometric means are not the only types of means. There are many other concepts of mean in the statistical literature. None of them, however, would fit the requirement in our present context. As was shown earlier, when we are averaging the annual growth rates of an economy for a finite number of years, what has to be ensured is that the *growth factor* corresponding to the average growth rate equals *the geometric mean of the growth factors* corresponding to the growth rates of the different years. Thus, the notion of the geometric mean does enter the discussion after all. But it is to be applied to growth *factors* rather than to growth *rates* as such.

Finally, so far as the methodology is concerned, there is nothing special about averaging the growth rates of different *years*. The same remarks would apply if, instead, we were averaging these rates for a number of other time units such as months, weeks, decades and centuries.

References

Sheel, A. (2020): "Unravelling India's Growth Story", in Uma Kapila (ed.), *Indian Economy: The Great Slowdown?*, Academic Foundation, New Delhi, 117–120.

Subramanian, A. (2019): 'India's GDP mis-estimation: Likelihood, magnitudes, mechanisms and implications', Faculty Working Paper No. 354, Centre for International Development, Harvard University.

World Bank (2022): *Global Economic Perspectives*, World Bank, Washington, DC.

4 What caused the slowdown?

4.1 Objective of the chapter

In the previous chapter, we noted that there was a slowdown in the pace of economic growth in India in the second decade of the century. In fact, in the last few years of the decade, if not throughout the decade, there was a *monotonic* fall in the annual growth rate. The objective of the present chapter is to find a plausible answer to the obvious question that arises. What *explains* these observed facts? We show that the explanation is to be sought in a combination of (a) the problems of *poverty* and of *inequality* in the distribution of income and wealth in India and (b) the depressed state of the economies of countries that are important trading partners of India.

4.2 Investment is the prime mover

We start by noting that the prime mover of economic growth is *investment* (or *capital formation*). Why that is the case is intuitively obvious both from the demand and the supply sides. It is investment that creates new job opportunities which, in turn, increases demand in the market. Hence, for an economy where the growth rate is low because of *demand deficiency*, the way out of the economic stagnation would be to find a way to increase investment. On the other hand, if the problem is on the *supply* side, that is if the growth rate is low not because there is any lack of demand but because the economy's *productive capacity* is not increasing fast enough, then, too, investment is crucial. It is investment that increases the capital stock of the country and enables it to produce more. This is particularly the case in developing countries such as India where it is the scarcity of capital that is the binding constraint on productive capacity.[1]

The importance of investment for economic growth is borne out by data. We may take the investment to be given by what, in the national income accounts, is called *gross fixed capital formation* (GFCF). Fixed capital is essentially the stock of *physical capital* and comprises such things as machines, buildings, roads and bridges. that are used for the purpose of producing and supplying goods and services. As in the case of GDP, the prefix

DOI: 10.4324/9781003350514-4

gross here means that it *includes* the depreciation of capital. We could, instead, choose to consider *net fixed capital formation* (i.e. to exclude depreciation). However, since, as explained in Chapter 1, GDP includes depreciation of capital, it seems all right to include depreciation in capital formation when we are talking about its relation with GDP.

GFCF, however, *excludes* such things as changes in stocks and expenditure incurred in acquiring valuables. The sum of GFCF, changes in stocks and expenditure on valuables is known as *gross capital formation* (GCF) and is to be distinguished from GFCF. The reason for taking GFCF, rather than GCF, of a year to be the indicator of investment in an economy in the year should be obvious. For instance, an increase in the accumulated stock of a produced commodity is not a part of an addition to the productive capacity of the economy that is achieved in the given year.

Since the purpose here is to understand the importance of investment in determining the growth *rate*, we consider the *rate of investment* rather than investment itself. The rate of investment is investment (i.e. GFCF) expressed as percentage of GDP. The investment rate, thus, is a measure of the percentage or proportion of the current year's output in the economy that is set aside for the purpose of adding to the capacity of the economy to produce commodities in future.

From national income accounts we also get information on *private* and *public* investment separately. The *rates* of private and public investment are taken to be given by GFCF in the private sector as percentage of GDP and GFCF by the government as percentage of GDP, respectively.

The close relation between GDP growth rate and GFCF (as percentage of GDP) is verified from data if we look at the values of these two variables across countries. Table 4.1 displays these values for a few selected countries in the year 2019.

The data in Table 4.1 can be used to argue that the ranking of countries by GDP growth rate is quite similar to their ranking by GFCF as percentage of GDP. Spearman's rank correlation coefficient has a high value of 0.65.[2] We say that there is high *rank correlation* between the rate of economic growth and the rate of investment.

Table 4.1 Annual GDP growth rate (per cent) and GFCF as percentage of GDP in selected countries, 2019

Country	*Bangladesh*	*China*	*India*	*Pakistan*	*Sri Lanka*	*UK*	*USA*	*EU*	*Russian Federation*
Growth rate (%)	7.9	6.0	3.7	3.1	2.3	1.7	2.3	1.8	2.2
GFCF (% of GDP)	30.47	42.82	28.75	13.72	27.11	17.72	20.96	21.85	21.13

Source: www.data.worldbank.org and World Bank (2022)

Table 4.2 Private, public and total GFCF as percentages of GDP and the rate of growth of GDP in India, 2011–12 to 2019–20

Year	*Private GFCF (% of GDP)*	*Public GFCF (% of GDP)*	*GFCF (% of GDP)*	*Growth rate of GDP (%)*
2011–12	26.97	7.54	34.31	5.2
2012–13	26.42	7.02	33.44	5.5
2013–14	24.20	7.08	31.30	6.4
2014–15	23.08	7.00	30.08	7.4
2015–16	21.28	7.45	28.73	8.0
2016–17	21.27	6.92	28.19	8.3
2017–18	21.46	5.72	28.18	6.8
2018–19	22.11	7.08	29.19	6.5
2019–20	21.82	6.93	28.75	3.7

Source: For Private GFCF and GFCF, www.data.worldbank.org, and for GDP growth rate, Table 3.2 of Chapter 3 in the text. Public GFCF has been calculated as the difference between GFCF and Private GFCF.

In Table 4.1, we compared the rate of investment of *different* countries with their growth rates in a *given* year. We may also compare the values of these two variables in a *given* country in *different years*. Table 4.2 displays GFCF as percentage of GDP and GDP growth rate in India in the second decade of the present century. We have, however, deliberately left out the outlier year 2020–21. For later reference, the table also shows private and public GFCF, again as percentages of GDP, separately.

The calculated value of the Spearman rank correlation coefficient now is about 0.6. Again, therefore, we conclude that in India, over the years shown in the table, the rate of investment has been significantly positively correlated with the growth rate.

It is necessary, of course, to remind ourselves that *correlation* does not imply *causation*. The fact that the data show that, both across countries at a given time and across time in a given country, the rate of investment and the growth rate have a tendency to move in the same direction does not constitute a proof of the assertion that investment causes growth. As far as the data shown here are concerned, it may as well be the case that it is growth that causes investment. Then, too, we would have a high and positive rank correlation coefficient between GFCF as percentage of GDP and the growth rate of GDP.

It is in view of this possibility that we started our discussion in this section with the *theoretical* reasons for expecting investment to be the *cause* of growth. The data came later as a *verification* of these theoretical reasons. In other words, our methodology has been to use the fact that. while correlation does not imply causation, causation certainly implies correlation. Therefore, we *expect* the data to reveal a positive correlation. Tables 4.1 and 4.2 show that this expectation is conformed.

Moreover, even without referring to economic theory, one can, in such cases, also make of use of purely statistical techniques, called *causality tests*.

These tests are particularly useful in *time series analysis*. If, over time, two variables move in a manner that in some sense *related* (or *cointegrated*, to use the technical term), then by applying these tests it is possible to say which of the variables *causes* the other or whether there is *two-way dependence* between the variables (i.e. each causes the other). This type of research has been done on Indian data on the relation between investment rate and growth rate. A detailed discussion of this type of work would, however, necessarily be of a rather technical nature. We take the liberty of merely reporting the main result relating to Indian data. The curious reader may see, for instance, the paper by Jangili (2011) By considering the time period from 1950–51 to 2007–08, the paper shows that the causation runs more from saving and investment to growth than in the reverse direction. While a strong point of the paper is the long span of the time series, the period considered does not include the specific years of our special interest (i.e. the pre-Covid years of the 2010s). However, Saxena and Fouzdar (2020) consider data for the period from 1992 to 2018 to reach a similar conclusion regarding the direction of causality. Higher saving and investment lead to higher economic growth but the reciprocal causality is not observed.

Before ending this section, however, we note that what we have shown here is the importance of the rate of investment in determining the rate of economic growth. It is not the intention to suggest that it is the *sole* determinant. If that was the case, the rank correlation coefficient between these two variables would always be exactly 1. Thus, there may be other factors, including social and cultural ones, that may also have effects on the growth rate. It is the crucial role of the rate of investment in this context that is the main lesson of this section.

In a sense, however, our discussion in this section has only served to replace one question by another. In answering the question why there was a slowdown in the growth rate of the Indian economy even before Covid arrived on the scene, we must now ask why the rate of investment declined in these years. That there *was* a significant fall in this rate is evident from Table 4.2 itself. As is seen from the fourth column of the table, GFCF as percentage of GDP fell continuously from 34.31 per cent in 2011–12 to 28.18 per cent in 2017–18. It rose to 29.19 per cent in the next year but fell again to 28.75 per cent in 2019–20 which was the last pre-Covid year. In the year 2020–21 (not shown in the table), it fell further to 27.09 per cent. The next section is devoted to the task of explaining the decline in the rate of investment.

4.3 Explaining the fall in the investment rate

4.3.1 Fall in the rate of private investment

Total investment is the sum of private and public investments. However, it is private investment that has long been the dominant part of total investment in India and has continued to be so in recent years. For instance, as is seen from Table 4.2, in 2011–12 while the percentage of private GFCF in GDP was 26.97, that of total GFCF was 34.31. It follows that the ratio of private GFCF to total GFCF in that year was 26.97/34.31 = 0.79 (approximately). In other words, private investment constituted about 79 per cent of total investment in that year. In 2019–20, it was (21.82/28.75) × 100 = 76 per cent of the total. Similar exercises for all other years (including years in the earlier decades not shown in the table) would lead to similar findings.

Table 4.2 also shows that the rate of public investment (i.e. public GFCF as percentage of GDP) has gone through year-to-year fluctuations in the past ten years. But no clear downward or upward trend is discernible. The pronounced downward trend observed in the rate of *total* investment must, therefore, be the consequence of a similar trend in the rate of *private* investment which is its dominant component. Indeed, in the table we see the same picture of a nearly monotonic decline in the private investment rate as is the case with total investment.

For this reason, in looking for the reasons behind the persistent decline in the rate of investment, we shall concentrate on the factors causing the similar trend in the rate of *private* investment.

4.3.2 *The role of growth of demand in inducing private investment*

At one stage, in 2017–18 to be precise. it was noticed that the rate of *public* investment had been falling for a couple of years. It was 5.72 per cent in that year while it had been 6.92 per cent in 2016–17 and 7.45 per cent in 2015–16. At that time, it was argued by some observers that the explanation of the falling rate of *private* investment lay in the *complementarity* between public and private investments. When public investment falls, so does private investment. Stated in this form, however, this explanation does not seem to be adequate because, as we have just remarked earlier, no persistent decline in the rate of public investment has been observed in India over the period considered in Table 4.2. It was more a case of cyclical fluctuations.

The more important reason behind the sluggish behaviour of private investment is to be sought in the role of *aggregate demand* in the economy in inducing investment. The important point here relates to the *dual* nature of investment. Investment is related both to *current demand* and to *future demand*. On the one hand, investment is a component of the *current year's* aggregate demand because a part of the current year's output has to be set aside for the purpose of investment. On the other hand, the *purpose* of investment is to add to the capacity to produce commodities *in future*. Now, investors will be induced to make investments *in the current period* only if they feel confident that there will be enough demand for the commodities that would be produced *in future*. Thus, investment is motivated by *anticipated* future demand conditions. Moreover, private producers most often base their anticipations about the *future* on their *present and past* experiences.

The upshot of all this is that while investment itself is one component of aggregate demand, it is also *derived* from aggregate demand and, therefore, it depends on the *other* components of aggregate demand. Hence, if the process of a falling rate of private investment in the Indian economy that has been observed in the past decade is to be arrested, attention must be paid to the factors inhibiting the growth of these other components. Note that it is not enough to ensure that demand does not fall. It must actually *increase*. To repeat, investment adds to the capacity to produce. Hence, private producers would be induced to invest only if demand is expected to increase in future.

4.4 Factors constraining the growth of consumption demand

4.4.1 *Importance of* private *consumption in total consumption*

In order to identify the factors constraining the growth of aggregate demand, we look again at the components of demand. By far the most important part of the aggregate demand for GDP in India is *private consumption*. For instance, in the year 2019–20 as much as 57 per cent of the aggregate demand came from this source alone. Government consumption accounted for roughly 11 per cent of aggregate demand while the contribution of total (i.e. private plus public) investment was about 33 per cent. (The careful reader will notice that these three percentages add up to more than 100! This is explained by the fact that the contribution of the other component of demand, net exports, in this year was *negative*, i.e. our exports fell short of our imports.)

We, therefore, start with private consumption and devote the major part of this section (Section 4.4) to this component. For this reason, we shall often drop the prefix "private" and simply call it "consumption."

4.4.2 *Inequality of income and wealth distributions*

For quite some time now the *main* constraints on the growth of consumption in India have been the problems of *inequality* and *poverty*. We shall discuss these issues in some detail blow. Section 4.4.2 is devoted to the matter of inequality. Start by noting that even if total income or GDP remains fixed (or rises very slowly), consumption demand in an economy can be boosted considerably by transferring income from the rich to the poor and the lower middle classes (i.e. by *reducing* the inequality of income distribution) because the poor and the middle class spend a greater proportion of their income on consumption than the rich. Similarly, since consumption of an individual depends not only on his or income but also on accumulated wealth, reducing the inequality of the distribution of *wealth* will also boost total consumption in the economy. There is, however, no unique measure of inequality of a given distribution. The most widely used measure is the so-called Gini coefficient. It is a number computed by applying a statistical formula. The number lies between 0 and 1. The closer it is to 1, the greater is the inequality of the distribution. But the statistical literature contains many other measures of inequality.

Most economists are of the opinion that the pre-Covid years witnessed an *increase* in the inequality of income distribution. Until recently, however, there were no official data on the distribution of *income* in India. What we had (at least for the years up to 2011–12) were data on the distribution of *consumption expenditure*. According to one estimate the value of the Gini coefficient of the distribution of consumption expenditure in India was 0.357 in 2011. By international standards this was not too high a degree of inequality. The catch, however, is that most other countries report the Gini value of the distribution of *income* while the Indian Gini is that of consumer expenditure. Only a part of household income, however, is spent on consumption. The other part is saving and since the distribution of saving is expected to be even more unequal than that of consumption, common sense tells us that the income Gini would be higher than the consumption Gini. As per one estimate, the income Gini for India in 2011–12 would be about 0.50 (see Chancel and Piketty, 2019). This places India among the most highly unequal economies of the world at that time. Among the least unequal of the countries were the Scandinavian countries where the Gini coefficient ranged between 0.25 and 0.29. Many other AEs, including the UK, Germany and Japan, also had income Gini values between 0.31 and 0.37. For the USA, the values was about 0.40. Some of the Asian neighbours of India follow the system of reporting the Gini coefficients of consumption rather than income. But most of these countries too, including Bangladesh and Pakistan, had lower values of Gini at the time and continues to do so up to the present moment.

All this is about the situation in 2011–12. For the years *after* 2011–12, there are no official data in India even for consumer expenditure! The standard sources of data on consumer expenditure in India are the five yearly large sample surveys conducted by the NSO (previously called the National Sample Survey Office (NSSO)). *After* 2011–12, the next survey was scheduled for 2016–17. It was delayed by a year and carried out in 2017–18. For some reason, however, the government has not yet made the report of this survey public.

Unavailability of estimates of the Gini coefficient, however, does not mean that absolutely nothing can be said about the direction of change in the inequality of income in India in recent years. In fact, it can be argued that not too much should be read into the values of any *particular* measure of inequality, whether it is the Gini coefficient or any other measure of inequality. As we have already remarked, Gini is not the only measure of inequality, although it is the most popular one. There are many others. It is quite possible that *different* measures of inequality not only may give different estimates of the level of inequality in a country at a *given* time but can also give *different answers to the question whether inequality has increased or decreased over time*. It is possible, for instance, that in India between two given years the Gini coefficient *decreases* while the value of another measure of inequality *increases*.

It turns out, however, that it is possible to say *some* useful things about the time trend of inequality of income or wealth even if the Gini coefficient (or some other particular measure of inequality) cannot be calculated. Consider any two years. If, for each of these years, we know what percentages of the total income goes to, say, the richest 10 per cent, the middle 40 per cent and the poorest 50 per cent, then, by comparing between these percentages in the two years, it is sometimes possible to get *some* idea about the *direction of change* of inequality, that is about whether overall inequality has *increased or decreased*, even though it is not possible to say exactly what the degree of inequality is in each of the two years. For instance, if we see that the richest 10 per cent of the people are now getting a *greater* percentage of total income than before (which *means* that the bottom 90 per cent of the population is getting a *smaller* share), then, in an intuitive sense, inequality has increased.

This type of judgement about the *directions of change* in the inequality of income distributions over time has now been made possible for many countries by a new body of research that has come into existence in recent decades. The findings of this line of research are now available on the website of World Inequality Database. By making ingenious use of various unconventional data sources (such as income tax returns), this type of research has been able to reconstruct large parts of the income distribution in India for a long series of years starting from the second decade of the twentieth century. To a large extent this has solved the problem of non-availability of income distribution data. (As we have seen earlier, what we had in India before was *consumer expenditure* data and that too for only the years for which there were published reports of consumer expenditure surveys.) We say that the problem has been solved "to a large extent" but not entirely. For some years, especially for those that are now in the remote past, it has not been possible to reconstruct the whole income distributions covering the entire population. Nevertheless, the *broad* trends of changes in the distributions of income and wealth in India over the years and decades have now become much clearer from the findings of this line of research.

In Table 4.3, we show the percentage shares of different population groups in total income in India in 2001, 2011 and 2019. We have, again, deliberately focused on the state of affairs prevailing *before* Covid hit the economy in 2020.

As is seen from the table, both between 2001 and 2011 and between 2011 and 2019, the share of total income going to the *top* 10 per cent of the population in the income hierarchy *increased* while the share of the *middle* 40 per cent as well as that of the *bottom* 50 per cent *decreased*. Obviously,

Table 4.3 Income inequality in India: percentage shares of population groups in total income in 2001, 2012 and 2019

Year	*Top 1%*	*Top 10%*	*Middle 40%*	*Bottom 50%*
2001	16.3	42.0	39.9	18.1
2011	21.5	55.2	31.1	13.7
2019	21.7	57.1	29.8	13.1

Source: www.wid.world

there was an *increase in the inequality of the income distribution* in the first two decades of the present century. This conclusion is not dependent on the use of any particular inequality index. In other words, in this case, whichever inequality index we use, whether it is the Gini index or not, we shall reach the same conclusion regarding the *direction of change* of inequality. The possibility (noted earlier) that using different inequality indices may, in some cases, result in different conclusions regarding the direction of change does not arise in the present context. The Indian case is such that *all* inequality indices will yield the same conclusions. They may, of course, differ in their answers if we ask *exactly* what the *degree of inequality* was in each of the three years. Note, however, that our main interest is in the direction of change. What we mainly want to know is whether inequality *increased* or *decreased* over the time period considered in the table. To that question we get a definitive answer: it increased.

As additional information, the table also shows the share of total income going to the top 1 per cent of the population. It is quite dismaying to note that just 1 per cent of the people of the country cornered as much as 16.3 per cent of the total income in 2001 and that their share increased even further in course of the following two decades. In the last pre-Covid year, 2019, they got 21.7 per cent.

At the moment 2019 seems to be the last year for which there is reliable information regarding the distribution of income in India. There are, however, indications that inequality of income has tended to increase after this date. This, course, is not surprising since the country has been in the grip of Covid in this phase and it goes without saying that at times of such widespread disasters the poor suffer greater economic damages than the rich (see Chancel et al., 2022). Oxfam (2022) states that as many as 84 per cent of the Indian households witnessed a decline in income in the period from March 2020 to November 2021 while over the same period the number of Indian billionaires rose from 102 to 142.

Consumption of an individual, however, depends not only on his or her current income but also on accumulated wealth. While the point is valid in general, it is of particular importance in a country such as India where the majority of the population does not have the benefits of a social security network. It is private wealth that a person has to fall back upon in case of

Table 4.4 Wealth inequality in India: percentage shares of population groups in total household wealth in 2001, 2012, 2019 and 2021

	Top 1%	*Top 10%*	*Middle 40%*	*Bottom 50%*
2001	23.9	55.1	36.6	8.3
2011	31.6	63.1	30.5	6.4
2019	31.7	63.9	30.1	6.0
2021	33.0	64.6	29.5	5.9

Source: www.wid.world

an emergency. Under these circumstances, the inequality in the distribution of *wealth* also is an important constraint on aggregate consumption in much the same way as the inequality of income.

It has to be remembered, however, that just as, in the case of income, it is *household* income (rather than company income) that is important as a determinant of private consumption, in case of wealth it is household wealth that we have to concentrate on. Table 4.4 shows the percentage shares of various population groups in the total household wealth in India in selected years. In this case we have information for the year 2021 also.

As is seen from Table 4.4, the direction of change in the inequality of wealth distribution in India in the first two decades of the century was exactly similar to that in the inequality of income distribution. The share of total wealth going to the *top* 10 per cent of the population in the wealth hierarchy *increased* monotonically while the share of the *middle* 40 per cent as well as that of the *bottom* 50 per cent *decreased* monotonically. There was, thus, an *increase in the inequality of the wealth distribution*. Commentators have expressed particular concern with the fact that the share of the wealthiest 1 per cent of the population in total wealth has not only increased monotonically but also reached an unusually high level, about one-third of the total, even before the Covid pandemic. Again, these conclusions are not dependent on the use of any particular inequality index.

4.4.3 *Other dimensions of inequality*

We have discussed inequality of the overall distribution of income and wealth in detail because these had major impacts on the level of aggregate private demand in India in the 2010s. However, some special aspects of the issue of inequality (such as inequality of the probability of retrenchment, inequality of financial inclusiveness and gender discrimination) were also at work and made things worse. For instance, among wage earners it was those who worked at the lowest wage levels that faced the highest probability of being thrown out of jobs when demand for the produced goods nosedived because of the increase in overall inequality of income and wealth. Skilled workers enjoying relatively high wages escaped the first rounds of retrenchment because skills were in short supply and employers were wary of losing contacts with those who had them. Thus, along with the increase in overall inequality, there was increased inequality *within* wage-earners. Similarly, inequality of financial inclusiveness implied that, among producers, those who were most in need of loans for their working capital needs were precisely those that did not have access to such loans. Gender discrimination explains why female workers were affected more severely by the growth slowdown caused by overall inequality than their male counterparts.

4.4.4 Unemployment

While official inequality estimates are not available for the years after 2011–12, there are official estimates of *unemployment*. An increasing trend in unemployment is a pointer towards the likelihood of a similar trend in inequality. As per official estimates, the rate of unemployment in India was 2.3 per cent in India in 2004–05 and 2.2 per cent in 2011–12. In 2017–18, however, as per the Periodic Labour Force Survey of that year (published in 2019), it soared to 6.1 per cent. (see Acharya, 2020, p. 122). These are figures for the rate of "open" unemployment. Economists distinguish between "open" and "disguised" unemployment. A person is a disguised unemployed if he or she *apparently* is employed but the income earned is too low for a decent living. An open unemployed has no income at all and lives by what economists call *transfer income* (i.e. money received as charity from friends, relatives or the government), by borrowing and dissaving or by illegal activities.

4.4.5 Poverty

While precise data on disguised unemployment are not available, note that total number of the two types of unemployed persons (open and disguised) can be taken to be the number of *poor* people on the country. So far we have been talking about inequality. One special aspect of the problem of inequality is *poverty*. While inequality refers to the distribution of income or wealth among all sections of the population, the notion of poverty focuses on those individuals whose incomes fall below a specified minimal amount called the *poverty line*. The most widely used measure of poverty in an economy is the Head Count Ratio (also called the *poverty rate*) which is simply the proportion of poor people in the population of the country. This will do for our purposes although, again, the literature contains other, technically more sophisticated measures of poverty. Obviously, a reduction in poverty will also increase aggregate consumption in the economy.

Poverty in India is, again, measured in terms of consumption expenditure rather than income. Poverty line is the level of *expenditure* required to reach a specified minimal level of living. One's actual expenditure is then compared with the required minimal level in order to determine whether one is poor or not. Now, up to 2011–12, India's record in alleviating poverty was considerably better than that in reducing inequality. At least, this was the case so far as poverty rate, that is the Head Count Ratio was concerned. In the years 1993–94, 2004–05 and 2011–12 this rate was 45.3, 37.2 and 21.9 per cent, respectively. Thus, there was a steady and significant decline in the incidence of poverty in India over these years.

By contemporary international standards also, we see that while both in 1993–94 and in 2004–05, the poverty rate ratio *was* quite high in India, that was not the case in 2011–12. Most of the *developing* economies, including Bangladesh, were in an even worse situation in 2011–12. Pakistan had about the same poverty rate as India. Sri Lanka had a much lower value of 1.9 per cent in 2012. It, however, had a much smaller population than India. A given percentage reduction in the poverty rate calls for a much greater effort (in terms, for instance, of government budget allocations for poverty alleviation measures) in a country with a larger population. From that point of view, a comparison with China (whose poverty rate was 12.7 in 2011) is more meaningful here. The AEs, of course, also had lower poverty rates than India. Altogether, therefore, it seems fair to say that in the first decade of the twenty-first century India's record of poverty alleviation was considerably better than that of inequality reduction.

However, this was only true of the 2000s. What can we say about the *subsequent* trend of poverty in India? Again, the non-availability of the report of the NSO Consumer Expenditure Survey of 2017–18 in the public domain means that there is no official estimate of the Head Count Ratio of poverty for that year. An unofficial version of *some* parts of the report, however, has appeared in a section of the media. As per this version, the proportion of the poor among the population in India increased between 2011–12 and 2017–18 from 21.9 per cent to about 22.8 per cent. Actually, even in the reports of the previous surveys, NSO did not report the poverty rates (i.e. the Head Count Ratio) for the country as a whole. It reported this rate for the rural and the urban sectors separately. Researchers then calculated the country-wide poverty rate as the weighted average of the two rates by using the proportions of the rural and the urban populations in the total population as the weights. For 2017–18, the finding, based on the unofficial version of the report, was that since the previous survey there had been a *fall* in the urban poverty rate and a *rise* in the rural poverty rate. However, since the majority of the population was in the rural sector, the effect of the rise in rural poverty dominated and there was a rise in the overall poverty rate of the country.[3]

Moreover, work based on the unofficial version of the findings of the 20217–18 survey also reports that there was been a *fall* in the *aggregate private consumer expenditure* in the economy between the years 2011–12 and 2017–18. A fall in aggregate consumption between two successive surveys of the NSO (or the NSSO as it was previously known) is something that had never happened in India over a very long period. As we have had occasions to note more than once, the Indian economy contracted (i.e. GDP itself, not just the *growth rate* of GDP, declined) in 2020–21 and this was something that had not happened in a long time before that year. Although we are now talking of aggregate *consumption* (rather than aggregate income or output which is measured by GDP), what we now see is a pointer towards the *possibility* that *contraction* in the Indian economy might have started as early as in 2017–18 or even earlier than that. At least, this strengthens the suspicion of overestimation in the official figures for the growth rate of India in the years following 2013–14 that we have already discussed in Chapter 3.

Be that as it may, no information on poverty in India seems to be available for the intervening years between the 2017–18 and 2020–21. It is generally known, however, that in 2020–21 Covid brought untold economic misery to large sections of the population.

Altogether, therefore, it seems reasonable to conclude that while, in the first decade of the present century, the Indian economy witnessed an *increase* in inequality but a *decrease* in poverty, in the second decade both inequality and poverty has *increased*. This has acted as a constraint on the growth rate of private consumption expenditure in India in recent years. In fact, between the years 2015–16 and 2019–20 this rate *fell* almost continuously from 7.86 per cent to 5.91 per cent, barring a slight increase in the year 2018–19. In 2020–21, it was -7.25 per cent, almost the same as India's GDP growth rate in that year.

4.5 Slowdown in the growth rate of government expenditure

Since government expenditure is a part of aggregate demand, it is also pertinent to note the slowdown of the growth rate of this particular source of demand over a large part of the second decade of the century. Although this slowdown was not a continuous one, the basic downward trend is clear enough. Data are available on the growth rate of the government's total consumption expenditure. This type of expenditure includes all *government purchases of goods and services* (including wages and salaries of government employees) and also most types of expenditure related to national defence and security. However, it does not include any type of capital expenditure. The growth rate of this variable was 7.6 per cent in 2014–15. It fell to 7.5 per cent in 2015–16 and fell further to 6.1 per cent in 2016–17. There was a surge to 11.9 per cent in 2017–18 because that was the year of implementation of the central government's Seventh Pay Commission recommendations. But in the very next year, 2018–19, the growth rate plunged again to just 6.7 per cent. In the last pre-Covid year of 2019–20, it fell further to 3.4 per cent. In the Covid year 2020–21, there was a marginal rise to 3.6 per cent. All the growth rate figures mentioned here are in sharp contrast to the high growth rate of 14.2 per cent in 2009–10.[4] Thus, while it was the constraints on the growth of *private* consumption that were the major factors behind the slowdown of the GDP growth rate, deceleration in the growth of government expenditure also played a role. Needless to say, this deceleration was caused by the government's policy decision to limit its fiscal deficit.

4.6 External demand: falling growth rate of exports

As we have seen earlier, inequality in India has been high and increasing not only in the *second* decade but also in the *first*. How, then, do we explain the fact that India was in a phase of relatively *high* rate of GDP growth in the 2000s? *One* possible explanation can be that, as noted before, there was considerable progress in *poverty reduction* in India in those years. To some extent, this may have *counteracted* the effect of increasing inequality.

Most economists, however, are of the opinion that the creditable growth performance of the of the 2000s was more importantly due to the creditable *export* performance. So far, in our discussion, we have restricted ourselves to the constraints on the demand for goods and services *within* the country. It is this *domestic* demand that is constrained by the problems of inequality and poverty prevailing in the economy. What happened in the 2000s was that, faced with this problem of the domestic economy, the producers turned increasingly towards *external* markets and were able to export a good part of their output. Recall that *net exports* (i.e. exports minus imports) is also a component of the aggregate demand. Exports, therefore, served, at least partly, to get around the domestic demand-deficiency problem.

Data seem to lend support to this view. As per World Bank data, between the years 2001–02 and 2010–11 the value of India's exports of goods and services as percentage of GDP increased steadily from 12.6 per cent of GDP to 22.4 per cent. It is unlikely to be accidental that the 2000s were a decade of fast GDP growth in India. Clearly, exports constituted an important source of demand for Indian producers and made up for the deficiency of domestic demand to a significant extent. The 2010s, on the other hand, saw a decline in these percentage figures. From a high point of 25.4 per cent in 2013–14, exports declined to 18.4 per cent of GDP in 2019–20.[5]

The increasing importance of exports in the Indian economy in the 2000s was also reflected in the figures for the annual *growth rates* of the value of India's exports. The picture, however, changed sharply in the 2010s. Table 4.5 displays the growth rate of exports for all the years from 2001–02 to 2020–21. Despite the year-to-year fluctuations of the growth rate, the sharp contrast between the upbeat picture of the 2000s and the relatively lacklustre performance in the 2010s is brought out quite clearly by the numbers in the table. The average growth rate of exports in the 2010s turns out to be *by far smaller* than that in the 2000s. Note also that the export deceleration started long before the Covid pandemic.

Table 4.5 Annual growth rates (per cent) of India's exports of goods and services, 2001–02 to 2020–21

Year	*Growth rate (%)*
2001–02	4.31
2002–03	21.09
2003–04	9.58
2004–05	27.18
2005–06	26.09
2006–07	20.39
2007–08	5.87
2008–09	14.78
2009–10	-4.83
2010–11	19.48
2011–12	15.49
2012–13	6.81
2013–14	7.79
2014–15	1.78
2015–16	-5.64
2016–17	4.98
2017–18	4.57
2018–19	12.35
2019–20	-3.31
2020–21	-4.68

Source: www.data.worldbank.org

The deceleration in the growth rate of exports in the 2010s would have been easy to explain if there was a significant deceleration in the *growth rate* of the *world economy* in these years because that would have an obvious negative effect on the foreign demand for India's exports. However, as we saw in the previous chapter, there was no significant difference between the average growth rate of the world economy in the 2000s and that in the 2010s.

To explain the fall in the growth rate of Indian exports, therefore, we have to look *specifically* at countries that were important *export destinations* for India. The country with the largest share in India's exports both in the 2000s and in the 2010s was the USA. The UAE, China, the UK and the European countries were (and continue to be) among her other important export destinations. In some of these countries (notably, China, the UK and some of the European countries), there *was* a deceleration of the GDP growth rate in the 2010s. This had a negative effect on the growth of their demand for India's exports.

So far as the largest single purchaser of Indian goods and services, the USA, was concerned, however, the explanation was a little different. While there *was* a fall in the US demand for Indian exports in the 2010s, the reason did not lie so much in any growth deceleration in the USA. The US growth rate fluctuated but there was no significant deceleration. The explanation, rather, lay in some changes in the ways in which major US producers, especially the large multinational companies headquartered in the USA, organised their production.

In the 2000s and also in the first few years of the 2010s, an important part of the system was the so-called "international value chain." This term refers to the production system under which a company breaks up its production process into different parts and carries out each part in a country where some input crucial to that particular part is in abundant supply. The different parts are then put together to finish the production process. (Needless to say, it is technological progress and the consequent dramatic reduction in the costs of international transport of goods and of international communication that made this system profitable.) Thus, a US company may carry out in India those parts of its production process that are labour-intensive or that require the writing of software programmes because unskilled labour as well as software development skills are available in India at cheaper rates than in the USA. Typically, some Indian company would be engaged under contract for these purposes. Note that when the Indian company sends the (possibly semi-finished) product to the US company, the consignment would be India's export. From the US viewpoint, this would be an example of "off-shoring." For a fuller discussion of international value chains, see, for instance, Coe and Yeung (2015). In the impressive phase of her export performance, a good part of India's exports, especially to the USA, was of this type. There came a stage, however, when the US policy planners noted that this system was exacerbating the problem of unemployment in the USA. Off-shoring began to be discouraged. The growth rate of India's exports to her most important export destination began to fall.

4.7 Demonetisation and GST: faulty implementation of policies?

Some economists have expressed the opinion that in some cases well-meaning policies have had adverse effects on the growth rate of the economy because of the ill-planned way in which these have been implemented. The demonetisation of high-denomination (Rs. 1000 and Rs. 500) currency notes announced in November 2016 and the Goods and Services Tax (GST) implemented in 2017 have been cited as examples of good policies that have been badly implemented.

The main motivation behind the 2016 demonetisation was the belief that a huge amount of black money was held by dishonest businessmen in the form of high-denomination notes. It was thought that declaring these notes to be illegal and, at the same time, giving everybody the opportunity to deposit such notes in bank accounts would serve two purposes at the same time. On the one hand, the holders of black money will be penalised because they would not dare to deposit the money in bank accounts lest they be asked to explain the sources of the money. Their black money hoardings will be effectively destroyed. On the other hand, innocent persons who happened to hold some high-value notes would be protected since they could always put the money in their own bank accounts. Gone would be the so-called "black economy" which had so long kept a large part of the economy outside the sphere of influence of economic policies and which had been a source of funding for various kinds of unlawful activities. Moreover, the increase in bank deposits could be a source of investible resources and could boost economic growth. There will also be additional benefits in the form of inculcation of banking habits among the people and of a greater degree of digitisation of the economy.

What happened in practice, however, was different. A large part of the Indian economy was (and still is) the so-called informal sector in which cash transactions were the major part of total transactions. The sudden announcement of the demonetisation of the high-denomination notes (which constituted as much as 86.9 per cent of the total amount of currency in circulation) subjected a large part of the country's economy to a very severe and abrupt cash crunch. There were widespread disturbances to the productive and marketing processes. The growth rate of the economy, instead of rising, actually fell.

Doubts have also been expressed as to how far (or whether at all) the main objective of destroying the black economy was achieved. What had been overlooked was the fact that only a small part of black money was held in the form of caches of currency notes locked away in hidden chests. The major part was invested within the black economy. This part brought profits at rates much higher than the bank interest rates. The small part that was *not* invested now started being deposited into bank accounts. The depositors apparently was under the impression that, since the amount of money was relatively small, it would be relatively easy to explain its source if explanation was called for. Moreover, at a time when everybody was queuing up at the banks to deposit demonetised notes, this was actually a good opportunity to turn black money into "white money" by depositing it into bank accounts without raising doubts.

Be that as it may, our main concern here is with the question whether demonetisation was a cause behind the long growth slowdown in India. The matter has now been rigorously studied. The answer that emerges is in the *negative*. One authoritative study, RBI (2017), shows that while demonetisation did affect growth adversely, the effect was *transitory* in character. An analysis of *quarterly* (rather than annual) growth rates reveals that while a significant negative effect was felt in the immediate aftermath of the event in the third quarter of the financial year 2016–17, the impact started moderating in January 2017 and, with an increase in the pace of *remonetisation* (i.e. the issue of new currency notes), vanished completely by the later part of the fourth quarter. It seems safe to conclude that although the *annual* growth rate continued to slide downwards in the subsequent years, this trend was more an expression of the underlying pattern of *long* slowdown that we are discussing here rather than the consequence of demonetisation.

Similar remarks apply to GST. Since the purpose of introducing GST in India was discussed in detail in Section 2.6 of Chapter 2 in connection with the discussion of indirect taxes, we can be brief at this point. For the producers of those goods and services that came under GST, there were some initial problems in adjusting to the new system. Businessmen complained about procedural difficulties. This led some observers to doubt whether the objective of GST, viz bringing about a greater degree of regional integration in the economy, was achieved in practice. Academic research, however, has laid these doubts to rest. It has been shown that, in all countries where GST has been introduced in place of the traditional sales tax, there have been some initial procedural problems. Over time, however, as the problems get sorted out, the growth-inducing effects of the change-over assert themselves. India has been no exception (see, for instance, Rao and Mukherjee, 2019). Thus, the negative effects of GST have been temporary and this policy intervention, too, does not seem to have a role in explaining the long economic slowdown in India in the pre-Covid years.

4.8 Special problems of the Covid year: lockdowns and problems of global supply chains

Since our main objective is to explain the slowdown of the growth rate of the Indian economy that began long *before* Covid year 2020–21, we have so far abstained from discussing the special problems that arose in that year. For the sake of completeness of the discussion, however, we now mention the two most important of these problems. One of these was the *lockdown* that had to be imposed in order to contain the spread of the pandemic. For obvious reasons, the lockdown disrupted production processes and was directly responsible for the steep decline in the output of all sorts of goods and services. This was obviously a problem that originated on the supply side but that, like all supply-side constraints, indirectly contributed to demand-side problems by throwing people out of jobs and by forcing small producers and self-employed persons to suspend their productive activities, thus reducing their consumption and investment drastically. The second problem was similar in nature to the first one but operated on an international scale. Since almost all countries had to impose lockdowns, production processes in all countries suffered. We have already discussed earlier how the *international value chain* was facing difficulties even before the Covid year. Now, with the lockdowns, the value chain was completely destroyed and the export performances of all countries were adversely affected. India's exports which, as we have seen earlier, were already facing difficulties now suffered a further setback.

4.9 The relative importance of demand and supply constraints

The reader has by now surely noticed that the main line of our explanation of the growth slowdown in the Indian economy in the pre-Covid years has emphasised demand-side constraints on the growth rate rather than supply-side ones. To be sure, supply-related factors can also turn out to be major explanatory factors, depending on the nature of the slowdown faced by an economy at a particular time. The economic literature emphasises four *physical* determinants of economic growth from the supply side: (1) labour and human capital. (2) physical capital, (3) infrastructure and (4) total factor productivity. There also are *financial* determinants among which *credit supply* is the most important. All of these are major supply-side drivers of economic growth since they determine the *productive capacity* of the economy.

Obviously, there *can be* situations where a country fails to grow at a high rate because its productive *capacity* is limited and not because there is a lack of demand in the market for what is actually produced. In our context, however, the crucial question is whether this was the case in India over the particular stretch of time under consideration (i.e. in the second decade of the present century and, more particularly, in the years immediately before the Covid). The answer seems to be in the *negative*. While, in the Covid year 2020–21, the major issue was the supply disruption caused by the lockdowns (although these gave rise to demand disruptions also), in the pre-Covid years the main issue was the inadequacy of demand. Supply bottlenecks played only a subsidiary role. For instance, it is true that some banks were beset with the problem of *non-performing assets* (NPA). Loans given by banks to businessmen are the banks' *assets* because they get returns from the loans in the form of interest. If the businessmen fail to pay interest (or to repay the principal), the banks face a crisis. Their assets become *non-performing* and they become weary in the matter of giving new loans to *other* businessmen. This creates a credit supply problem in the economy and reduces the growth rate. At the time that we are talking about here, *some* Indian banks did suffer from this problem. Most economists are, however, of the opinion that this was not the *main* reason behind the slow growth of credit supply in the economy. The principal problem was not that banks did not want to *give* loans. Rather, it was that businessmen were unwilling to *take* loans because of a lack of demand in the market for goods and services. The whole matter is summed up succinctly in a remark in a research paper written in the *pre-Covid* year 2019: facts and figures "prove sufficiently that what the Indian economy is going through is essentially a demand problem" (Anand and Azad, 2020, p. 55). Another paper, written in the Covid year 2020, remarks, "Earlier, Indian economy was primarily experiencing a demand slowdown whereas now both demand and supply have been disrupted" (see Mahendra Dev and Sengupta, 2020, p. 4).

4.10 Summary and conclusion

The previous chapter noted that there was a persistent deceleration in the growth rate of the Indian economy in the 2010s, especially in the latter half of that decade. The present chapter asks why that was the case. The special problems of the Covid year obviously did not have much to do with it since the problem *preceded* the pandemic. Neither did the reason lie so much in the problems of unplanned implementation of some policy interventions because these problems were transitory. To some extent, the decrease in the growth rate of government expenditure did play a role. Government expenditure, however, is a relatively minor part of aggregate expenditure in the Indian economy.

The main reason behind the deceleration in the growth rate of the economy is to be sought in the combination (i) the problem of inequality and poverty in the economy and (ii) the growth deceleration in some of the countries that are important trading partners of India. The chain of argument behind this assertion is as follows. It is the rate of *investment* that drives the rate of economic growth. Since *private investment* is the dominant part of total investment in India, the *decline* in the rate of private investment that was observed in the 2010s must be judged to be the proximate cause of economic deceleration in India.

We are, thus, led to ask why the rate of private investment has fallen. On a closer look, it transpires that although private investment itself is one component of aggregate demand, it is actually a *derived* demand. It is derived from an expected increase in the *other* components. In India, the most important of these other components of demand is *private consumption*. The problem of inequality and poverty has been a major constraint on the growth of private consumption in the country in recent years. There was a time (in the 2000s) when the Indian economy could bypass this particular constraint by making use of yet another component of demand, namely *external* demand, i.e. the demand of *other countries* for Indian goods and services. Creditable *export* performance saved the day. In the 2010s, however, the growth of external demand has also weakened. One major reason here has been the stagnating growth rates in some of India's important trading partners. The problem has been exacerbated by the breakdown of the international value chain that had been built in the preceding decades on the basis of the system of off-shoring by large producers in the USA and some other countries.

Notes

1 In countries where agriculture is an important contributor to GDP, *land* is also an important input. But land is in fixed supply, and nothing can be done about that. Measures to increase the *productivity* of land (such as increasing irrigation facilities) can, of course, be taken. But that is, again, a matter of investment. On the other hand, a country with a large and growing population such as India does not face any problem with supply of *labour*. *Skilled* labour may be in short supply, but transforming unskilled labour into skilled labour is a matter of investment in *human capital*. Strictly speaking, human capital is also a kind of capital. Moreover, investment in human capital involves investment in physical capital as well. For instance, increasing health, education and training facilities requires investment in constructing buildings, acquiring equipment, etc.

2 There is a statistical index for measuring the rank correlation between two variables, say, x and y. It is called *Spearman's Rank Correlation Coefficient*. It is a number lying between –1 and 1. If it is positive and close to 1, that means that there is a high and positive correlation between the two variables (i.e. that the higher is x, the higher is y too, and vice versa). We do not enter into the technical discussion of exactly how close to 1 it has to be in order for this judgement to be valid. However, a rule of thumb is that there is a high positive rank correlation if the coefficient is greater than 0.5. Similarly, we say that there is a high negative correlation (i.e. the higher is x, the lower is y and vice versa) if the coefficient is less than –0.5. If it is close to 0, then, whether it is positive or negative, there is negligible correlation between the ranks of the values of x and y. As stated in the text, for the data shown in Table 4.1, Spearman's Rank Correlation Coefficient is calculated to be 0.65 approximately. We may, therefore, conclude that there is positive correlation between the rate of investment and the growth rate of GDP.

3 The 2017–18 poverty rate mentioned in this paragraph was obtained from the website www.livemint.com/news/india/rural-poverty-has-shot-up-nso-data-shows-11575352445478.html last accessed on 21 January 2022.

4 The growth rates of government expenditure mentioned in the text have been sourced from the website www.data.worldbank.org/indicator/NE.CON.GOVT.KD.ZG?location=IN last accessed on 7 June 2022.

5 Since it is *net exports* (i.e. value of exports minus value of imports), rather than exports as such, that is a component of aggregate demand in a country, it may seem that we should have talked here about *net* exports as percentage of GDP. However, since the value of imports depends not only on the *quantities* of the imports but also on their *prices* and since import prices are determined in global markets, the value of imports of a country is often influenced by forces operating *outside* the domestic economy. For instance, for India the single most important import item is crude oil. Global crude oil prices, however, are unrelated to India's domestic economy. For this reason, *net* exports as percentage of GDP are often seen to be unrelated to the strength of the domestic economy. Net exports of goods and services are essentially what is called the *balance of payments on current account* (or the *current account balance*, for short) of the country. In the case of India, the rate of GDP growth and the current account balance as percentage of GDP have often moved in *opposite* directions. Broadly, in the high-growth decade of the 2000s the percentage *fell* and in the deceleration years of the 2010s it *rose*. The rise in the rate of *oil price inflation* in the 2000s and the fall in this rate in the 2010s may have had something to do with these observed trends. To be sure, the value of *exports* is also dependent on both prices and quantities. However, export prices are related more closely to domestic factors (such as domestic cost of production) than are import prices. Moreover, GDP is also expressed in value terms. Hence, when we express the value of *exports as percentage of GDP*, what we get is more closely related to the strength of the economy than is net exports (i.e. current account balance) as percentage of GDP. It is in view of such considerations that in the text we have concentrated on exports (rather than on net exports).

References

Acharya, S. (2020): "The job crisis worsens", in Uma Kapila (ed.), *Indian Economy: The Great Slowdown?*, Academic Foundation, New Delhi, 121–124.

Anand, A. and Azad, R. (2020): "What it is and what can be done", in Uma Kapila (ed.), *The Indian Economy: The Great Slowdown?*, Academic Foundation, New Delhi, 49–64.

Chancel, L. and Piketty, T. (2019): 'India's income inequality, 1922–2015: From British Raj to Billionaire Raj?', *Review of Income and Wealth*, 65(S1), 33–62.

Chancel, L., Piketty, T., Saez, E. and Zucman, G. (2022): *Global Inequality Report 2022*, Belknap Press, Cambridge, MA.

Coe, N.M. and Yeung, H.W. (2015): *Global Production Networks*, Oxford University Press, New York.

Jangili, R. (2011): 'The causal relationship between saving, Investment and economic growth in India-What does the relation imply?', *Reserve Bank of India Occasional Papers*, 32(1), 25–39.

Mahendra Dev, S. and Sengupta, R. (2020): 'Covid 19: Impact on the Indian economy', Working Paper No. 013, Indira Gandhi Institute of Development Research, Mumbai.

Oxfam (2022): *Inequality Kills-India Supplement 2022*, Oxfam India, New Delhi.

Rao, R. and Mukherjee, S. (2019): *Evolution of Goods and Services Tax in India*, Cambridge University Press, Cambridge.

RBI (2017): *Macroeconomic Impact of Demonetisation-A Preliminary Assessment*, Reserve Bank of India, Mumbai.

Saxena, S. and Fouzdar, A. (2020): 'Connection between saving, investment and economic growth in India', *SCHOLEDGE International Journal of Business Policy and Governance*, 7(4), 63–69.

World Bank (2022): *Global Economic Perspectives*, World Bank, Washington, DC.

5 Arresting the slowdown

The policy issues

5.1 Plan of the chapter

In the previous chapter, we sought to obtain an *explanation* of the persistent deceleration in the growth rate of GDP over the past several years. It is high time we used our understanding of the problem to answer the *policy question* of what can be done to set things right or, at least, to reduce the severity of the problem. This is the task that this chapter is devoted to.

I argue in this chapter that the details of the required policy package would depend mainly on which of two alternative economic scenarios would unfold in the coming months and years. We need to do contingent planning, that is to be ready with alternative plans of policy action contingent upon the actual scenario and to act in accordance with the exigency of the situation. The alternatives hinge mainly on the question whether *inflationary pressures* will arise or persist in the Indian economy in the future. Literally, there is inflationary pressure in the economy whenever there is a positive rate of inflation, that is whenever the aggregate price level rises. In practice, however, the inflation rate is almost always positive in a growing economy. In such an economy, *deflation* (i.e. a *fall* in the aggregate price level) is an extremely rare phenomenon. For this reason, what economists usually worry about is *accelerating inflation*, that is the case where over time there is an increase in the rate of inflation (so that it is not only the price level but also the *rate of increase of the price level* that rises). Thus, what policy planners aspire for is *non-accelerating inflation*, that is for a situation where the inflation rate falls or, at least, stays constant over time.

To see whether the inflation rate is accelerating or not, we need, of course, to measure the rate of inflation. Since inflation is defined as an increase in the price level, to measure inflation we have to measure the price level in the first place. Now, measuring the price level is by no means as trivial a task as it may seem at first. The main problem is that there are many commodities in the economy. So, what do we mean by *the* price level?

Economists answer the question with the help of what they call a *price index*. Crudely, it is an aggregate of the prices of the different commodities. There are, however, different price indices in use. The measured price level

DOI: 10.4324/9781003350514-5

and, therefore, the measured rate of inflation will depend on which particular price index we decide to use. In Section 5.2 we discuss the specific price index that is mostly used in India for the purpose of formulation of monetary policies. In Section 5.3, we show that if we look at the record of the rate of inflation (as measured by this index) in India in recent times, no clear indication seems to emerge as to whether this rate is going to rise or fall in the near future. This is why contingent planning enters the picture. Let us say that the scenario in which there is demand deficiency in the market and inflation remains under control (i.e. the rate of inflation does not accelerate) is called Scenario 1, while Scenario 2 refers to the case where there is, again, a deficiency of demand but there is accelerating inflation at the same time. In Sections 5.4 and 5.5, I discuss the economic policies that would be called for under Scenarios 1 and 2, respectively.

The reason why both Sections 5.4 and 5.5 refer to the problem of demand deficiency is that, as discussed in the previous chapter, most economist are of the opinion that this is the root of the problem of the long economic slowdown in India. For the sake of completeness, however, we briefly discuss in Section 5.6 some of the policies that have been suggested for India on the basis of the assumption that economy as a whole is supply-constrained. Section 5.7 sums up the discussion of the chapter. An appendix to the chapter describes how inflation rates are calculated in India.

5.2 Inflation of the consumer price index

5.2.1 The consumer price index

Essentially, what is done for calculating the rate of inflation is to first construct some kind of *average* of the prices of the different commodities and consider it to be an overall indicator of the price level in the country. This indicator is called the *price index*. The rate of inflation is then defined to be the rate of increase of the price index.

One important question in this context is which commodities we should consider for the purpose of this calculation. Clearly, the choice of the commodities depends on the *purpose* for which we wish to use the price index. If our interest is in the effects of economic policies on the standard of living of the people (as it is in this book), the *Consumer Price Index* (CPI) would be the relevant price index for us. CPI is calculated by taking into account the commodities that the *consumers* buy in the market. It is also called the retail price index since it is obviously the retail (rather than the wholesale) prices of the commodities that are of relevance here.

Depending, again, on our purpose, we can think of different specific CPIs. For instance, if our main interest is in the prices that have to be paid by consumers located in the rural sector, we should focus on the commodities that are purchased by rural consumers. The CPI based on such a choice of commodities is called CPI (Rural). Correspondingly, there is a CPI (Urban) that focuses on commodities consumed by urban consumers. Again, instead of distinguishing between consumers on the basis of their location, we can also distinguish between them from the point of view of their occupations. This leads to the notions of CPI (industrial workers) (or CPI (IW), for short) and CPI (agricultural labourers) (or CPI (AL), for short). The names of these indices tell us about what type of commodities each of them focuses on.

Needless to say, however, our main interest in this chapter is in the rate of inflation in the economy as a whole and, therefore, in a CPI that would have country-wide significance. A CPI of this type is, in fact, used in India. It is called CPI (Combined). However, since this is the *only* CPI that we shall be concerned with, we shall, for simplicity, just call it *the* CPI. Actually, it is calculated by combining CPI (Rural) and CPI (Urban) but we shall not enter here into the computational details of how this combination is achieved.

5.2.2 CPI inflation

Since the CPI is our measure of the price level, by inflation we shall mean the rate of change in CPI. To distinguish it from the rate of country-wide inflation measured on the basis of *other* types of price indices (such as the wholesale price index), it is also called the CPI inflation rate.

Since the objective is to measure *changes* in the price level, we need to fix a *base* (or *reference*) point of time so that prices at the *current* time can be compared with those at the base point and we get an idea about how prices have changed between these two points in time. In India currently the base year for calculation of CPI is 2012. The government publishes CPI figures for every *month* with that fixed base year. The *monthly* CPI inflation rates are calculated on the basis of these indices. However, we also need to know the *annual* rates of inflation. There are two methods of calculating these. A rough and ready method is very often used. The annual rate of inflation for a year is taken to be the simple average of the 12 monthly inflation rates for the different months of the year. For technical reasons which we do not discuss here, a theoretically better method would be to first calculate the annual CPI *index* which may be taken to be the simple average (i.e. the arithmetic mean) of the 12 monthly values of the price index. The annual rate of CPI inflation would then be the rate of change of the annual index. In reality it is seen that the estimates of the annual inflation rates obtained from these two methods are approximately the same.

Calculation of inflation rates is an important exercise. Many interesting nuances are involved here. For the curious reader we describe the procedure in detail in the Annexure to this chapter.

5.3 CPI inflation in India

5.3.1 Inflation targets

Needless to say, we wish to see the inflation rate under check. Inflation targeting as a statutory objective of monetary policy was introduced in India by an agreement between the government and the RBI signed in February 2015. It was formally put into practice by an amendment to the Reserve Bank of India Act of 1934 in May 2016. It was specified that it is the CPI inflation rate (rather than inflation measured by other price indices) that would constitute the target inflation rate. Keeping the annual CPI inflation rate at or below 4 per cent, with an "upper tolerance limit" of 6 per cent and a "lower tolerance limit" of 2 per cent, was set as the objective. In other words, while it would be ideal to have a 4 per cent rate of inflation, slight variations from the ideal should not cause panic. If the rate exceeds 6 per cent, the Reserve Bank should take appropriate monetary policy actions to bring it down, Similarly, if the inflation rate falls 2 per cent, it should be pushed up. It was also announced, that the inflation targets would be valid for a period of 5 years after which they would be revised if necessary. A government notification issued in May 2021, however, has extended the validity of these target values for another 5 years. Thus, these specific inflation targets are going to remain valid at least until May 2026.

While the term "upper tolerance limit" is self-explanatory, a "lower tolerance limit" may seem odd if inflation is a bad thing. However, in economies where there is an important *private sector*, it has been noticed that from the point of view of economic growth a low but positive rate of inflation is actually better than zero (or negative) inflation. This is because economic growth is primarily driven by investment and investment by private producers depends on their expected future returns. Expected returns look rosier if some inflation is expected. The expected *future* rate of inflation, in turn, depends on the actual rate of current inflation. This is the link between inflation and growth. Needless to say, this link is operative only if the rate of inflation is moderate. If it is too high, it will adversely affect the purchasing power of the consumers and cause demand-side problems for the producers.

5.3.2 Monthly CPI inflation

As stated earlier, the inflation targets are set in terms of the *annual* CPI inflation rate. As explained in the previous section, however, it is the *monthly* CPI values published by the government that usually constitute the basic information from which annual inflation rates are calculated in India. We, therefore, start by looking at the recent record of *monthly* CPI inflation rates in India. Monthly inflation data are also important information from the viewpoint of the central bank. Obviously, the annual inflation rate in a year cannot be calculated until the year has ended. It is the movements of the monthly rate that can give an advance indication of what is going to happen to the annual rate (since the annual inflation rate is calculated from the annual CPI values and the annual CPI for a year is the average of the monthly CPIs).

The monthly CPI inflation rates for the 62 months from April 2017 to May 2022 are shown in Table 5.1. As is seen from the table, over the time period considered here the monthly CPI inflation rate was relatively low in the sub-period from April 2017 to November 2019. It was consistently below 6 per cent, the upper tolerance limit for the *annual* inflation rate. In many of these months it was close to 4 per cent. In fact, in several cases it was below that level. In one particular month, June 2017, it was even below the *lower* tolerance limit of 2 per cent for the annual rate. This time span of approximately two and a half years was witness to what was probably the phase of lowest inflation rates in India in the recent past.

While some observers are prepared to give some credit for this to the statutory inflation targeting introduced in 2016, many others point towards the problem of aggregate demand deficiency that has plagued the Indian economy over the past decade and that we have discussed in detail in the previous chapters. Indeed, it is when deceleration of the growth rate of the economy is accompanied by a simultaneous easing of inflationary pressures, that the growth deceleration can be unambiguously attributed to demand deficiency. If the inflation rate surges while the growth rate is still stagnating, it is either a case of economy-wide stagflation or one of aggregate demand deficiency coupled with sector-specific inflationary pressure. In such cases economists look for supply-side factors to explain inflation.

A surge in the monthly CPI inflation rate occurred in December 2019 and retained momentum till November 2020. Since the lockdowns were imposed in April 2020 *after* Covid appeared on the scene, the inflationary pressure in the last four months of the year 2019–20 must be attributed to *other* supply-side factors such as increase in the prices of petroleum products. In the first half of the financial year 2020–21, however, the increase in the prices of food articles and other essential items of consumption (caused by the lockdown-induced disruptions in production processes and, more importantly, in supply chains) was superimposed on the rise in petroleum product prices. No wonder the inflationary pressure was very high in this phase. The monthly CPI inflation rate was consistently above the 6 per cent level from April 2020 till November of that year. During the rest of the year inflationary pressure eased marginally. However, it remained above 4 per cent. Moreover, since September 2021 inflation rate has been accelerating. The 7.8 per cent inflation rate of April 2022 is the highest figure in the table as a whole. It should also be noted that, prior to this latest phase of acceleration, there were quite sharp month-to-month fluctuations in the rate of CPI inflation in India. In May 2022, however, there was a moderation in the inflationary pressure.

Table 5.1 Monthly CPI inflation rates in India, April 2017 to May 2022

Year	*April.*	*May*	*June.*	*July.*	*August.*	*September.*	*October.*	*November.*	*December.*	*January.*	*February.*	*March.*
2017–18	3.0	2.2	1.5	2.4	3.3	3.3	3.6	4.9	5.2	5.1	4.4	4.3
2018–19	4.6	4.9	4.9	4.2	3.7	3.7	3.4	2.3	2.1	2.0	2.6	2.9
2019–20	3.0	3.0	3.2	3.1	3.3	4.0	4.6	5.5	7.4	7.6	6.6	5.8
2020–21	7.2	6.3	6.2	6.7	6.7	7.3	7.6	6.9	4.6	4.1	5.0	5.5
2021–22	4.2	6.3	6.3	5.6	5.3	4.4	4.5	4.9	5.6	6.0	6.1	7.0
2022–23	7.8	7.0										

Source: RBI (2021, Table 235, p. 376) and www.mospi.gov.in

Table 5.2 Annual CPI inflation rates in India, 2012–13 to 2021–22

Year	*12–13*	*13–14*	*14–15*	*15–16*	*16–17*	*17–18*	*18–19*	*19–20*	*20–21*	*21–22*
CPI inflation	10.0	9.4	5.8	4.9	4.5	3.6	3.4	4.8	6.2	5.5

Source: The annual inflation rate for a year is calculated as the average of the monthly inflation rates of the year and may differ a little from that calculated as the rate of change of the annual price index RBI (2022a, Table II. 2.1)

5.3.3 Annual CPI inflation

Since official inflation targets are stated in terms of *annual* rates, it is also important to look at the time pattern of the behaviour of these rates in India. Since we are now talking of annual rates, we look back a little farther than in the case of monthly rates (so that the data set does not become too small). Table 5.2 displays the annual CPI inflation rates from the years 2012–13 to 2021–22.

The pattern of the movement of annual CPI inflation rates presents a much neater picture than that of the monthly rates. This is but to be expected since the annual CPI values from which these rates are calculated are *averages* of the monthly CPI values of the respective years and smoothen out the month-to-month fluctuations of the monthly values. As is seen in Table 5.2, the annual CPI inflation rate decreased continuously from 2012–13 to 2018–19. Thereafter, it registered an upward trend. Although the latest figure of 5.5 per cent for 2021–22 is lower than that of 6.2 per cent for 2020–21, it is higher than the figures for all of the five years from 2015–16 to 2019–20.

Recall from our discussion in Chapter 3 that there are good grounds for suspecting that the deceleration phase of the path of the growth rate in India began in the early years of the second decade of the century (although the official estimates of the growth rate would put this date at the year 2017–18). The data in Table 5.2 can, therefore, be interpreted to indicate, roughly, that up to the year 2018–19 the growth deceleration phase coincided with the phase of decreasing inflationary pressures. It is in 2020–21 that growth rate and the inflation rate have moved in opposite directions.

5.3.4 Alternative future inflation scenarios

The main conclusion that emerges from the discussion in the previous subsections of this section is that it is difficult to make any prediction about the future path of the CPI inflation rate in India. This is especially true of the *monthly* inflation rate. As is seen from Table 5.1, in any given month within the time period considered in the chart, it would have been nearly impossible to foresee even the *direction* of the movement in the inflation rate in the next month, let alone the precise *magnitude* of the change in this rate. While the pattern of *annual* inflation rate (in Table 5.2) is neater, it is again obvious that any definitive prognosis would be problematic. While there has been a decrease in the annual rate of inflation in 2021–22, there is no telling whether the next few years will see a similar moderation of inflationary pressure.

Accordingly, our discussion of economic policy in the rest of this chapter will be divided into two parts. The first of these will presume a scenario of a falling trend in the inflation rate while the second will allow for a rising trend.

5.4 Scenario 1: demand deficiency with non-accelerating inflation

5.4.1 Short-run policies

We now come to the question of policy formulation under the two alternative scenarios. Under each of these scenarios, we discuss policies in the short and the long runs separately. The phrases "short run" and "long run" have been standard terms in Economics ever since Marshall (1890) distinguished between four different lengths of time: (i) the very short run, (ii) the short run, (iii) the long run and (iv) the very long run. A change that takes place in the very long run is also called a *secular* change. These different lengths of time have never been very precisely defined. We shall follow this somewhat dubious tradition. In most cases, however, we shall talk only about the short and the long runs, without bothering to specify exactly how short the short run is. Informally, however, the reader may think of the short run as "the next few months" and the long run as the "next few years."

Consider Scenario 1 where the decelerating trend in the rate of economic growth in India is accompanied by a similar (or, at least, a non-accelerating) trend in the inflation rate. As we know by now, this is the standard case of an economy where the main economic problem is one of inadequate demand in the market.

In *theory*, the policies that are available to the government of a country with a demand-deficient economy are well-known. We have discussed them in detail in some of the previous chapters (especially, in Chapter 2). In *practice*, however, in a country like India policy options *in the short run* seem to be limited. First of all, since the *global* economy is likely to remain depressed in the short run, trying to boost *external* demand is unlikely to bring the desired results.

Turning to policies directed at *domestic* demand, it may be noted that most of the usually practised *fiscal* policies are known to have a time lag problem. For instance, cuts in *income* tax rates take time to bear fruit. Usually, they have to be approved by the Parliament. Even if the government takes recourse to ordinances or other types of administrative orders in order to avoid delays in implementation, their effects on the disposable income at the hands of people will be felt only at the time when tax payments fall due (rather than immediately). Moreover, *income* tax rate cuts are irrelevant for the vast majority of people in the low and lower-middle income groups since this section of the population is below the exemption limit anyway. Cuts in the rates of GST and the various other types of *indirect* tax will be more effective. By reducing the market prices of goods and services they would help in boosting demand. Again, however, practical considerations put limits on the extent to which this particular policy can be relied upon. The major part of the total tax revenue of the government in India comes from indirect taxes. Usually, therefore, governments are averse to proposals for cuts in the rates of indirect taxes. Again, as in the case of direct taxes, the structure of indirect taxes too is usually sought to be made as progressive as possible by either exempting the mass-consumption goods or taxing them at relatively low rates. Therefore, usually there is not much scope for *further* reductions in the rates of these taxes. Yet, it is the purchasing power of the poor and the lower-middle classes that is of relevance here. It is these classes that constitute the overwhelming majority of the population and it is the deficiency of purchasing power of these classes that is the main cause behind the over-all demand deficiency problem in the economy. Other sections of the population do not face such severe limitations on their capacity to spend.

While the policy of increasing *government expenditure* can, in general, be expected to work better as a way of increasing the purchasing power of the people, the time lag problem may again play the spoiler in the short run, at least so far as the usually practiced ways of implementing public projects are concerned. In particular, it takes time to formulate and execute proposals for public *infrastructure* projects. The process of recruiting personnel in government offices is also notoriously slow.

The only type of government expenditure that can have an *immediate* impact on people's purchasing power would be to put money directly in their hands. The most obvious way of doing so would be to give cash dole-outs. This would be equivalent to what Friedman (1969) referred to as the proposal of "helicopter money": bags of money would be dropped from helicopters. It is as if money will descend on people like the Biblical "manna from the heaven" with the government playing the role of God. However, apart from the fact that there are obvious administrative problems of implementing such procedures, it would be difficult to ensure that the money given out in this way goes to the people who need it most. The many dubious ways in which the rich and the powerful grab other free gifts of nature (such as natural resources) for their exclusive use do not leave one very confident that the lion's share of this particular free gift of the government will not be cornered by them.

A more sensible form of the same policy would be to credit the money to people's bank accounts. In fact, the mechanism required for such programmes seem to be already in existence. As of August 2021, there were more than 43 crore (i.e. 430 million) bank accounts in India under the Prime Minister's Jan Dhan Yojana. This scheme was launched in 2014 with the objective of achieving a greater degree of *financial inclusion* in the economy by granting low-income people the access to banking facilities *and* giving them an easy way of receiving benefits under various government schemes. There is no minimum balance requirement for accounts under this scheme and procedures for checking identifications at the time of account opening are relatively easy. Indeed, even without any official identification, one can open a "small account" under this scheme on the basis of self-attested statements. Since there is only one account per *family*, it is obvious that a large part of the low and lower-middle income people of India is already covered under this scheme.

However, while the objective of extending the usual banking facilities to the poorer sections of the society seems to have been achieved to an extent through this scheme, critics have questioned whether it is these facilities as such that the account-holders (most of whom have zero savings) are in need of. Jan Dhan accounts would be of much greater utility if these are used for crediting the public benefits due to the account holders. The use of the accounts for this purpose, however, seems to have been limited. So far only five crore of the accounts are being utilised for the purpose of crediting the amounts due under the Direct Benefit Transfer (DBT) scheme. DBT was launched in 2013 even before the Jan Dhan Yojana scheme was inaugurated so that subsidies due to people under various public schemes could be credited to people's bank accounts and leakages and delays could be avoided. Its main limitation was the limited reach of banking facilities in the country. Now that the Jan Dhan Yojana has extended these facilities to a much greater number of people, there is now a greater opportunity of realising the original goal of DBT.

The proposal that we are currently discussing, however, involves not only a much more intensive use of the Jan Dhan accounts for the purpose of DBT but also a substantial extension, albeit on a temporary basis, of the scope of DBT itself by crediting money to Jan Dhan accounts for the general purpose of ending the demand deficiency problem in the macroeconomy in addition to the payments made under the already existing welfare schemes.

Schemes like the one advocated here are usually thought to have inflationary consequences. Note, however, that we are talking here about a demand-deficient economy. Since we are discussing short-run policies here, if there is a demand deficiency problem to start with, the problem is likely to persist within this time frame. In such an economy if there is inflation in the short run, it must be due to supply-side factors. The problem facing the economy would then be one of stagflation. This case belongs to what we have called Scenario 2 and will be taken up separately in the following section.

On the side of more conventional *monetary policies*, again, possible short-run policy actions seem to be few in number. As we have explained in detail before, the main instrument of monetary policy in India, namely changing the repo rate, has so far proved ineffective. The G-SAP programme of the RBI under which the central bank purchases government bonds in the open market has also had little effect so far. The common weakness of these measures derives from the fact that they are aimed merely at increasing the lendable funds at the hands of the financial institutions. It is, however, the stagnant *demand* for loans in the market (which, in turn, derives from the stagnant demand for consumer goods), rather than paucity of investible funds at the disposal of the producers, that prevents investment and job creation.

To summarise, the menu of workable policies for solving the problem of recession in a demand-deficient economy is a severely limited one in the short run. Putting money directly into the hands of people in the lower-income classes by making use of the Jan Dhan accounts in the banks seems to be the only type of policy that will have an unambiguous positive impact on the economy within this time horizon. In India the point has been emphasised not only by academic economists but also by a section of the business classes (for instance, the Confederation of Indian Industry (CII)) that has to bear the burden of an accumulating stock of unsold goods in the godowns. Somewhat surprisingly, however, the government has so far steadfastly refused to adopt this type of policy.

5.4.2 *Long-run policies*

If we look beyond the short run, however, all of the demand-increasing policy measures that we discussed in Chapter 2 become relevant. If the growth rate of the world economy picks up in the long run, there would be some prospect of an increase in *external* demand. Available projections of the growth rates of the global economy for the next couple of years, however, give little hope.

Even within the time horizon of the next two years, of course, there is the possibility of increasing the exports of a number of *specific* commodities even in the existing situation of a global stagnation. For instance, in the fight against the Covid-19 pandemic the goal of achieving a 100 per cent vaccination rate is a far cry in many countries of the world. If, on top of that, booster doses of the vaccines at regular intervals turn out to be necessary, it seems likely that there is going to be a high and enduring demand for Covid vaccines in the global market in the next two years and probably even after that. India is likely to have a comparative advantage here. After all, India currently produces more than 60 per cent of the global output of all sorts of vaccines and is rightly regarded as the vaccine manufacturing capital of the world. Similar is the case with other commodities that are needed in the vaccination programme (such as cold chain facilities needed for storing the vaccines and injection syringes)

In general, however, as long as the global slowdown continues, policies aimed at boosting *internal* demand are likely to work better. The policy of directly putting money in the hands of the less well-to-do sections of the population which we have advocated earlier as a short-run policy, however, is difficult to continue indefinitely. In the long run, it is likely to strain the government's resources. Indeed, if that was not the case, in any economy the problem of poverty would be a much rarer phenomenon than it is in reality.

The problem of time lags in the operation of fiscal policy, of course, becomes less important in the long-run context. So far as tax policies are concerned, however, for the same reasons as were discussed earlier in the short-run case, in practice there will again be little elbow room for actions aimed at easing the burden of either the direct or the indirect taxes on people in the low or lower-middle income groups. Tax burden on the well-to-do can, of course, be lightened. But, again as in the short run, that is not likely to have much of an impact on demand since these sections of the population do not have the problem of paucity of money to spend. Moreover, it will increase the inequality in the distribution of post-tax income.

Past experience, however, does permit us to be more optimistic about the effects of increase in government expenditure. Way back in 2003, when the economy was on the upswing, the Indian Parliament had enacted the Fiscal Responsibility and Budget Management (FRBM) Act with a view to limiting the ratio of fiscal deficit to GDP to a maximum of 3 per cent. In 2008–09 and 2009–10, however, when the ripples of the global financial crisis of 2007 reached the Indian shores, the government of the day, quite rightly, deliberately flouted the FRBM Act and undertook a massive expansion of public expenditure. In 2008–09, the fiscal deficit was Rs. 3.36 lakh crore while GDP was Rs. 56.3 lakh crore (see RBI, 2016). Thus, the fiscal-deficit-to-GDP ratio for the year came to 5.9 per cent. In 2009–10, it climbed even further to 6.5 per cent. One suspects that it was this, rather than the repo rate cuts that were also carried on during this time, that was responsible for the surprisingly quick recovery of the growth rate at this time. The suspicion is strengthened by the fact, noted before, that the growth rate started nosediving again from 2011–12 when public expenditure cutbacks began (while the repo rate cuts continued).

We may also mention here that *international* experience in this regard also points in the same direction. The US experience of the 1930s as well as of the Global Financial Crisis of 2007 have already been discussed in detail in Chapter 2. Historically, there is hardly *any* instance of a successful battle against demand deficiency fought *exclusively* on the basis of interest rate policy. Government investment in various infrastructural projects can play a most effective role in this time frame. In fact, if such investment is in social infrastructure such as health and education, it will not only add to total investment demand in the current period but will also reduce inequality by relieving the poorer sections of the population of the need to undertake such expenditure on their own. The fall in inequality, in turn, will boost consumer demand. Moreover, it will increase the *future* productivity and, hence, the future earning potentials of those who are underserved by private institutions in these sectors.

5.5 Scenario 2: demand deficiency with accelerating inflation

5.5.1 The structure of inflation in India

Consider now the *stagflation* scenario where we have stagnation in the growth rates of output and employment and, at the same time, an acceleration in the rate of inflation. There is, however, a difference between the type of stagflation that is often seen in AEs and the one that has been experienced in India from time to time. In the AEs, stagflation is often caused by supply-side constraints *alone*. It is because of supply bottlenecks that output stagnates. Because of the same reason supply tends to fall short of demand and there is inflation. In such cases demand-boosting measures will obviously make the inflation problem even worse without solving the output stagnation problem. That is why *short-run* solutions to the problem of stagflation are difficult, if not impossible, to find. The real solution is to remove the constraints on production and supply and that usually takes time.

For countries like India, it may seem that the problem is even more complicated. Output stagnation in India in recent years has been basically a demand-side problem and its solution lies in boosting demand. When such an economy faces accelerating inflation at the same time, we have a hotchpotch of demand- and supply-side issues rather than a purely supply-side problem. It seems that inflation control in such an economy would be even more difficult than in an advanced economy in stagflation.

It turns out, however, that there is a saving grace also. If we look at the *structure* of inflation in India, we see that there is considerable variation in the inflation rates of different commodity groups. In such cases, *microeconomic* policies aimed at those sectors that have high inflation rates can be combined with *macroeconomic* policies boosting economy-wide demand.

To achieve such a combination, however, it is necessary to start by identifying the sectors in which sector-specific inflation control measures are most urgently called for, that is by identifying the commodities (or commodity groups) whose prices are contributing the most to inflation in the country. Common sense suggests that it is these commodity groups that inflation control measures should be directed at.

In this context, we may refer to the distinction between overall inflation and inflation in the prices of particular commodity groups. For a long time economists believed that an overall price index (such as the CPI) changes very often because many of its component prices are very *volatile* in nature, i.e. these components rise and fall very frequently. But even if the price index rises (or falls) for some time, it will eventually revert to some kind of natural or trend level. Policy-makers should not be particularly bothered about overall CPI inflation because it is a temporary and volatile phenomenon. This led to the emergence of the concept of *core inflation*. It was claimed that *food and fuel* prices were particularly volatile in nature. A distinction, therefore, was made between *headline CPI inflation* and *core CPI inflation*. Headline CPI inflation is simply the over-all CPI inflation that we have been talking about so far. *Core* CPI inflation is inflation in CPI calculated by *excluding* food and fuel prices from consideration. The idea was that core inflation was the *stable* rate of inflation and that in the long run this was the rate of inflation to which headline inflation converged. It is, therefore, core inflation that should be taken to be *the* rate of inflation in the country. While food and fuel inflation would obviously contribute to headline inflation because headline CPI includes food and fuel, it was argued that the important question was whether or how much these prices contribute to core inflation. Data for some countries (including the USA) and the analytical methods available at the time seemed to indicate that the food and fuel inflation did *not* have a high impact on core inflation. The policy conclusion that seemed to emerge was that there was no need to worry too much about food and fuel inflation. These were *transitory* in nature. As long as the *core* CPI inflation rate was under control, there was no cause for worry.

More recent data on inflation in India, however, do not support this view. If food and fuel inflation rates were *volatile*, that should mean that they are as likely to rise as to fall. In reality, they often tend to change in one direction for some time at a stretch. Therefore, under the influence of these important components, the *headline* inflation rate also changes in the same direction at a stretch. Now, when the headline rate rises continuously for some time, people *expect* it to continue to rise in the future and *behave* accordingly. As a result, the headline rate would *actually* rise in the future. Future inflation becomes a self-fulfilling prophecy. Moreover, accelerating inflation now becomes a more pervasive phenomenon, no longer confined to food and fuel. At that stage, therefore, the *core* inflation rate also rises. Thus, the rates of headline inflation and core inflation often move parallelly. There is no convergence of the headline rate towards the core rate. The actual empirical demonstration with Indian data has been given only with data on food prices inflation (see Patnaik (2019)). However, the same arguments should apply for fuel prices also.

The upshot of the above discussion is that food and fuel inflation *is* a cause for worry. Furthermore, this is true whether it is the headline inflation rate or the core inflation rate that is taken to be the overall rate of inflation in the country. Thus, no additional mileage is gained by focusing on core inflation. In our policy discussion that follows, therefore, we shall follow the usual practice of considering the headline CPI inflation as the relevant rate of CPI inflation in the country.

Let us take a look at the observed behaviour of the headline and the core inflation rates in India in recent months. In India, core CPI inflation rate excludes "food and fuel." However, "fuel" here refers only to fuel used by *households* for purposes of cooking and lighting. Thus, LPG cooking gas, kerosene and firewood are included in fuel but consumption of petrol and diesel is not. Hence, core CPI inflation which is inflation calculated by *excluding* food and fuel actually *includes* petrol and diesel. The government, however, also publishes figures for the rate of CPI inflation of commodities *excluding* food, fuel, petrol and diesel.

Table 5.3 Monthly headline and exclusion-based CPI inflation rates in India in some recent months (year-on-year, per cent)

Month	*Headline CPI*	*Core CPI*	*CPI Excluding Food, Fuel, Petrol and Diesel*
June 2019	3.2	4.1	4.6
September 2019	4.0	4.2	4.9
December 2019	7.4	3.8	3.7
March 2020	5.8	3.9	NA
June 2020	6.2	5.4	5.3
September 2020	7.3	5.4	5.2
December 2020	4,6	5.6	5.3
January 2021	4.1	5.5	5.2
February 2021	5.0	6.0	5.5
March 2021	5.5	5.9	NA
April 2021	4.2	5.3	NA
May 2021	6.3	6.6	NA
June 2021	6.3	6.1	5.3
July 2021	5.6	5.8	5.1
August 2021	5.3	5.8	5.1
September 2021	4.4	5.9	5.2
October 2021	4.5	5.9	5.0
November 2021	4.9	6.2	5.5
December 2021	5.6	6.1	5.6
January 2022	6.0	6.0	5.6
February 2022	6.1	5.8	5.6

Core CPI, CPI excluding food and fuel; NA, Not available.

Source: Table 5.1 in the text and RBI (2022b, Table II.1)

Table 5.3 displays the monthly rates of headline CPI inflation, core CPI inflation and CPI inflation excluding food, fuel, petrol and diesel for 21 months. There are breaks in the series for the last of these three rates of inflation since for 4 of the 21 months this rate was not available at the time of constructing this table. It is seen that, starting from December 2019, the core inflation rate has been consistently *above* the inflation rate that excludes food, fuel, petrol and diesel. Since core inflation excludes the inflation in food and fuel prices but includes the inflation in the prices of petrol and diesel, this is expected. Note, however, that the path of the headline inflation rate has been neither consistently above nor consistently below either of the two other types of inflation. Moreover, there is no convergence of headline CPI inflation to either of the two types of core inflation.

To emphasise the fact that acceleration of inflation in India in recent times has been a sector-specific (rather than an economy-wide) phenomenon, we show, in Table 5.4, the CPI inflation rates for three major groups of commodities, (1) food and beverages, (2) fuel and light and (3) all commodities

Table 5.4 Monthly CPI inflation rates (per cent) for selected groups vis-à-vis headline CPI inflation rates in India in the last four months of 2021

Groups	*Weights*	*September 2021*	*October 2021*	*November 2021*	*December 2021*
Food and beverages	45.86	1.6	1.8	2.6	4.5
Fuel and light	6.84	13.6	14.3	13.3	11.0
Core CPI	47.30	5.9	5.9	6.2	6.0
All groups (i.e. Headline CPI)	100.00	4.3	4.5	4.9	5.6

Source: GOI (2022, Table 2, p. 163)

other than those in in the first two groups (i.e. the core CPI group) as well as the overall (i.e. headline) CPI inflation rate for the last four months of the calendar year 2021. The weights on the various commodity groups in the construction of the CPI are also shown. As is seen from the table, while there has been a steady acceleration in the headline inflation from 4.3 per cent in September 2021 to 5.6 per cent in December 2021, all commodity groups have not contributed equally to this process. In particular, while food and beverages registered steady *acceleration*, fuel and light underwent a *deceleration* in the last three of these four months. Core CPI remained constant between September and October, accelerated between October and November and decelerated slightly between November and December 2021. Clearly, the observed acceleration of headline inflation was driven by the steady acceleration in the inflation rate of food and beverages (which had a high weight of 45.86 in the commodity basket of the typical consumer).

What is the role of inflation in the prices of *petroleum products* in driving headline inflation? Popular perception in India considers these prices to be major sources of inflation. The perception is based on the fact that in recent years these prices have increased by leaps and bounds. Government spokespersons, however, have sought to downplay this view by pointing out that while these prices have, indeed, increased, the impact on the headline CPI inflation has been negligible. At first sight, data seem to support this official view. The major petroleum products are petrol, diesel, LPG and kerosene. The commodity group "fuel and light" does not include petrol and diesel. LPG and kerosene are included in fuel and light and their prices, too, have, of course, increased. However, as is seen in Table 5.4, the fuel and light inflation rate has come down in recent months. Moreover, fuel and light carry a weight of only 6.84 in the consumption basket. On the other hand, while petrol and diesel *are* included in Core CPI, their weight (not shown in the table) is negligible because these items are not directly consumed by households in significant amounts. As per the official view, therefore, petroleum products as a group does not seem to be a major driver of CPI inflation. While these prices may be important from the viewpoint of *producers*, CPI is concerned with the *consumption* basket of the typical consumer.

This view, however, does not seem to stand up to closer scrutiny. The important point here is that while the *direct* effect of inflation in petrol and diesel prices on CPI inflation may be limited, it has indirect "cascading" effect on many other components of CPI. The most obvious of these other components is the group *transport and communication* which is included in Core CPI. This group carries a weight of 8.59 (not shown in Table 5.4). However, this weight is higher than the 6.84 weight given to fuel and light in the construction of CPI. Moreover, in recent times inflation in this group has accelerated. What is even more important is that increased transport costs tend to increase the prices of almost everything that a consumer buys the market. This is particularly true in a large country such as India where products often have to be transported over long distances between the points of their production and consumption. This is as true of agricultural products as of industrial ones. Thus, while at first glance it is food and beverage prices that gets most of the blame for accelerating headline CPI inflation, petroleum product prices, particularly the prices of petrol and diesel, are, on a closer look, seen to be of considerable importance in this context. It seems that in this respect the public perception is quite right after all. Unfortunately, however, precise quantitative estimates of these indirect effects of petroleum prices are hard to come by. Nevertheless, from an intuitive point of view these effects seem to be too important to be neglected when it comes to formulating policies for controlling inflation.

5.5.2 Checking inflation in food prices

Short-run policies

We have now identified two commodity groups at which the inflation control measures (under Scenario 2) should be directed. Broadly, these are *food* and *petroleum products*. For food products, however, there does not seem to be much leeway for policy action *in the short run*. The only course of action that is open in this time frame is to impose *price controls and rationing*. Under the traditional price control system, the government sets the price of the commodity at a level which is *below* the free market price. Since free market price is the price at which demand equals supply, this means that at the price fixed by the government there would usually be some unsatisfied demand. People would be unable to buy as much of the commodity as they would like to at the (relatively low) price fixed by the government. For this reason, price control usually has to be backed up by *rationing*. The government fixes not only the price but also the *quantity* in which any one person can buy the commodity.

This conventional model of price control, however, is now out of fashion because of the well-known practical problems of administering such a control system. A variant of this model that is currently followed in India is based on the idea of *modified rationing*. Under this system, the government does not control the prices in the market. However, it buys the commodities (mainly, cereals and pulses) from farmers. The farmers do not necessarily have to sell their produce to the government. They are free to sell it to any other purchaser. The government, however, is supposed to make its purchase prices sufficiently attractive to the producers. It then sells the procured amounts through ration shops at relatively low prices to those consumers whose incomes do not exceed a specified level. It also fixes the *quantities* of these commodities that any one consumer would get from the ration shops. No consumer, however, is under any compulsion to make use of this ration system. Anyone can purchase any amount of the commodities in the open market. Some other essential items of consumption (such as kerosene) that are not agricultural products are also supplied through this system.

The chief merit of the modified rationing system, of course, is that it gives some support to the living standards of the poorer sections of the society. In our present context, the more important point is that it puts a leash on CPI inflation since CPI is constructed by using the actual prices paid by the consumers. Since the ration system operates alongside the open market, the inflation rate may not be fully controlled by this method. But the prices paid by at least *some* of the consumers is kept under check. Needless to say, operation of the rationing system involves net government expenditure since the prices at which the commodities are supplied through the ration shops are less than the procurement prices. In this sense, it falls under the category of government expenditure policy. In the present context, however, the focus is on the use of expenditure policy in this particular *sector-specific* way rather than on increasing the *aggregate* amount of government expenditure (which would fall under *macroeconomic* policy).

Continuation of the modified rationing system is certainly to be recommended. It should be noted, however, that the main source of supply here is *government* procurement of the commodities. There have recently been some attempts at facilitating large scale purchases of agricultural products by *private* corporate houses. Three legislations were enacted in 2020 towards this end. While it was not clear at that stage whether government procurement would continue, farmers were apprehensive that it might not do so and that, in that eventuality, they would have to face the market power of the big private companies. They would not get remunerative prices because they will be in a weak bargaining position against the companies. This apprehension led to a strong farmer movement, the longest one in recent memory. Faced with the agitation, the government has declared its intention to repeal the acts. While the government professes to continue its procurements, critics are sceptical about the course of action that government intends to pursue in future. The relevance of the matter to our present context consists in the fact that discontinuation of government procurement will have *inflationary* consequences for *two* reasons. On the one hand, it will mean discontinuation of the rationing system and will deprive a large section of the population of the opportunity to purchase food-grains at subsidised prices. CPI will increase. On the other hand, because, again, of their market power, large corporate houses will be able to extract higher prices from the consumers. *All* consumers, including those who were hitherto buying food-grains and agro-based products from the open market rather than from the ration shops, will be paying higher prices. The upward pressure on the CPI inflation rate will, thus, be reinforced. Discontinuation of the government procurement programme and the consequent discontinuation of the modified rationing system are *not* recommended.

Long-run policies

Needless to say, however, a rationing system can only be a short-term expedient for checking inflation of food prices. In order to find a more satisfactory solution of the problem one has to look into causes underlying the long-run trends in the relevant economic variables. A comprehensive investigation into the matter (Sasmal, 2016, pp. 203–220) shows that some of the factors that are often mentioned in this context (for instance, increases in global prices of food-grains, government interventions such as the minimum support prices guaranteed to the farmers and upward revisions of minimum wages of agricultural workers) do not actually have much role in explaining the *long-run* trends in food inflation in India. A more transparent picture emerges from demand-supply comparisons. Sasmal notes that per capita demand for agricultural goods can be taken to be driven by per capita income in the country. Taking real per capita net national product (NNP) as an indicator of real per capita income, the study shows that there has been a sea change in the relative rates of growth of demand and supply between the era of the Green Revolution and the more recent decades. Over the period from 1970–71 to 1990–91, the heydays of the Green Revolution, the growth rates of both cereal and non-cereal items far outstripped the growth rate of per capita income. While real per capita NNP increased by about 43 per cent over this 20-year period, production of cereals, oilseeds, potato, milk and eggs increased by 103, 94, 217, 145 and 242 per cent, respectively.

To be sure, these were growth rates of *total* outputs. However, results of a comparison of real per capita NNP growth with growth rates of *per capita* outputs of the food items would not be much different. Per capita output is simply total output divided by population. Hence, the *growth rate* of per capita output is the growth rate of total output *minus* the growth rate of total population. India's population at the time was growing at the rate of roughly 3 per cent per year. Deduct 3 from the growth rates of the total outputs and result of the exercise remains roughly the same.

Things changed dramatically, however, in the period from 1990–91 to 2011–12. Over this period real per capita NNP grew by 165 per cent. However, the growth rates of the outputs of the same five food items *fell* to 22, 61, 206, 137 and 215 per cent. Clearly, the supply of food items in India has failed to grow hand in hand with demand not only in the time of Covid (when the lockdowns played havoc with the supply lines) but also over a much longer time span since the 1990s.

It would, of course, be ridiculous to try to solve this problem of excess demand by reducing the rate of growth of demand (because that would mean *reducing* the rate of growth of real per capita NNP). Increasing the growth rate of agricultural output would be the way to go.

Sasmal identifies resource degradation and technological stagnation on the one hand and lack of public investment in infrastructure on the other as the key constraints on agricultural growth (and, therefore, the key drivers of food inflation in India in the long run). It is now generally acknowledged that while the rapid rise in output per acre of agricultural land during the Green Revolution brought much-needed relief from the food scarcity of the 1960s, the story had a flip side. The indiscriminate use of groundwater resources and the heavy doses of chemical fertilisers and pesticides destroyed much of the natural fertility of the soil. This is borne out by the fact that those states of India that witnessed the most dramatic increase in output per acre in the first two decades following 1970 were precisely the states where it fell most steeply in the two *following* decades. In this sense, there has been *resource degradation* in Indian agriculture. The need of the hour is a new technology that would increase output per acre *without* damaging the environment. While agricultural scientists are seized of the matter and much research is under way, widespread use of the required type of technology at the ground level, something that may deserve to be called a *new* Green Revolution, does not seem to be on the horizon. This is the problem of *technological stagnation*. Availability of technology, however, is not the whole of the matter. Successful *adoption* of appropriate technology depends crucially on the availability and accessibility of the necessary infrastructure. Both physical and socio-economic infrastructure are of importance. Physical infrastructure includes the supply of such crucial inputs as irrigation and fertilisers as well as transportation facilities for the farmers' produces. Socio-economic infrastructure includes finance, crop insurance and basic health and education facilities for farmer households. That there are large differences between demand and supply in these areas are too well-known to need elaboration. What is relevant in this context is that it is *public investment* that is needed in these fields. Since these types of investment involve long gestation lags and since the rate of return on them (in money terms) is relatively low, *private* investors do not usually find them attractive. For these reasons, public investment in technological and infrastructural development is our recommended policy for control of food price inflation in the long run.

5.5.3 *Checking inflation in petroleum product prices*

The global oil market

We now come to the question of controlling petroleum prices inflation. Since almost all of India's need for *crude* petroleum are met by imports, we start with a brief discussion on the global supply of crude which is the raw material that is extracted from the underground (or undersea) oil reserves and is refined into various petroleum products (such as petrol, diesel, kerosene and LPG). Many countries of the world, about a hundred, produce crude oil. (India, too, produces some.) However, this does not mean that the crude oil market is perfectly competitive. A handful of countries produce the major part of the global supply. The 13 countries that make up the Organization of Petroleum Exporting Countries (OPEC) currently produce about 40 per cent of the total supply. There are also a few large producers of crude (such as Russia and Brazil) that are not in the OPEC. Together, OPEC and these other countries produce the lion's share of the total annual crude production in the world. The location of the USA in this picture is worth commenting on. For a long time, the USA produced a negligible percentage of the total supply. After the so called "shale oil revolution" of the 2000s, however, the country has emerged as the *largest* producer of crude oil. (Currently, Saudi Arabia is the *second* largest while Russia is the *third*.) Yet, the demand for crude oil in the USA is greater than supply. Thus, so far as matters relating to crude oil price in the global market is concerned, the economic interests of the USA lie on the side of the *consumers*.

Overall, therefore, the structure of the global crude oil market can be said to be *oligopolistic* in the sense that while there are many *consuming* countries, a handful of countries wield controlling power on the *supply*. This means that a handful of countries control the market price of crude oil. The control, however, is *indirect*, rather than direct. No producing country can dictate to any other producing country the price at which the latter would sell its crude to a consuming country. However, in matters relating to the quantity of *production*, the major oil-exporting countries take joint decisions. Hence, when they decide to reduce production, global supply goes down. If demand remains the same, price tends to increase.

There are, however, various grades (i.e. qualitative classes) of crude oil. Their prices differ. Two of the high-quality crudes are called Western Texas Intermediate (WTI) crude and Brent crude. Originally, the name Brent crude was given to crude oil obtained from Brent area of the North Sea oilfields. It now refers more generally to oil produced by countries in Africa, Asia and Europe. WTI, as its name indicates, originally meant crude produced in the western parts of the state of Texas in the USA. It now refers to oil produced in the two continents of North America and South America. Within each of these two grades there are sub-grades. For instance, Brent crude includes

Dubai crude and Oman crude. Because of India's geographical proximity to the major Brent-producing countries (such as those in the Middle East) and the consequent transport cost advantage of this type of crude, it is Brent crude that India mostly imports.

Short-run policies

In view of the crucial importance of oil in energy production, most countries try to hold some buffer stock of oil to guard against the possibility of sudden disruptions of global supply (such as those caused by wars or natural calamities). Countries (such as India) that have refining capabilities of their own hold the stocks in the form of crude. As a policy measure, some of these countries have released a part of these strategic reserves with the intention of increasing global crude supply. The proposal was originally mooted by the USA and was subsequently acted upon by some other countries. In November 2021, the USA which had a reserve of 727 million barrels of crude released 50 million barrels. Other countries took similar decisions. India released 5 million barrels from its stock of 38 million barrels. Most observers, however, are of the opinion that, in practice, this policy measure is unlikely to have more than a marginal impact on global crude prices. Because of the very nature of the objective of holding these strategic reserves, it is unlikely that large amounts of these reserves will be released. Moreover, because of the same reason, such releases are likely to be once-for-all (or, at least, infrequent). On the other hand, faced by the drop in oil demand (caused by the Covid-induced world-wide economic deceleration) and the resulting drop in oil prices, the oil-exporting countries, especially, the members of OPEC, have cut down on their *daily* crude oil production in the hope of arresting the declining trend in prices. This is likely to have a *continuing* impact on global supply even when global demand picks up. For these reasons, this particular policy measure does not seem possible to be a very potent weapon in the battle against petroleum price inflation.

In search of a more effective policy, we note that petroleum product prices in India depend on four factors (1) the import cost of crude oil, (2) the domestic cost of refining crude into the finished products, (3) the mark-ups over cost charged by the petroleum companies (most of which are government-owned) and (4) indirect taxes imposed by the central and the state governments. For the rise in petroleum product prices experienced in India in recent years, accusing fingers have often been pointed at the import cost part since Brent crude oil prices have indeed been rising over quite some time. It should be noted, however, that there have been stretches of time when Brent prices were actually *falling*. In fact, the most dramatic fall took place in the year 2020–21. Under the impact of the sharp global economic deceleration caused by the Covid pandemic, demand for crude oil fell sharply in the global market. All crude oil price including the Brent prices nosedived. Even in that phase, however, petroleum product prices in the domestic market in

India were *rising*. The excuse that it takes time to revise the domestic prices of the finished products when import cost of crude oil changes does not seem to bear scrutiny. As has been pointed out, the government companies take little or no time to revise prices *upwards* whenever crude import cost *rises* but have not revised prices downwards when import cost has fallen. Moreover, there does not seem to be any reason for believing that over the past few years there has been any significant rise in the cost of *refining* the crude. Clearly, the main factor behind the acceleration in the rate of inflation in petroleum products prices in India at times of a fall in global crude prices is the series of hikes in indirect taxes on these products. These taxes, in fact, rose consistently over the period from 2013–14 to 2020–21. There may also have been an increase in mark-ups. (Information on mark-up rates of the oil companies do not seem to be in the public domain.) Cuts in the mark-ups and the rates of indirect taxes would, therefore, be warranted. These would have an immediate impact on the market prices. Moreover, indirect taxes are a very substantial part of the petroleum price paid by the consumer in India. In case of petrol and diesel they constitute more than half of the price. Thus, there seems to be considerable elbow room for this type of policy action. (That may not be case, however, with countries such as the USA where the rates of indirect taxes on these products are considerably lower.) At the very least, the government should allow the pass-through of the benefits of falls in the global crude prices (when such falls do occur) to the consumers. All that this would entail would be keeping the rates of indirect taxes and mark-ups *unchanged*.

Long-run policies

Needless to say, in the long run, it is the price of crude oil that is the basic driver of the pattern of the movement of domestic prices of petroleum products. One obvious policy recommendation in the long-run context, therefore, would be to increase domestic crude production. While there is some scope for intensifying drilling operations in the existing oilfields, there is an even more urgent need for much greater efforts at exploring for crude reserves than is seen at present. The Oil and Natural Gas Corporation (ONGC) which does the major part of oil explorations and crude oil production in India should receive adequate funding for the purpose. The cost of domestic crude is likely to be less than the cost of procuring crude in the oligopolistic global crude market and of transporting it to India. In the long run, the price difference is likely to over-compensate for the initial investments in exploration. That is why this is recommended as a *long-run* policy. At the moment, however, the government seems to be more interested in *privatising* the exploration and drilling operations than in funding new explorations by ONGC. In fact, ONGC has recently been advised by the government to consider leasing out its largest producing oil and gas fields to *foreign* companies. Not much is known at present about what the effects of such arrangements on price of Indian crude would turn out to be. Previous experience with leasing PSEs in other industries to *domestic* private companies, however, does not seem to permit one to be optimistic. Nowadays, however, oil *companies* (whose main job is oil *refining* rather than exploring) are also expanding their activities into the field of exploration. This is true of the publicly owned Indian Oil Limited (IOL) (which is India's biggest oil company) as well as of some of the private companies in the field. Needless to say, while we do not recommend privatisation of public sector units, all of these companies, whether public or private, should be supported in their oil exploration and drilling activities.

A related policy would be to encourage the use of *natural gas* for the purpose of producing energy. Natural gas usually comes together with crude oil (although there are some reservoirs that contain natural gas but no oil). For this reason, producers of crude oil such as ONGC also produce natural gas. Like crude oil (and coal), natural gas is also a fossil fuel but it does not need refining and can be delivered straight to users. In India, it is the Gas Authority of India Limited (GAIL), a public sector unit, that does most of the business of transporting natural gas from the gas fields to the users through pipelines. Recently, IOL has entered into the business of delivering compressed natural gas (CNG) in cylinders to users located in areas where GAIL is yet to extend its pipelines. (CNG is not to be confused with liquefied petroleum gas (LPG). Petroleum gas is not a natural gas. It is produced in the oil refineries by cracking naphtha which is a by-product of the crude oil refining process. While many oil companies produce LPG and sell them in cylinders, so far (in end-2021) in India it is only IOL that also procures *natural* gas from ONGC and sells it in the form of CNG in cylinders.) An additional justification for encouraging increased production and use of natural gas is that in many uses its cost to the consumer per unit of energy obtained is less than that of petrol and diesel.

To state our third (and last) policy recommendation in the long-run context, we recall the oligopolistic nature of the global crude oil market. The exporters of crude oil operate as a group but the oil-consuming countries do not. As a result, each consuming country is in a weak bargaining position with respect to the exporters. In fact, it is often the case that within each consuming country the different oil companies act individually in the matter of negotiations over their purchase contracts, thus weakening their own bargaining position even further. Some countries now have woken up to this last problem. India is presently (in December 2021) in the process of drawing up a strategy under which all of its oil companies, public and private, would join hands and act as *one* purchaser in bargaining with the foreign oil-producers. This is a move in the right direction. Our recommendation here is that it should be taken a step further. All oil-importing *countries* should come together to form a buyers' group and confront the oil cartel as a single buyer. This would increase the bargaining power of the oil importers and prevent the oil cartel from exerting exclusive control over global crude oil price. The kind of international understanding among the oil-importing countries that this would involve would take time to come about. That is why this is recommended as a long-run policy. A beginning in the direction of building up the required consensus can, however, be made in the foreseeable future if the biggest oil-importing countries of the world (such as the USA, China, Japan and India) take the initiative in the matter. That they have recently collaborated in the matter of releasing parts of their strategic oil reserves raises hopes for the proposal that we have put forward.

5.6 Supply-oriented policies: *Atmanirbhar Bharat Abhiyan*

In May 2020, when Covid 19 was raging in full fury in the country and it was obvious that the problem of economic slowdown which had already been a severe one was soon going to get even worse, the government announced an economic stimulus package for the purpose of arresting the slowdown. The package was called *Atmanirbhar Bharat Abhiyan*, literally meaning *Self-reliant India Mission*. Although the objective of self-reliance was popularly interpreted to mean reducing India's dependence on imports, the government emphasised that this was not an import substitution strategy. Rather, the idea was to boost indigenous production for the purpose of catering to both domestic demand and the need for exports.

The total value of the package was the impressive figure of more than Rs. 20 lakh crore. This was about 10 per cent of India's GDP of a year. The total amount was to be spent in five different tranches directed towards different sectors of the economy. Small and medium enterprises, small farmers and migrant workers, agricultural infrastructure sectors, crucial infrastructural industries credit supply through measures adopted by the Reserve Bank, etc., were covered under the different tranches.

Critics, however, have pointed out that almost the entire amount of the package was planned to be spent on giving *loans* to the beneficiaries (i.e. the producers and the workers). This was the basic limitation of this policy intervention. As we have seen before, so far as the producers were concerned, the main problem of the time was *not* one of *availability* of loans. Rather, it was one of *unwillingness* of producers to take loans for the purpose of investment because of inadequacy of demand for the produced goods. For the workers, on the other hand, what was needed was *grants* rather than loans. In a situation of widespread unemployment and poverty, workers would naturally be wary of taking loans that have to be repaid with interest in the future.

No wonder the objective of the stimulus package was not fulfilled. While the package was announced in the early part of the financial year 2020–21, very little new investment took place in the economy during the rest of the year. As we now know, the growth rate of GDP for that year was negative.

Needless to say, it is not the intention here to suggest that broad-based supply-side interventions such as the *Atmanirbhar Bharat Abhiyan* would be irrelevant for India under all circumstances. They would obviously be appropriate if and when the economy faces *aggregate* (rather than sector-specific) supply constraints.

5.7 Concluding remarks

The basic message of the policy discussion in this chapter is that if inflation is under check in the coming months and years, macroeconomic policies would constitute the main weapon in the fight against economic deceleration in the Indian economy. Whenever inflationary pressures arise, however, it would be necessary to combine them with microeconomic policies aimed at those specific sectors that turn out to be the main sources of such pressures. In connection with the second scenario, it may be noted that, so far as CPI inflation in India is concerned, the importance of the effects of *global* price movements is sometimes over-emphasised. As has been shown in a recent report of the RBI, an analysis of monthly inflation rates over the years from 1992 to 2021 reveals that global inflation has only a moderate impact on Indian inflation. A 1 per cent change in global commodity prices leads to a 0.02 per cent change in CPI inflation (see RBI, 2022a). Thus, it is the domestic economy that must be judged to be the main driver of CPI inflation in India. This underlines the importance of the role of *domestic* economic policies to contain any inflationary pressures that may arise in the Indian economy in the future. Finally, the remark on the necessity of contingent planning that we made at the beginning of the chapter bears repetition: economic policy must be dovetailed to the need of the hour. There is no "one size fits all" policy remedy for all eventualities.

Appendix to Chapter 5: calculation of the CPI inflation rate

In this annexure, we discuss how the rate of CPI inflation is measured. We start with some of the basic things about how any price index (whether a CPI or not) is calculated. First of all, since our objective is to measure *changes* in the price level, we need to fix a *base* (or *reference*) point of time (time t_0, say) so that prices at the *current* time t_1 can be compared with those at the base point and we get an idea about how prices have changed between these two points in time. How do we calculate the change in prices? If there was only one commodity in the market and if p_0 and p_1 are the prices at the base time and the current time, respectively, we could simply consider the ratio p_1/p_0 or, as is the convention, express p_1 as the percentage of p_0, that is take $[(p_1/p_0) \times 100]$. We could say that this is the value of the *price index* at time t_1. Note that the value of the price index at base time t_0 is always 100 since then the "current" time is also the base time so that p_1 is the same as p_0. If the value of the price index at t_1 is 110, we say that there has been a 10 per cent increase in price between t_0 and t_1; if it is 80, we say that there has been a 20 per cent *decrease* in price and so on.

The fact that there are many commodities in the market is, however, a complication. For each commodity there would be one price ratio (or *price relative*, as it is often called). The main thing to decide is how to combine the different price relatives into a single one. What is usually done is to take an *average* of the price relatives. Taking a *simple* average (i.e. one that treats all commodities equally and does not pay attention to the fact that all commodities do not carry the same importance for the consumers), however, would not be advisable. A *weighted* average is, therefore, taken. We first multiply the price relative of each commodity by a number that indicates the *proportional importance* of the particular commodity for the consumers. This number is the *weight* on the price relative of that commodity. We thus obtain the *weighted* price relatives of the different commodities. Then we calculate the *weighted average of the price relatives*, that is the sum of the weighted price relatives divided by the sum of the weights. However, since the weights are *proportions*, the sum of the weights would be 1. Hence, the weighted average of the price relatives is simply their weighted *sum*. Finally, as in the case of a single commodity discussed in the previous paragraph, we multiply this sum by 100 to get the price index. The interpretation of the index remains the same as in the case of a single commodity. The value of the price index at the base time will again be 100.

How do we determine the weights? So far we have been talking about price indices in general. Consider now the case of a CPI. Usually, the weight (i.e. the importance) of a commodity for a *consumer* is taken to be the proportion of the *total expenditure* of the consumer that is spent on the particular commodity. For any given commodity this proportion will, of course, be different for different consumers. But if we have data on the expenditure patterns of a sufficiently large number of consumers, then an estimate of this proportion for the *typical* consumer (i.e. some kind of an average over all the different consumers) can be obtained. In India, such data on expenditure patterns are generated by expenditure surveys conducted from time to time by the National Statistical Office (NSO), previously known as the National Sample Survey Office (NSSO). While it is not possible to observe the expenditure pattern of literally *every* consumer, a sufficiently large sample of consumers is drawn at random for the purpose.

We have said that the weight on a commodity is the proportion of a consumer's expenditure that is spent on that commodity. But these proportions can (and usually do) change over time. Hence, the values of these weights at the base time t_0 may not be the same as those at the current time t_1. Even if we have the data to estimate the weights at both of these two points of time, the question arises as to which of these two sets of weights to use. There is no universally accepted answer to this question. In India it is the weights estimated with data relating to the base time t_0 that is used. We shall not pursue the matter further here. However, it will be good to remember that this particular choice of weights is merely a convention and that there are other possible choices (such as the weights estimated for the current time t_1 or some average of the two sets of weights).

From a practical point of view there are still a couple of loose ends. To compute price indices we need data on prices at the base time, those at the current time and the weights on the price relatives. As we have said earlier, the convention is to take the weights calculated for the base time and these are calculated from data generated by expenditure surveys. These surveys are, however, huge operations, involving interviewing lakhs of households and processing the data. Thus, even if we know that a survey was carried out in a particular year, it is difficult to say which precise point of time of the year the data relate to. This difficulty is usually avoided by *assuming* that the weights calculated from the data would apply to *all* time points in the year in which the survey was conducted. It is for this reason that we usually talk about a base *year* (rather than a precise base *time point*).

Again, because of their huge scales, it is difficult to conduct expenditure surveys every year. (In India currently the practice is to conduct them *every five years* although efforts are on to increase their frequency.) Thus, it may be that when a particular year is chosen as the base year, expenditure survey data (needed for calculating the weights on the commodities) are not available for that particular year. In such cases the weights needed for calculating the price index are computed on the basis of data available for an *adjacent* year.

The reader may recall from our discussion in Chapter 1 that the base year used for calculating *real* GDP is not fixed once for all. If the base year is too far back in time, this will lead to the problem that the list of commodities produced and consumed in the economy may differ between the base year and the current year. The price of a currently produced commodity may not be available for the base year. Now, exactly the same problem may arise in the context of price indices. For this reason, for the calculation of price indices, too, the base year is changed from time to time.

In India currently the base year for calculation of CPI is 2012. The government publishes CPI figures for every *month* with that fixed base year. Price data are collected every month. The value of CPI for *all* months of the base year 2012 are taken to be 100. Thus, for calculating the CPI for, say, January 2013 what is done is to calculate the price relative for each commodity by taking the ratio of the price prevailing in January 2013 to that prevailing in the same month of the base year 2012 and then to compute the weighted average of the price relatives by using the weights for the base year 2012 (computed on the basis of expenditure survey data for 2012 or for some adjacent year). Similarly, when we calculate the CPI for February 2013, the price relative for each commodity will be the ratio of price in February 2013 to price in February 2012. The weights needed for calculating the weighted average of the price relatives remain the same: these are the weights applicable for the whole base year 2012. Similar procedures apply for the calculation of the CPI indices for all other months of 2013 as well as for any other month of any subsequent year (until the government announces a change of the base year for CPI).

Now, the CPI values are used to obtain the rates of *monthly* inflation for every month. CPI inflation is the percentage change in the value of the CPI. In India, the convention is to do this calculation of *monthly* inflation on the year-on-year basis. Under this method, the CPI for the month under consideration is compared with the CPI *for the same month in the previous year* (and not with the CPI of the immediately preceding month). For instance, the CPI value for January 2013 (with 2012 as the base year) was reported to be 104.6. Since the CPI for January 2012 is, by definition, 100, this means that in January 2013 there was a 4.6 per cent monthly inflation in CPI in India in January 2013. Again, in January 2014, the CPI was reported to be 113.6. This means that over the *two-year period* from January 2012 to January 2014 there was CPI inflation at the rate of 13.6 per cent. But what was the *monthly* rate of inflation in January 2014? As per the "year-on-year" method, it is the percentage change in the value of CPI in January 2014 over its value in January 2013, that is $[\{(113.6 - 104.6) \div 104.6\} \times 100] = 8.6$ per cent. Similarly, since the CPI for February 2014 is also reported to be 113.6 and that for February 2013 is reported to be 105.3, the monthly rate of inflation in February 2014, under the year-on-year method is $[\{(113.6 - 105.3) \div 105.3\} \times 100] = 7.88$ per cent. The reader may recall from Footnote 6 of Chapter 1 that the year-on-year method is also followed in India for calculating the *quarterly* growth rates of real GDP. The argument for following this method was stated and commented upon there. We do not repeat the discussion here.

Often, however, we also talk about the *annual* rate of inflation. For that purpose, we need the value of the price index for the *year* under consideration. This, however, is taken to be the simple average (i.e. the arithmetic mean) of the monthly values of the price index. For instance, in the 12 months of the financial year 2013–14 from April 2013 to March 2014, the values of the CPI index (with base year 2012) were reported by the government to be 106.1, 106.9, 109.3, 111.0, 112.4, 113.7, 114.8, 115.3, 114.5, 113.6, 113.6 and 114.2. The average of these numbers which is 112.2 is, therefore, taken to be the CPI for the year 2013–14. The rate of annual CPI inflation in any year is then defined as the percentage change in the annual CPI between the year under consideration and the immediately preceding year. Since we are dealing here with *annual* CPI value, the year-on-year method now coincides with the usual method of calculating the rate of change in this value between consecutive years.

However, if monthly CPI inflation rates have already been calculated, then for simplicity, the annual CPI inflation rate in a year is often taken to be the simple average of the monthly CPI inflation rates of the 12 months of the year. The two methods of calculating the annual CPI inflation rate may not yield exactly the same figure. But they will be approximately the same, and the difference is usually found to be negligible.

References

Friedman, M. (1969): *The Optimum Quantity of Money and Other Essays*, Aldine, Chicago.

GOI (2022): *Economic Survey, 2021–22*, Government of India, New Delhi.

Marshall, A. (1890): *Principles of Economics*, Macmillan, London.

Patnaik, A. (2019): 'Impact of food inflation on headline inflation in India', *Asia-Pacific Sustainable Development Journal*, 26(1), 85–111.

RBI (2016): *Handbook of Statistics on the Indian Economy, 2015–16*, Reserve Bank of India, Mumbai.

RBI (2021): *Handbook of Statistics on the Indian Economy, 2020–21*, Reserve Bank of India, Mumbai.

RBI (2022a): *Annual Report 2021–22*, Reserve Bank of India, Mumbai.

RBI (2022b): *Monetary Policy Report*, Reserve Bank of India, Mumbai.

Sasmal, J. (2016): *J. Resources, Technology and Sustainability: An Analytical Perspective on Indian Agriculture*, Springer, Singapore.

6 Economic policies and pandemics

The case of Covid-19

6.1 Plan of the chapter

In the previous chapter, we argued that macroeconomic policies should be the main weapons in the fight against the economic slowdown that India is currently experiencing although in some cases they need to be combined with microeconomic ones. Microeconomic policies become even more vital when we recognise that while the Indian economy has been decelerating for a fairly long period even before the Covid-19 pandemic, it is the pandemic that brought this lingering problem to the point of a full-blown crisis in the year 2020–21. It is important to consider the question of what type of policies would be appropriate for controlling such pandemics.

Apparently, the question lies in the domain of medical experts and epidemiologists rather than in that of economists. On a closer look, however, it is seen to have important economic aspects as well. These issues constitute the subject matter of this chapter. Since curative medicines for the disease are yet to be widely available, the only hope at the moment lies in preventing the spread of the disease. Vaccines constitute the main weapon in this war. Issues relating to the design and development of vaccines and to their production and distribution are, therefore, vitally important. Policies targeted specifically towards this particular sector of the economy take the centre stage in this discussion. Thus, the focus is now on *microeconomics*. Moreover, unlike in the previous chapter, it is *supply-side* policies that play the central role.

It is to be noted that it is because Covid-19 is the most recent pandemic and is still fresh in public memory that most of the discussion in the chapter is carried out in terms of policies relating to the supply of vaccines for this particular disease. It is emphasised, however, that the economics of the matter is quite general. The same analysis would apply to policies pertaining to the supply of *all* types of vaccines and, in fact, also to the development of *curative* medicines.

Before entering into a discussion of economic policies in this context, however, a word seems to be in order on the question why one should spend time discussing Covid-19 at this point of time when the worst phase of this

DOI: 10.4324/9781003350514-6

pandemic seems to be over, at least so far as the Indian economy is concerned. I discuss this matter in Section 6.2.

In Section 6.3, we note that since a pandemic, by definition, is a *global* problem, common sense tells us that it would have been in the best interests of all if mankind could stand up in unison to face it. It is not just the obvious health-related benefits of such a unified stand that we have in mind here. We cite facts and figures to show that in the case of the Covid-19 pandemic, it would have benefitted not only the *global economy* but also the *AEs* which have so far displayed a lamentable tendency to practise "vaccine nationalism" (i.e. to grab as much as possible of the limited global supply of Covid vaccines for their exclusive use).

If vaccine nationalism hurts the AEs in economic terms, why do they cling to it? Section 6.4 discusses two possible explanations of this apparent paradox. One explanation is based on the hypothesis that the AEs are simply unaware of the fact that they would gain by adopting a more cooperative attitude (or, at least, they underestimate the magnitude of these gains). The other explanation argues that a major stumbling block on the way to achieving global vaccination (or, at least, an equitable distribution of the *available* global supply of Covid vaccines) is the oligopolistic power of the major producers in the world market for vaccines.

In Section 6.5, we take the reality of vaccine nationalism for granted and make a number of policy recommendations from the point of view of the Indian economy. The broad contours of an optimal policy framework, of course, follow immediately from common sense: encourage the development and manufacturing of Covid vaccines in the country and ensure the availability of the vaccines at reasonable prices to the consumers (or to the central or the state governments who procure the vaccines on behalf of the consumers). However, the task of encouraging the development of a *new* product is a more difficult one than that of simply subsidising the producers of a good that is already there in the market. Similarly, the question of appropriate pricing of the vaccines that are to be developed is a more complex one than that of controlling the price of a good in an existing market. We argue, however, that despite these complexities a number of simple, yet useful, policy recommendations can be made on the basis of the lessons of experience. Some specific policy mistakes that have been made in India and the need to avoid them in future are also highlighted.

Section 6.6, the concluding section, summarises the lessons drawn from the policy discussion and emphasises that these lessons are likely to retain their relevance even when the Covid-19 pandemic becomes a thing of the past.

6.2 Why spend time discussing Covid-19?

India has by now achieved a relatively satisfactory rate of Covid-19 vaccination. As of 14 June 2022, 66 per cent of the country's population has received two doses of some vaccine while 74 per cent has received at least one dose. The corresponding figures for the USA are 67 per cent and 78 per cent, respectively. (In the matter of booster doses, however, the figure for India is an unsatisfactory 2.7 per cent. The US figure is 31 per cent.)[1] Mainly because of the vaccination programme, the spread of the disease has been controlled. By all accounts, the worst phase of the pandemic is over so far as India is concerned. Under the circumstances, should a book on the contemporary Indian economy devote space to a discussion of Covid-19? One reason why the answer is in the affirmative has already been mentioned before. To repeat, it was the pandemic that brought the pre-existing problem of economic slowdown to a full-blown crisis point.

The *additional* point that we wish to make at this stage is that even if we assume that the Covid-19 pandemic is on its way out, it is unlikely to be the last pandemic to hit the world. Moreover, while the last pandemic of comparable proportions was the influenza epidemic of the late 1910s and the 1920s, it does not follow that, in future, pandemics will be spaced in time about a century apart from each other. On the contrary, heath experts and environmentalists are apprehensive of more frequent recurrence of pandemics. Environmental degradation and the resulting ecological imbalance that our planet has witnessed in recent times play an important role in this context. It is true that this deleterious process began in the very remote past. In fact, its history may even be as old as that of human civilisation itself. However, there is no denying the fact that the process gathered momentum with the Industrial Revolution of the late-eighteenth and nineteenth centuries and has accelerated further with the progress of time. To be sure, industrialisation has played a very positive part in promoting mankind's material progress in general and in uplifting the standard of living of the masses in particular, especially in the countries that are today categorised as the AEs. Its negative impact on the environment did not matter so much as long as its magnitude was relatively small.

Recent decades, however, has seen a sharp acceleration of the rate at which ecological damage has been perpetrated. The way in which people and animals come into contact in today's world has increased the frequency of outbreaks of the so-called *zoonotic diseases*, diseases that originate in animals. When pathogens jump the species barrier that separates people from animals, their ability to spread among humans and the severity of the diseases that are caused in humans are seen to increase enormously. Such barrier jumps occur, for instance, when, because of population growth and displacement, people move into new areas in search of food and enter animal habitats that have never had human contact before. The process is abated and magnified enormously by the interaction among a whole gamut of factors such as an increasing rate of rural-to-urban migration in search of industrial employment, climate changes caused by deforestation and carbon emission and trade in animal products and wildlife.

In view of all this, health experts are now of the opinion that pandemics are going to be much more frequent in the future than they have been in the past. Marani et al. (2021), for instance, used a newly assembled record of past outbreaks, measured the intensities of the outbreaks and estimated the annual probabilities of their recurrence. It was found that the probability of a pandemic of a scale similar to that of Covid-19 was about 2 per cent every year. This implies that, by, say, 2026, it will be more likely than not that an individual born in the year 2000 will witness the occurrence of another Covid-19-like outbreak. To make matters worse, the annual recurrence probability of 2 per cent is not a constant. It may rise in future.

Experts associated with this type of research emphasise that it is not the purpose of such studies this type of research to create a scare. The purpose, rather, is to stress the need to take timely and effective *policy* actions to prevent recurrences of epidemics or, at least, to bring down the probabilities of their recurrence. Our motivation in reporting them here is the same. We are, however, referring here to the need for *economic* policies to minimise the impacts of future epidemics. Such policies are, therefore, of more than transient interest.

6.3 An ideal policy: united stand against the pandemic

6.3.1 The economic benefits of vaccine capacity creation

In order to emphasise the need for international cooperation in facing up to the challenge posed by the Covid-19 pandemic, we start by describing the benefits that can be reaped from such a unified stand. The potential *health* benefit of such a stand is obvious. We shall confine the discussion to its *economic* benefit.

Since the main weapon in fighting the pandemic is vaccine, we shall concentrate on the issue of the *rate of vaccination*. Now, the task of achieving a high global rate of vaccination can be divided into two parts: (i) creating adequate vaccine manufacturing *capacity* and (ii) *distributing* the global supply of vaccines as equitably as possible among the people of the world.

We first remark on the economic benefits from capacity creation. We start by asking just how large is the magnitude of the benefit from vaccine capacity. If it is a small matter, there would be little point in analysing the factors that limit this capacity and in discussing the possible ways of removing them. It turns out, however, that, far from being small, the benefits are, in fact, enormously large.

Look first at the economic *loss* emanating from the pandemic. Economists at the IMF have estimated that the sum of the global GDPs of the first two years after the outbreak of the pandemic in early 2020 would be less by $12 trillion than what it would have been, had there been no pandemic (see Gopinath, 2020). In other words, over this 24-month period, the pandemic would impose a GDP loss of $500 billion *every month* on the global economy. The enormousness of the economic loss hardly needs elaboration. Needless to say, the loss is mostly due to the disturbances caused to production and distribution of goods and services by the lockdowns and other restrictions that have had to be imposed for the purpose of containing the spread of the disease. This, of course, means that, had there been no pandemic, the global economy would have *benefitted* by way of *avoiding* the GDP loss.

It is more difficult to estimate the benefit from the production of Covid vaccines, taking the reality of the pandemic into consideration. A recent study estimates the benefit (in terms of global GDP) by first noting the vaccine capacity that is already in place (called *baseline* capacity) and then calculating the benefit from creating *additional* capacity. The baseline capacity is estimated to be 3 billion units where a "unit" of capacity is defined as the *fixed investment* necessary for producing one course per year of any Covid vaccine approved by a regulatory agency plus the *complementary investment* required for delivery of the vaccine to the consumer. (A "course" consists of the required doses of the vaccine. Most of the existing Covid vaccines require two doses. For these, 1 course equals two doses.) It is estimated that the benefit (in terms of global GDP) from this baseline capacity is $8.7 trillion. It is then estimated that if the capacity can be *increased* to 4 billion units, annual GDP benefit would increase to $9.4 trillion (i.e. that there would be an increase of $0.7 trillion in global GDP). If capacity increases to 5 billion units, the GDP benefit would rise to $9.8 trillion (i.e. there would be a *further* increase in GDP by the amount of $0.4 trillion). For further details, see Castillo et al. (2021).

Moreover, these estimates of the benefit to the world's GDP from the creation of additional Covid vaccine production capacity are actually estimates of only the *direct benefits*. This is because they do not take account of the facts that the disease would also generate large and accumulating losses to *human capital* by harming education and health and that these would also have a negative impact on the annual GDP of a year.

6.3.2 *Need for concerted effort to increase the aggregate supply of vaccines*

The large economic benefits from the creation of Covid vaccine production capacity obviously implies that it is in the interest of mankind as a whole that economic policies be directed towards creating a capacity level that would be adequate for the purpose of achieving a satisfactory *global* vaccination rate. Each country should promote research on the development of Covid vaccines and should ensure that the vaccines that are developed are produced in adequate quantities. Within each country this would involve promoting competition in the market for Covid vaccines by encouraging producers to enter this line of business since, as is well-known, the level of output of a commodity would be higher in a competitive market than in a monopolistic or oligopolistic one. Moreover, there should be *cooperation* among countries in these regards. In particular, the production technologies that are developed in a country should be disseminated globally so that other countries can participate in the efforts to increase global outputs of the vaccines.

Precious little, however, seems to have been done so far in these respects. As a result, full vaccination of the entire population of the world remains a far cry. Most of the Covid vaccines currently in use requires two doses for a person to be "fully vaccinated" (although in February 2021, the US Food and Drug Administration authorised a one-shot vaccine made by Johnson and Johnson for emergency use in that country). In addition, booster doses are recommended since the immunity given by the vaccine is seen to wane after some time. However, as of June 2022, as much as 30 per cent of the world population was yet to receive even a single dose of a vaccine, about 40 per cent was yet to be fully vaccinated and about 74 per cent was yet to get a booster dose.

6.3.3 Need for equitable distribution of vaccines

The need for international cooperation stands out even more starkly in the context of *distribution* of the available global supply of Covid vaccines among the countries of the world. Since Covid-19 is a hitherto-unknown type of disease, development and subsequent production of Covid vaccines involves massive investments of financial as well as knowledge resources. No wonder, the high-income countries of the world have an advantage here and, therefore, the bulk of the presently available total supply is produced in these countries. The governments of these countries have cornered the lion's share of the existing global supply of Covid vaccines. Moreover, there are allegations that governments of the rich countries are building huge stockpiles of the vaccines in order to be able to deal with possible *future* outbreaks of the disease. The US government is reported to be holding enough stocks to vaccinate the whole population of the country at least five times over.

It is no wonder, therefore, that the distribution of vaccines among countries has been greatly unequal. As of June 2022, in as many as 72 countries, at least half of the population is yet to get even the first dose of a Covid vaccine. In countries that are at the bottom of the distribution, the situation is truly alarming. For instance, in Burundi, a central African country, practically the entire population remains unvaccinated: 99.9 per cent of the population has not obtained even a single dose.

6.3.4 Not only an ethical issue but also an economic one

A very obvious question that arises at this point is the following. Why, at all, should we be interested in reducing the inequality in the distribution of Covid vaccines among the countries? Is it because the loss of human lives and of livelihoods in the relatively deprived countries of the world hurt our ethical values in general and our intuitive idea of natural justice in particular?

We wish to emphasise that while ethical issues are certainly important, they are *not* the whole story. (Indeed, if they *were*, there would not be much scope for discussing the matter in detail in an economics book.) There are *economic* costs of vaccine inequality. It has now been established with the help of data that the extreme inequality in vaccine distribution have imposed a high cost not only on the global economy but also on the high-income economies themselves. For instance, Oxfam International (2020) calculated that if the AEs bore the full cost providing vaccination to the *low-income countries*, they would have to bear an expenditure of $25 billion. Using this cost estimate, Hafner et al. (2020) calculated that, by *not* extending this help to these countries (i.e. by keeping them unvaccinated), the AEs would incur a GDP loss of $119 billion because they would lose the opportunity of engaging in profitable international trade with the low-income countries. In other words, by spending $25 billion on vaccine supply to the low-income countries, the AEs could obtain a benefit of $119 billion. The "rate of return" would be (119 ÷ 25) = 4.76. In other words, for every dollar that they spend on this particular act of philanthropy, the AEs would get back a benefit of about 4.8 dollars.

In a similar vein, Cakmakli et al. (2021) show that if the trade links between the AEs on the one hand and the *emerging markets and developing economies* (EMDEs) on the other are taken into account, it turns out that by practicing vaccine nationalism the AEs imposed on themselves a GDP loss of about $1.6 trillion up to the year 2021.

The interlinkages between the economies of the world are of crucial importance in these calculations. Suppose that Country A is fully vaccinated while Country B is unvaccinated and is a trading partner of country A. The pandemic hurts B economically by harming production. This reduces the purchasing power of the people in B and, therefore, its ability to pay for imports from A. Hence, A's *exports* to B and, thus, the *foreign* demand for A's products fall. Thus, what began as a supply-side problem in B creates a demand-side problem in A and has a negative effect on A's GDP. A supply-side problem may also appear in A since it is frequently the case that some vital intermediate inputs in the production process of an advanced economy are imported from other countries and the initial supply-side problem in B may hinder B's ability to supply A with the required inputs. Moreover, in addition to this direct interlinkage between exports and imports of A and B, there will be *indirect* linkages between them in the presence of a third country C if all the three countries trade with each other. In reality, as we have seen before, there are a large number of inadequately vaccinated countries although there are also a number of well-vaccinated ones. It is easily seen that there would be high overall (i.e. direct plus indirect) interlinkage. Thus, just as "nobody is safe from Covid-19 unless everybody is safe," no country, not even a fully vaccinated one, is immune from the deleterious *economic* effects of the pandemic as long as any of its trading partners is unvaccinated.

The meaning and significance of these estimates should be appropriately distinguished from those of the estimates of the *global* GDP benefit from *vaccine capacity creation* that we discussed earlier (in Section 6.3.1). There we were talking of the benefit derived from increasing the *aggregate* supply of Covid vaccines in the world. What the estimates referred to in the previous paragraph show, however, relates to the *distribution* of the given available supply of vaccines. The focus here is on the beneficial effect of a more egalitarian inter-country distribution of vaccine access rather than on that of an increase in the *aggregate* supply of vaccines.

6.3.5 *Attempts at putting up a united front*

It is not the case that no attempts have so far been made to address the twin issues of aggregate vaccine supply and its equitable distribution. One of the most notable among such attempts is the Covid-19 Vaccines Global Access Facility (COVAX) set up under the auspices of the World Health Organization (WHO), the Coalition for Epidemic Preparedness Innovations and the Global Alliance for Vaccines and Immunisation. The objectives of COVAX are to raise funds for the purpose of encouraging and assisting the development of Covid vaccines, to build up stocks of these vaccines and to distribute these among all countries of the world in an egalitarian way by giving priority to the need to vaccinate people in the high-risk groups. By January 2021, as many as 190 countries accounting for an overwhelming majority of the world's population had joined COVAX. A little later, the USA followed suit. It was decided that among the member-countries the low-income ones – there were 92 of them – would get the vaccines free of cost. The other countries would have access to the vaccines but would pay for them.

The vaccines were to be distributed in stages. In the *first* stage each member-country would get an allocation of a number of doses that would be proportional to its population. Care would, however, be taken to ensure that 3 per cent of the people in the country who are in the highest-risk groups (for instance, health workers) are vaccinated. Within this stage, additional allocations would also be made for covering 20 per cent of the population, giving priority to such groups as the elderly or those with comorbidity. In the *second* stage, the member-counties would receive further allocations but now the allocation to a country would depend on the urgency of its need as determined by factors such as the state of the country's health infrastructure and the speed with which the Covid virus is spreading in the country. In the *third* stage, the entire population of the world would be covered.

In practice, however, COVAX has been a non-starter. Underfunding has been the main problem. Even the modest fund-raising target of $6.8 billion for the year 2021 does not seem to have been fulfilled. As a result, COVAX has been unable to purchase vaccines in the needed quantities for distribution to low-income countries free of cost. A related issue is that the member-countries cannot be forced to procure vaccines *exclusively* from COVAX. They are free to make bilateral deals directly with the manufacturing companies. The AEs, in their eagerness to build as large stockpiles of Covid vaccines as possible, have found this very suitable for their purposes. Thus, in the year 2020 alone, as many as 44 bilateral deals were concluded between vaccine companies and governments of the rich countries. The trend continued into 2021. In fact, these countries started placing advance orders with the companies even before COVAX was formally started. For instance, as soon as Pfizer, Moderna and AstraZeneca, the first three Covid vaccines to be produced, received their regulatory approvals, the AEs, accounting for only about 15 per cent of the world's population, signed up advance purchase deals for as much as 85 per cent of the total *estimated* output of these three companies for the period up to the end of 2021. This has had a cascading effect on the COVAX programme. Having spent enormous amounts on stockpiling (and on giving research subsidies to vaccine companies in the developmental stage), the AEs did not have enough funds to spare for COVAX. The resulting underfunding meant that COVAX was unable to match the prices offered by the rich governments for their procurements from the companies. This, in turn, made the bilateral deals more attractive for the companies.

6.4 What explains the failure to take a united stand?

6.4.1 Failure to recognise inter-country economic linkages

In the previous section, we have seen that while mankind would gain enormously in economic terms if it could take a united stand against the pandemic, this ideal position has remained a utopia. In this section, we ask the obvious question that arises here, namely *why* that has been the case so far. In particular, we ask why the AEs have so far refrained from participating in programmes such as the COVAX, i.e. why they have adopted the policy of vaccine nationalism.

Two different explanations of this apparent paradox can be given. One of these is that the AEs are not *aware* of these cost-benefit calculations or, at least, they *underestimate* the benefits that they would get from a policy of international cooperation. These estimates, based on the inter-country economic linkages, are recent findings of research undertaken mostly by academic economists and are yet to be disseminated widely among governmental policy planners.

We are not, however, of the opinion that this hypothesis, by itself, constitutes an adequate explanation of the apparent paradox that we are discussing. We are talking about AEs here. Economic advisers of the governments of these countries are knowledgeable experts. In fact, many of them are well-known for their contributions to academic research in economics. It is unlikely, therefore, that AE governments would be uninformed about the magnitude of the potential economic benefits (to themselves) of helping the rest of the world in securing Covid vaccines. There is, thus, a need to look for other explanations.

6.4.2 *Market power of vaccine manufacturers*

A different (and more widely discussed) explanation of the paradox lays stress on what is loosely described as the "market power" of the vaccine manufacturing companies. To understand this explanation, start by referring to the classification of market forms on the basis of the number of producers in the market. At one extreme is the case of a *perfectly competitive* market where there are a large number of producers producing a homogeneous commodity and selling it to a large number of consumers. In such a market, each producer's output is so small a part of the total supply of the commodity that no single producer can significantly affect the total output or the market price of the commodity by his or her unilateral action. In this sense, no individual producer has significant *market power*. (A similar remark applies to individual consumers.) Each producer takes the market price as given. The actual price and the total output of the commodity are determined by the interaction of the forces of demand and supply in the open market. There is *free entry*, that is any producer can enter the market. Hence, in the long run, every producer earns only *normal profit*. If anyone earns supernormal profit in the short run by charging a higher price, this will induce the entry of new producers into the market and increased competition among producers will push down profits to its normal level in the long run.

At the opposite extreme lies the case of a *monopoly* where there are just one producer and a large number of consumers. Here the producer has complete market power in the sense that he or she controls the total supply and can set the price at any level without worrying about losing customers to other producers. He fixes the level of output at the level that would maximise his profit and sets the price at the maximum level that the consumers are willing to pay. A monopolist can (and usually does) earn supernormal profit even in the long run. It is also known that the price of the commodity would be higher and the quantity of output produced would be smaller in monopoly than in perfect competition

Despite these differences between perfect competition and monopoly, there is one point of similarity between them. Under perfect competition since each producer's output is a negligible fraction of the total output, at what level a producer decides to fix the output has no bearing on the output decision of any other producer. In monopoly the producer in question is the only one in the market and, therefore, there is no question of his output decision affecting anybody else's. For this reason, for both of these market forms, the question how market price and output are determined is a relatively simple one.

It is more difficult to deal with the intermediate case of *oligopoly* where there are a large number of consumers but only a *few* producers. (A special case of oligopoly is *duopoly* where there are just two producers.) Here each producer's output is a non-negligible part of the aggregate output. Hence, the output and pricing decisions of each producer have a bearing on the other producers' decisions. This interdependence between the decision-making processes of the individual producers makes it quite difficult to understand how market price and output are determined under oligopoly. Different assumptions regarding the behaviour of the producers lead to different theories of oligopoly. Among these, historically the first theory to be proposed was the one developed by Cournot (1838). To this day it remains the most widely used theory of oligopoly.

Informally, oligopoly seems to be closer to monopoly than to perfect competition. Indeed, according to most theories of oligopoly (including Cournot's), price is higher and total output smaller than in perfect competition. Therefore, the consumers (i.e. the people at large) are supposed to be better off under perfect competition than under oligopoly (or monopoly). For this reason, democratically elected governments are interested in promoting competition in all markets by encouraging *free entry* into markets. Anybody interested in producing any commodity should not face any barrier. It was Cournot's pioneering theory of oligopoly that later led to the enactment of anti-trust laws in the USA (for instance, the Sherman Anti-Trust Act of 1890). (In American parlance, a "trust" is a group of companies that collude among themselves in order to become what is effectively a monopoly.) The importance of a *theory* of oligopoly in this context comes from the fact that in order to take steps to prevent the formation of oligopoly in a market the government must understand the effects that the proposed steps are going to have on price and output levels and for that, in turn, it is necessary to understand how price and output are determined in the first place.

Examples of oligopolies are to be found as much in the markets for vaccines as in many others. Actually, most practical examples of oligopoly are those of what is called *oligopoly with product differentiation*. What happens is that although all the oligopolists produce basically the same commodity, each of them flaunts his or her own product as something special and uses brand names. Usually, however, the products of the different producers are close substitutes of one another. They serve the same basic purpose. The market for Covid vaccines is also of this type. In fact, in view of the scarcity of these vaccines at the present time and of the dire necessity for them from the health point of view, the consumers consider the different brands of Covid vaccines as more or less perfect substitutes. For them, any brand will do.

The market for Covid vaccines, however, has several special features in a number of other respects. Three of these are particularly important. *First*, this market came into being only after the Covid pandemic appeared on the global scene in late 2019. There was no history. Little, therefore, is known about the cost structure of Covid vaccines or about the profit markups on costs applied by the producers. As in any other market, the companies are not legally required to disclose these data to the consumers. They just bring the products to the market and set the prices. The purchasers have to take it or leave it. Whether they have to reveal the data to the *government* is not clear because the details of a bilateral deal between the government and a company are not in the public domain. In fact, they seem to be very closely guarded secrets. What is clear is that even if some cost figures are quoted, the government would have no way of judging their reliability. Since this is a *new* industry, there are no benchmarks (from previous records or from the practices prevailing in other countries) with which one can compare the companies' claims.

Secondly, Covid is a hitherto-unknown type of disease. Therefore, inventing Covid vaccines has involved a great deal of scientific research. Needless to say, the same is expected to be true of all of the several other Covid vaccines that are presently in various stages of development. The vaccine companies hold *intellectual property rights* (IPRs) on these vaccines. This is the main reason why the Covid vaccine market, as of now, is oligopolistic rather than perfectly competitive. The IPR of a company on its own Covid vaccine implies that no other producer can manufacture the same product by imitating the technology developed by this company. The vaccine companies consider their IPRs to be legitimate in view of the large amount of effort and financial resources that they have had to invest in developing the vaccines. Anyway, under the legal system of the USA (where the bulk of the presently available global supply of Covid vaccines is produced), IPRs (on all types of products whose technologies are based on research done by the producers) are legally protected. Moreover, the member countries of the World Trade Organization (WTO) (which includes all of the AEs of the world and many of the others) are signatories to the agreement on Trade-Related Aspects of Intellectual Property Rights (TRIPS) signed in 1994. TRIPS requires all of these countries to respect the IPRs of producers located in any of them.

Thirdly, in view of the public health emergency that the pandemic has caused, *most* of the governments (including those of the AEs) have, quite rightly, taken the responsibility of procuring these vaccines from the manufactures at negotiated prices and supplying them to the people of the respective countries free of cost. In most of the cases, therefore, within an economy the government is the sole purchaser of Covid vaccines. A *manufacturer*, however, is free to sell its vaccine to any buyer in the global market.

These features of the market for Covid vaccines have led to a situation where the vaccine companies are in a stronger bargaining position than the governments when it comes to negotiating the *prices* of the vaccines. The scarcity of vaccines implies that the companies do not have to worry about their *sales* prospects. In fact, in the USA, one of the *two* companies whose vaccines were the first to reach the manufacturing stage, Moderna, had received *advance* order from the US government for the lion's share of the output that the company planned to produce up to the end of 2021. The other company, Pfizer, did not have advance orders but received substantial government grants for research. One would, therefore, think that the government would have enough clout with the vaccine companies to obtain hefty discounts on prices. What has happened in practice, however, seems to be almost exactly the opposite. Because of the absence of any benchmark of comparison, the government had no way of judging the fairness or otherwise of the prices demanded by the companies. The companies have essentially dictated the prices. Exactly what prices were agreed upon is, of course, something of a mystery because, as have been noted earlier, the details of such deals are never made public. However, the fact that so far the companies have shown little willingness to sell the vaccines to COVAX at the relatively low prices offered by this WHO-sponsored programme implies that the companies have secured what, from *their* points of view, are better deals with the US government.

Moreover, the absence of benchmarks has combined with the IPRs of the companies to create a situation where the government in the USA has so far been unable to do much by way of promoting competition in this market. The anti-trust laws have been of little help in this regard since the companies have used the IPRs to prevent other producers from making use of the technology developed by them. Thus, they have been able to deter free entry *without* necessarily colluding among themselves for the purpose of creating a monopoly-like situation (which is what the anti-trust laws seek to prevent).

What do all these have to do with the explanation of paradox of vaccine nationalism? Unlike the explanation discussed in Section 6.4.1, the one that emerges here is more charitable to the governments of the AEs. It puts the blame on the vaccine companies. They refuse to sell vaccines to COVAX at the prices offered by COVAX since they are able to extract higher prices from the governments of their respective countries. Moreover, their restrictive policies prevent the emergence of a competitive market. This, in turn, restricts the global supply of vaccines. It is true that, as we saw in the preceding subsections, all this imposes a GDP loss not only on the global economy as a whole but also on the AEs. However, while the companies are located in the AEs, they are driven by the motivation of maximising *their* profits and are not concerned with what happens to the GDPs of even their own countries, let alone being concerned with global GDP loss.

While most observers find this second of the two explanations of vaccine nationalism to be more convincing than the first, some of them have pointed out that unseemly "vaccine-grabbing" by the AEs has also strengthened the machinations of the vaccine oligopolists. As have been noted before, the stocks of Covid vaccines that have been built up by the AEs are more than enough for achieving a hundred per cent vaccination rate in these countries (even if we take the need for *booster doses* into account). This is particularly true of the USA. It seems, therefore, that the AE governments had overestimated their procurement needs and this has strengthened the bargaining position of the vaccine companies.

6.5 Vaccine policy in India

6.5.1 Supply-side problem

So far in this chapter, we have tried to explain why vaccine nationalism has been practised by the AEs and how it has harmed the global economy as well as the AEs themselves. The time has now come to recognise the reality of vaccine nationalism and to turn to the important question what economic policy actions can be suggested for India under the existing circumstances.

The first thing that is to be noted in this connection is the fact that what we are discussing here is a *supply-side* problem. The issue here is not one of insufficiency of demand. On the contrary, there is excess demand for Covid vaccines and the reason is the shortage of supply of these vaccines in relation to demand. To be sure, the absolute magnitude of the supply shortage within the country has decreased over the recent months with an increase in the vaccination rate. Nevertheless, as mentioned before, we are still far from the ideal of one hundred per cent vaccination rate. The needs for *booster* doses and for stockpiling for the purposes of dealing with possible future outbreaks are also to be kept in mind. In cases of supply shortages of the usual types of consumer goods such as foodgrains, *rationing* is sometime introduced as a short-term measure for the purpose of reducing demand. Basically, this involves equal sharing of the available supply. Everyone gets *some* amount of the good although the amount is less than what one would like to have. In the present context, however, rationing (of this type) must be ruled out. The problem is that there are not enough *doses* of the vaccines and it would not do to give everybody a *fraction* of a dose.

There is also the *export* angle. India has, for long, been a leading producer of different kinds of vaccines. At a time when the rate of growth of demand for India's exports of *other* commodities is slackening because of the economic deceleration in India's trading partners and when there is a lot of unsatisfied demand for Covid vaccines in the world, there is an urgent need to develop and produce these vaccines for export purposes also. For all of these reasons, we now concentrate on policies directed at increasing supply of Covid vaccines.

6.5.2 Indigenous development is the way

The supply problem, in turn, can be divided into two parts: *development* of Covid vaccines and their *production*. We start with development. It is easily seen that in this connection the main thrust of policy planning should be towards *indigenous* development. While, as we have seen before, in the global context there is much to be said in favour of the abolition of IPRs on Covid vaccines, experience shows that dependence on Covid vaccines developed abroad is unlikely to be of much help for India. Most of these have been developed by vaccine companies in Western countries. While these companies hold IPR on the vaccines, it is unlikely that abolition of the IPR system would, by itself, have an immediate positive effect on the availability of the vaccines in India. There are reasons for this apprehension. As per the Doha Declaration of 2001 relating to TRIPS, in a public health emergency any member-country of the WTO already has the right to waive IPRs on any vaccine or medicine (no matter who holds these IPRs) and to issue *compulsory licence* to producers of this item *within* the country. Since Covid-19 certainly qualifies as an emergency, India can invoke this right. The catch is that while a foreign company's IPR on a vaccine can be declared to be inapplicable in India under this provision, there is no way of forcing the company to reveal the details of the *technology* that it has developed. The technology is the trade secret of the company and the company is under no legal obligation to put it in the public domain. In case of *medicines* it is sometimes the case that, by examining their chemical composition, pharmaceutical engineers can reconstruct the underlying technology by what is called "reverse engineering." A *vaccine*, particularly a *Covid* vaccine, however, is a highly sophisticated product and reverse engineering is virtually impossible. In fact, the Western vaccine companies seem to be aware of this. For instance, this is what seems to have emboldened the American vaccine company Moderna to announce that it would not enforce its patent rights if any other producer anywhere wishes to replicate the Covid vaccine developed by it. It appears that the company has voluntarily waived its IPR. The magnanimity may, however, be explained by the fact that in reality such replication would require a transfer of the actual technology. It cannot be done by imitation or reverse engineering.

Moreover, a country like India may face problems of *logistics* in organising the production and distribution of vaccines that have been developed abroad. Experience shows that when a new product is developed *indigenously*, the scientists involved in the process tend to pay attention to the question whether the *ingredients* that would go into the product are easily available in the country. This is an advantage when the product moves from the stage of development to that of production. A product developed abroad but produced in the country may not retain this advantage. For instance, the Covid vaccine developed by Pfizer needs about 280 different ingredients that are sourced from about 20 different countries. While a giant multinational such as Pfizer may have the organisational capability to handle a complex production process of this type, that may not be the case with an Indian producer. Similarly, there is also the matter of *storage, distribution* and *delivery* of the produced vaccines. The Pfizer vaccines needs to be stored in temperature ranging between –90 °C and –60 °C. The mid-point of this range, –75 °C, is colder than the typical *winter* temperature in the Antarctica. The Moderna vaccine is somewhat better in this respect but it, too, requires storage at sub-zero temperature (–20 °C). (The AstraZeneca and the Russian-origin Sputnik V vaccines, however, are reported to be storable at temperature varying from 2 °C to 8 °C.) This may prove to be a problem for tropical countries where there is scarcity of the required cold storage infrastructure. It is for all of these reasons that we recommend encouraging *indigenous* development of Covid vaccines.

6.5.3 Increase in funding of research and development

How do we go about this task of encouraging indigenous development? In this connection, the first point to note is that since Covid-19 is an entirely new type of infective disease in human experience, developing vaccines that would prevent its spread would obviously involve *research*. Moreover, in view of the fact that there are only a handful of Covid vaccines available in the country at the moment, it is also obvious that a big push in this direction is called for. Thus, a most natural policy that would suggest itself would be to *subsidise* research aimed at development of vaccines.

Very little in this respect, however, seems to have been done in India so far. Despite the raging pandemic, there was no explicit mention of subsidisation of research in this specific area in the Union budget for the year 2021–22. While there was an allocation of Rs. 35,000 crore for vaccines, it turned out that the sum was mainly meant to be transferred to the state governments for supporting their vaccination drives. This is a far cry from *adequate* funding of vaccine *research*. To be sure, it is not surprising that a developing country would be unable to match the records of the advanced nations of the west in this respect. (As per one estimate, the USA has so far *actually spent* $2.23 billion in research grants and subsidies for developing Covid vaccines. The corresponding figures for Germany, UK, the European Union and Canada are, respectively, $1.51 billion, $500 million, $327 million and $283 million.[2] However, a *near-zero* budgetary allocation for Covid-19 vaccine development could certainly have been bettered. The official agency in India that funds research for this purpose is the Indian Council of Medical Research (ICMR). ICMR initially got a pathetically small sum of Rs. 25 crore earmarked for this specific purpose. In November 2020, it got an additional sum of Rs. 900 crore from the Department of Biotechnology (which is a part of the Ministry of Science and Technology) as a stimulus package under Mission Covid Suraksha. However. a major part of even this small amount seemed to have remained unutilised till the end of the financial year 2021–22.

Of course, inadequate allocation for the explicit purpose of supporting Covid vaccine development does not mean that ICMR (or other official agencies) cannot fund *any* research in this field. They can *divert* funds towards this line of research from their own total allocations. However, in the 2021–22 budget little seemed to have been done to increase the total allocations to these agencies, rendering such diversions difficult. In fact, while there had been an increase in these allocations in the budget for 2020–21, in the 2021–22 budget there was a *decrease*. The budgetary allocations that are relevant here are those earmarked for the Department of Health Research under the Ministry of Health and Family Welfare. (That is where ICMR gets its own allocations from.) The *actual* allocation to this Department was Rs. 1,861 crore in 2019–20. In the 2020–21 budget, the figure increased to Rs. 4,062 crore (as per the Revised Estimates of that year's allocations). In the 2021–22 budget, however, the allocation (as per Revised Estimate) was decreased to Rs. 3,080 crore. It may also be noted that since the budget for 2020–21 was presented to the Parliament on 1 February 2000, that is *before* the so-called first wave of Covid-19 in the country, it is not clear whether the increased allocation to health research in that budget, however commendable it might be on other grounds, was made with an eye to funding of Covid vaccine development. Moreover, in the budget for 2022–23, there was only a marginal (4 per cent) increase in the budgetary allocation over the Revised Estimate figure of the previous year. If we take account of inflation, it follows that there was actually a slight *decrease* in the allocation *in real terms*.

We reach the conclusion that there is a clear case for a substantial increase in government funding of research in the field of vaccine development.

6.5.4 Research in publicly funded organisations—the best bet

One crucial difference between subsidy policy decisions of the type that we are now discussing and those that were analysed in course of our overview of economic policies in Chapter 2 is that the discussion in that chapter concentrated on increasing subsidies to (and reducing indirect taxes on) producers of commodities that were already in the market. Presently, however, we are talking about encouraging the development of *new* products. To whom, then, should these subsidies be given?

In this connection, it is important to note that the products in question are vaccines that would immunise the recipients against a disease that is potentially life-threatening and was hitherto completely unknown. This has two important implications. *First*, the development of these products would be much more dependent on *fundamental* scientific research than the development of ordinary run-of-the-mill new consumer (or even investment) goods that would typically be improved versions of goods already in the market. *Second*, the development of vaccines would generate what economists call *external economies*. Essentially this means that the benefit accruing to the country or the society as a whole from the development of such a vaccine would exceed the *private* benefit (in the form of profits in terms of money) that it would bring to the persons or the companies that would develop it.

In view of the *first* of these two implications, the job of developing Covid vaccines are better entrusted to research institutes, universities and other organisations that have *research capacities* in fields related to vaccine development (such as virology and related sciences) than to companies whose expertise usually lies more in *manufacturing* vaccines. There may be exceptions. But, as a general rule, research institutions have greater interaction with *fundamental* research than do companies whose primary aim is to maximise profit. The *second* implication tells us why private sector companies cannot be expected to exert themselves enough in basic research relating to Covid vaccine development. In other words, if the matter is left to these companies, the necessary research efforts will be *undersupplied*. For these reasons we recommend that the major part of the subsidies for Covid vaccine development should go to research institutions that (a) have the interest and the expertise in the relevant fields of research and (b) are *socially oriented* rather than "for-profit" organisations. Needless to say, among institutions that have characteristic (a), it is the ones that are either publicly funded or funded by non-profit organisations that are likely to have characteristic (b). In this connection, the decision of the UK government to support Covid vaccine research at Oxford University at the earliest stages of the spread of the disease must be judged to be a right one and stands in contrast to policies followed by governments of some of the other countries including the USA.

6.5.5 Timing of research funding

There is also the crucial question of *timing* of the funding of research and development. Development of a safe and effective vaccine is a long process. Moreover, investment of time, energy and financial resources on a particular development proposal is risky since at the end of the day it may turn out that the money and the time have been wasted. *Alternative* lines of research, therefore, have to be pursued at the same time. It follows that the *sooner* the research and development efforts begin, the better are the chances of being able to develop a vaccine early in the process of spread of the disease. What happened in India in fact, however, was that, for a long time, we were content with permitting the Serum Institute of India (SII) to produce the brand of Covid vaccine known as Covishield in India under licence from AstraZeneca, the British-Swedish multinational that holds the IPR on the technology (by virtue of their agreement with Oxford University whose scientists were the original inventors of the vaccine). The IPR on the vaccine prevented widespread use of the technology. Moreover, the licensing arrangement should have been looked into carefully. It was too late when it was discovered that the licence contained clauses requiring the local producer to supply a significant part of the output to AstraZeneca to meet the demand in other countries.

On the other hand, *after* waking up to the exigency of the situation, we have had to speed up the regulatory process of vaccine *approval*. The circumstances forced us to approve the indigenously developed vaccine called Covaxin *before* the usually mandatory clinical trials were completed. While the fact that the vaccine has worked well in practice speaks highly of the inventive skills of our scientists, the hasty approval has cost us dearly in terms of export possibilities. It has attracted criticism in the international arena. In fact, a survey revealed that in a large number of countries people reported that they would not agree to being administered Covid vaccines manufactured in some specified countries including India. The moral is obvious: the research funding should have started right from the time when the pandemic started.

6.5.6 From development to manufacturing: production in the public sector

Needless to say, it is not enough to develop a vaccine; it must also be manufactured in adequate quantities and supplied to consumers at reasonable costs. What role can policies play in this regard? Since manufacturing is not the forte of research institutions, it goes without saying that vaccine companies would play a vital role here.

There is much to be said in favour of producing Covid vaccines in public sector undertakings (PSUs). The main economic argument here is well known. A private sector company would not produce a Covid vaccine in *socially optimal* quantities. This is because it would be, quite understandably, interested in maximising its *private* profit. Now, at any level of output, profit is revenue from sales (i.e. the private producer's *benefit*) minus cost. The benefit accruing to *society* as a whole, however, is *greater* than the private producer's benefit because it includes not only the private benefit of the producer but also the health and the economic benefits that all the *other* members of the society get from preventing the spread of the disease. In other words, private sector manufacturers would *underestimate* the *true* benefits from vaccine production and, therefore, the quantity of vaccines produced by them would be *less* than what is socially desired.

In this context, it should be noted that India has long been a major producer of vaccines. It produces about 60 per cent of the global output of all types of vaccines and is often called the "vaccine manufacturing capital" of the world. Just a decade or so ago, most of this output came from PSUs. Today, however, the bulk of the output is produced by the private sector producers. One may wonder whether, in these heydays of privatisation in India, the recommendation of public sector production of Covid vaccines is a realistic one. On a closer look, however, it is seen that the most of the PSUs in the field of vaccine production have *not* yet been privatised. Essentially, they have been left to rot. Repair and maintenance of their plant and machinery have been neglected. They are also deprived of government orders. About 90 per cent of vaccines needed for the Government of India's own Universal Immunisation Programme is today sourced from private manufacturers. On the other hand, there are still at least seven PSUs with previous experience in the field of vaccines. These are the Central Research Institute (CRI) in Himachal Pradesh; the BCG Vaccine Laboratory, the Pasteur Institute of India and HLL Biotech in Tamil Nadu; Bharat Immunologicals and Biologicals Corporation in Uttar Pradesh; Haffkine Bio-Pharmaceutical Corporation Limited in Maharashtra; and Indian Immunologicals Limited in Telangana. Even more lamentable is the case of the Integrated Vaccine Complex (IVC), inaugurated as recently as in 2016 as a state-of-the-art PSU that was supposed to *combine* development and manufacturing of vaccines. It was declared an "Institute of National Importance." Till now, however, it has not developed any vaccine and its only contribution to the fight against Covid-19 has been production of hand sanitisers! What we recommend is that the PSUs be pressed into service for manufacturing the indigenously developed Covid vaccines. Provisions should be made for the infrastructural upgrading that this may require.

6.5.7 Production in the private sector: the IPR issue

While we have argued for manufacturing of Covid vaccines in PSUs, it is possible that in the near future the PSUs alone may not be able to produce these vaccines in quantities that would be required for vaccinating the entire adult population of India. Moreover, given the facts that vaccines constitute an important export item for the country and that the global demand for vaccines for Covid-19 and similar other zoonotic diseases is likely to increase in the future, it seems advisable to try to increase the output of these vaccines beyond our domestic requirements. For these reasons the participation of the private sector in this field must also be given due importance.

Since we have recommended subsidisation of developmental research on Covid vaccines in publicly funded institutions, the very first issue that arises in the context of *private sector production* relates to how the matter of IPR would be handled. In Sections 6.3 and 6.4, we discussed how imperfection in the market for Covid vaccines and, in particular, the existing IPR regime in the advanced countries has been responsible to a large extent for the existing sorry state of affairs so far as global vaccination rate is concerned. In the present context, therefore, it is important to look at how the IPR issue has so far been dealt with *within* the country and whether there is scope for an IPR policy that would be better from the social point of view.

While there are now more than a hundred vaccines in the world at various stages of development and regulatory approval, India has so far approved seven vaccines. At the time of writing these lines (end-February 2022) five of these have actually been used: Covishield, Covaxin, Sputnik V, ZyCoVD and Corbevax. (Most of the people who have been vaccinated so far in India have been administered either Covishield or Covaxin. Covishield alone accounts for 85 per cent of them). While Covaxin and ZyCoVD have been developed indigenously, Sputnik V was developed in Russia. However, the Russian inventor has voluntarily abolished its IPR rights on the vaccine. Corbevax needs a special mention. It was developed in the USA but is patent-free. I shall have more to say on this vaccine below. The Pfizer and Moderna vaccines are also likely to be available in India in the future.

We now take a look at the framework in which production of indigenously developed Covid vaccines have proceeded in India. Covaxin was developed by Bharat Biotech Ltd. (BBIL), a vaccine manufacturing company, in collaboration with the National Institute of Virology (NIV), Pune, a research institute that receives funding from the ICMR. The company used a sample of coronavirus, the virus that causes Covid-19, isolated by researchers at NIV. The *rest* of the process of development as well as the trials that are mandatory for regulatory approval were carried out by BBIL in close collaboration with the experts at NIV and ICMR. It also received a grant of Rs. 35 crore from ICMR towards the cost of development. ZyCoVD has been developed by Cadila Healthcare with developmental as well as financial support from the Department of Biotechnology, Government of India. It also has the production right.

What kind of IPR arrangement was followed in cases of Covaxin and ZyCoVD, however, is difficult to decode from the information that is publicly available. Information regarding ZyCoVD in this regard is virtually non-existent. So far as Covaxin is concerned, in May 2020, ICMR announced that the virus strain isolated by NIV has been "transferred" to BBIL. It is not clear whether this means that BBIL holds the exclusive right to the technology that has been developed. There are contradictory signals. On the one hand, a NITI Ayog official announced that "there is only one Indian company (Bharat Biotech) that has the IP." On the other hand, ICMR has claimed that it "shares" the IPR with BBIL and will receive royalty at the rate of 5 per cent when sales begin. It also claimed that it was free to share the technology with *other* companies.[3] It is true that the government has subsequently also roped in three public sector vaccine companies to produce Covaxin. These are Bharat Immunologicals and Biologicals Corporation, Haffkine Bio-Pharmaceutical Corporation Limited and Indian Immunologicals Limited. However, this still fails to clear the confusion. Covaxin, apparently, is a brand name owned by BBIL which is not a public sector company. It is not obvious how any other company, whether in the public or the private sector, can produce this brand excepting under some kind of licensing arrangement with BBIL. It has also been asked why only three PSUs would produce this particular vaccine if the ICMR is really free to share the technology with *any* other company. Even the Integrated Vaccine Complex in Tamil Nadu has not been enlisted for the purpose. One explanation that has been proffered is that the technology of Covaxin uses the so-called "inactivated virus" of Covid-19 while some other vaccines use the "active" virus. While this may make Covaxin *safer* than the other vaccines from the point of view of the consumer, its *technology* is a new one and not many of the existing vaccine-making PSUs can be equipped for the needed technological re-orientation at short notice. Not all observers are, however, convinced by this explanation since, as noted before, of all these existing PSUs are more or less in the same state of neglect and disrepair. If the real reason is the inadequacy of budgetary allocations, the solution can only lie in increasing the provision of funds for the purpose.

One would think that the government's policy in this regard would be more consistent with its professed opposition to the existing IPR regime in the international arena, had it been the case that once a technology for a new vaccine is developed in (or with support of) a public institution in India, any Indian company with experience in manufacturing vaccines would be free to use it under some kind of royalty arrangement. It is this type of policy that we recommend.

It may be of interest to note that this is precisely the type of arrangement that Oxford University *initially* intended to adopt with respect to the vaccine that was developed by scientists at the University's Jenner Institute and that *later* came to be known as the AstraZeneca. Initially the idea was that the University would make the technology available to *any* producer under a royalty arrangement. When the development (including the required clinical trials) was complete, However, the University suddenly made an about turn and transferred the *sole* manufacturing right to AstraZeneca. Most surprisingly, Oxford would not even get any royalty from AstraZeneca! (It may, however, get some returns *indirectly* by virtue of some patents owned by VacciTech, a spin-off company of the Jenner Institute.)

The reason for the abrupt change of mind on the part of the University has, naturally, been speculated about. While no official explanation has been given, one speculation is that it was the Gates Foundation, a philanthropic organisation founded by the American billionaire Bill Gates, that had suggested this new arrangement. The Foundation had clout with Oxford University by virtue of a huge $700 million research grant that it had just then given to the university, one of the biggest research grants that the university had ever received from any source in its long history. The speculation is based on the fact that, despite his reputation as a philanthropist, Mr. Gates is known to be committed supporter of the *existing* IPR regime in the USA under which it is the vaccine companies which develop the vaccines with the help of government support that hold the IPRs.) To be fair to AstraZeneca, however, it should be mentioned here that this British-Swedish company has agreed to permit two companies based in the developing world, one in India and the other in Brazil, to produce the same vaccine under licensing arrangements. The Indian company is SII. This is how Covishield, the Indian brand name of the Oxford vaccine, has come into being.

It is possible to argue that the relatively liberal IPR policy that we have recommended earlier is still not liberal enough. Ideally, the technology that is developed should be treated as a *public good* and should be available to *all* for *free*. The research institutions that are the original inventors should not even demand any royalty or licence fee because, under the recommended policy, the research would be done in publicly funded institutions and, therefore, the cost of research will be borne fully by the government.

On practical grounds, however, this ideal system does not seem to be attainable in the Indian context in the near future. The government's limited support to developmental research has already been noted earlier. Under the existing circumstances, some kind of royalty arrangement seems to be unavoidable. However, as discussed earlier, that should not mean granting *exclusive* right to use the technology to one particular company.

So far, the nearest approximation to the ideal of *free* availability of technology has been the type of *philanthropic* arrangement under which Corbevax, one of the latest Covid vaccines, is reported to be made available by the developers. Corbevax was developed by academic researchers in Texas, USA, associated with the Baylor College of Medicine and the Centre for Vaccine Development at the Texas Children's Hospital. Their research made use of previous knowledge about vaccines for other diseases and was, consequently, much less expensive than the research underlying the Pfizer or the Moderna vaccines. The US government, however, did not provide any financial support, preferring, instead, to back the big pharmaceutical multinationals. The Corbevax developers had to manage with a research fund of just $7 million, a paltry sum compared to the huge government support given to the multinational companies. Even this small amount did not come from the government. It was contributed by individual donors and small philanthropic organisations. What is most laudable is that the developers have pledged to forego any royalty income. They have not only waived patent rights but also pledged to actually transfer the technology *for free* to *any* company with a proven track record in manufacturing vaccines. (The Baylor College of Medicine, however, will charge a small licence fee.) So far India is the only country that has evinced interest. An Indian company, Biological E Limited, with government support in the form of advance orders, has acquired access to the technology and has started producing the vaccine. The per dose cost of this vaccine is reported to be much less than that of either Covishield or Covaxin. Moreover, like most of the other vaccines that are available in India, Corbevax can be stored in ordinary refrigerators.

While attempts such as this to tackle the problem of vaccine availability on the basis of philanthropy are certainly laudable, government intervention would continue to be essential if the problem is to be effectively solved. (Indeed, if *private* philanthropy could be counted upon to solve the myriad problems of scarcity and deprivation afflicting the less developed parts of the world, economic policy would be largely superfluous.) Besides, it is unclear whether the Corbevax technology will be made available for free to *other* Indian companies too. No single company, however, is likely to have the production capacity required to produce the vaccine in sufficient quantities. This is particularly true if the need to achieve a hundred per cent vaccination rate and the need for booster doses are to be kept in mind, not to mention the need to be able to export the vaccines to other developing countries.

6.5.8 Procurement and pricing

The system of procurement of Covid vaccines from the private manufacturers and the procurement prices fixed by the government have changed frequently over the past few months. As of February 2022, the system in place is that the Government of India would procure 75 per cent of the total number of doses of any Covid vaccine manufactured in the country and would distribute these among the states and the union territories free of cost. The producer is free to sell the remaining 25 per cent to the private sector (for instance, to hospitals and other health care facilities in this sector and corporate houses). In practice, private hospitals have rarely used up the 25 per cent quota. Hence, the government has often procured more than 75 per cent of the production.

Currently, the procurement prices paid by the Government of India is Rs. 215 per dose of Covishield and Rs. 225 per dose of Covaxin. Presently, it is not procuring Sputnik V, leaving the entire output to be sold to the private hospitals or to the state governments. For sales to the private sector the maximum per-dose prices of Covishield, Covaxin and Sputnik V have been set at Rs. 600, Rs. 1200 and Rs. 948, respectively. A 5 per cent GST is applicable. The government has, moreover, fixed Rs. 150 as the upper limit for per-dose service charge that private sector hospitals can levy on the consumers for any of these vaccines. The manufacturers of both Covishield and Covaxin have, however, applied for regular market approval (i.e. for permission to sell directly to the public). At the time of writing these lines (end-February 2022) no decision on these applications has been taken. However, there are unconfirmed reports that a favourable decision is likely and that a price cap of Rs. 275 per dose for both of these two vaccines may be imposed. The system of government procurement is. however, likely to continue.

So far as Corbevax is concerned, the government has placed an order for 5 crore doses. The procurement price has been fixed at Rs. 145 sans taxes. At the moment (February 2022) no sale to private hospitals in envisaged.

Covishield and Covaxin have so far constituted the major part, more than 90 per cent, of Covid vaccine supply in India. The procurement pricing for these two vaccines has, therefore, attracted the attention of economists. It has been noted that in almost all other countries of the world (including the USA) the government procures the entire output of the Covid vaccines at agreed prices and there is no provision of sales to the private sector at higher prices. Dual pricing is a unique feature of the Covid vaccine pricing system in India. Actually, it seems to be a concession to the demands of the vaccine companies. As noted before, starting from around 2008, the majority of the PSUs producing vaccines and drugs and pharmaceuticals in India have been in a state of neglect. Consequently, the private corporates producing Covid vaccines are in a strong bargaining position when it comes to negotiating the procurement prices. Left to themselves, they would have sold their entire output in the open market at prices higher than the price offered by the government. Dual pricing seems to be a compromise that would induce them to accept the procurement prices. The important question is how good a compromise it is from the social point of view.

A clear answer seems to be difficult to find. On the one hand, the private sector prices of the vaccines are clearly too high in comparison to the monthly income of an *average* Indian family. Moreover, the private hospitals would add their own service charges and profit markups on these prices. In effect, it is only the rich and the upper middle classes that would be able to afford to get Covid vaccination at private hospitals at these prices. On the other hand, attempts have been made to defend dual pricing by pointing out that it charges the higher price only to those consumers who are able and willing to pay for their vaccination at these rates. This would be an egalitarian system in the sense that it would preserve the government's financial resources for the purpose of making vaccination available to the poor and the lower-middle class consumers free of cost. Some critics, however, are of the view out that while that may be true in theory, in practice dual pricing would create an incentive for the manufacturers to give *priority* to their private sector clients in the *time scheduling* of supplies and this would give rise to inequality in the distribution of the vaccines among the population. They also point out that this apprehension seems to be borne out, at least indirectly, by whatever little information is available about the vaccination rates for different income classes and for different geographical locations. For instance, the average income of a family in an urban area in India is known to be significantly higher than that in a rural one. Private sector hospitals cater to the relatively well-to-do and are concentrated in the urban areas and it may not be an accident that, so far, much higher rates of vaccination have been achieved in the urban than in the rural areas. While it is understandable that, at times of scarcity, supply of a commodity may need to be rationed on the basis of urgency of *needs*, fragmenting the market on the basis of *purchasing power* does not seem to be socially desirable.

On balance, therefore, it seems difficult to find strong arguments for dual pricing. It is not surprising, therefore, that very few among the other countries of the world have adopted this system. (One exception is Egypt.) At any rate, most commentators are of the opinion that 25 per cent seems to be too high a percentage of total output to be earmarked for sale to the private sector.

Finally, we comment briefly on the question of *fairness* of the procurement prices. The main problem in evaluating the fairness or otherwise of the announced prices lies in the absence of reliable *information*. As noted before, it is difficult to get information on costs of production and on the profit mark-ups that the companies apply on costs. Moreover, since all of the vaccines are *new* products to appear on the scene, there is no *benchmark* against which the negotiated procurement prices can be compared. In fact, even for the indigenously developed Covaxin there are no data on even the cost of *development*, let alone the total cost of development and manufacturing and the profit mark-ups. (The magazine *India Today* dated July 20, 2021, reports that a query under the Right to Information Act filed with ICMR elicited the response that while ICMR spent Rs. 35 crore on the development of Covaxin, it has no information on the expenditure incurred by BBIL.) Similar is the case with the cost of *production* of Sputnik V in India. (Since the Russian inventor of this vaccine has waived IPR and has transferred the technology free of cost, the cost of its *development* is immaterial in the present context.) The development cost of ZyCoVD, the only other vaccine that has so far been developed indigenously, is also unknown.

Regarding Covishield, the price of the AstraZeneca vaccine (of which it is the Indian brand name) in the global market can be used as some kind of a benchmark. However, there is no single global procurement price. It is procured in different countries at different prices. As per the latest information available in September 2021, in the UK, it is procured at the equivalent of $3 per dose, while the EU pays $2.5 per dose. These are the two lowest procurement prices for this vaccine in the world. If these are the benchmarks, then, at the prevailing exchange rate, the procurement price of this vaccine in India does not seem to be wide off the mark. (It is another matter that the countries (such as South Africa) to which the company is supplying the vaccine at much higher prices must then be judged to have agreed to set the procurement prices at unduly high levels.) It may, however, be noted that there is no dual pricing in the EU. Critics who have doubted the necessity of earmarking as much as 25 per cent of the output of Covishield for sales to private hospitals in India do, therefore, seem to have a point.

6.6 Summary and additional remarks

The lessons from the discussion in this chapter can now be summarised. While vaccines are the main weapon in the fight against the Covid-19 pandemic, today's world is characterised by a shortage in the aggregate production of vaccines as well as by a high degree of inequality in the distribution of the vaccines among countries. The reason is to be sought in mankind's failure to adopt a unified stand against the pandemic. The failure is due largely to vaccine nationalism practiced by the AEs. This, in turn, is mainly due to the market power of the oligopolists dominating the world market for vaccines and to the existing IPR regime.

Given this reality, the planning of vaccine policy in India must be approached from the viewpoint of her own national interests. Given India's experience in *manufacturing* vaccines in the *public sector units*, there is a lot to be said in favour of revitalising these units for the purpose of making vaccines. *Development* of vaccines is, however, prior to manufacturing. Since fundamental scientific research is involved here, the distinction between social and private returns from investment implies that *exclusive* reliance on research by private sector companies would lead to undersupply of research efforts. Research in publicly funded institutions is the best bet.

In the matter of *procurement* and *pricing* of the most widely used brands of Covid vaccine, India has followed a dual system under which the government procures 75 per cent of the outputs and the producers are free to sell the rest to private sector hospitals and corporate houses. There is a price differential. Prices charged to private sector buyers are higher. In almost all other countries, the entire output is procured by the governments. While theoretical arguments can be given both for and against the Indian system, the ground realities of the Indian economy seem to point towards the hypothesis that the universally followed model of 100 per cent procurement by the government would have been better.

One major policy mistake that has been made in many countries of the world (including India) and that should be avoided in the event of recurrence of pandemics in the future relates to the *timing* of the policy actions. Development of new vaccines (especially for hitherto-unknown types of diseases such as Covid-19) and their production is a time-consuming process. These processes have to be started, and the necessary budgetary allocations should be made as early in the process of the outbreak as possible. In the Indian context, timely actions in these directions were lacking. Early and stray signs of the ensuing pandemic were ignored. Valuable time was lost. As a result, when the pandemic struck with mind-boggling ferocity, there were knee-jerk reactions and other policy mistakes.

One tragic consequence of all this has been the avoidable loss of human lives and livelihoods on a large scale. In this connection, it may also be noted that recent epidemiological and demographic research has called into question the credibility of governmental claims of low number of Covid deaths in the developing countries (in comparison with that in some of the AEs such as the USA). It has been argued that the relatively low rate of officially reported mortality in these countries is due simply to *undercounting*. For the case of India, see, for instance, Guilmoto (2022). Expectedly, however, government spokespersons have not accepted these findings.

Finally, the lessons drawn from the policy discussion of this chapter are likely to retain their relevance even if and when the Covid-19 pandemic becomes a thing of the past. Medical experts warn us that coronavirus pandemics may recur in the future. More importantly, the *economics* of what the chapter says about *Covid vaccines* applies, in principle, to *all* vaccines in general. In fact, much of it applies to curative *medicines* as well. Economic policy for the *vaccine* sector, however, is particularly important for developing countries such as India because vaccines constitute the main weapon for *preventing* diseases. Prevention is better than cure not only in the obvious health-related sense but also in the economic sense since it is by far cheaper.

Notes

1 See www.nytimes.com/interactive/2021/world/covid.vaccinations-tracker last accessed on 7 August 2022.
2 See www.statista.com/chart/24808/ last accessed on 7 August 2022.
3 See www.scoll.in/article/994763/ last accessed on 7 August 2022.

References

Cakmakli, C., Demiralp, S., Kalemli-Ozcan, S., Yesiltas, S.K. and Yildirim, M.A. (2021): 'The economic case for global vaccinations: An epidemiological model with international production network', Working Paper No. 28395, National Bureau of Economic Research, Cambridge, MA.

Castillo, J.C., Ahuja, A., Athey, S., Baker, A., Budish, E., Chipty, T., Glennerster, R., Kominers, S.D., Kremer, M., Larson, G., Lee, J., Prendergast, C., Snyder, C.M., Tabarrok, A., Tan, B.J. and Więcek, W. (2021): 'Market design to accelerate COVID-19 vaccine supply', *Science*, 371(6534), 1107–1109.

Cournot, A.A. (1838): *Recherches sur les Principes Mathematiques de la Theorie des Richesses*, Hachette, Paris.

Gopinath, G. (2020): 'Reopening from the great lockdown: Uneven and uncertain recovery', *IMF Blog*. https://blogs.img.org/2020/06/24.

Guilmoto, C.Z. (2022): 'An alternative estimation of the death toll of the Covid 19 pandemic in India', *PLoS One*, 17(2), 1–14.

Hafner, M., Yerushalmi, E., Fays, C., Dufresne, E. and Van Syock, C. (2020): *Covid 19 and the Cost of Vaccine Nationalism*, Rand Corporation, Santa Monica, CA.

Marani, M., Katul, G.K., Pan, W.K. and Parolari, A.J. (2021): 'Intensity and frequency of extreme novel pandemics', *Proceedings of the National Academy of Sciences*, 118(35), e2105482118.

Oxfam International (2020): *Vaccinating poorest half of humanity against coronavirus can cost less than four months' big pharma profits*, 14 May. www.oxfam.org/en/press-releases last accessed on 6 July 2022.

7 Where will the money come from?

7.1 Financing of government expenditure

The time has now come to consider the most obvious question that we have so far swept under the rug. In most cases, our recommended policies would involve increases in government expenditure. Where will the money come from? If, to start with, there is a surplus in the government's budget, this is not a problem. The government simply incurs the additional expenditure without any difficulty though this will reduce the size of the budget surplus. Unfortunately, like the governments of most other countries of the world, the Government of India too has to start from a situation of a deficit budget, with expenditure already in excess of income. Under the circumstances how is the *increase* in the deficit that would result from our recommended policies to be financed? In this chapter, I discuss the more important among the different ways of doing so. We start by discussing briefly, in Section 7.2, the policy of taxing the richer sections of the population. The longest section of the chapter, Section 7.3, however, is devoted to a detailed discussion of what is known as the modern monetary theory, which proposes limitless currency printing as the way of financing government expenditure. The reason why this proposal needs to be analysed in detail is that it has a direct popular appeal and that, therefore, its limitations in the Indian context needs to be highlighted. This discussion will also unravel some of the main constraints that a developing economy such as India faces in today's world when it comes to formulating policies for ensuring inclusive growth. Sections 7.4–7.6 are devoted, respectively, to public borrowing, privatisation of public sector units and leasing-out of public assets. (There will be some unavoidable overlaps between these sections.) Section 7.7 concludes the discussion.

7.2 Taxing the rich

An obvious way of financing additional government expenditure is to increase tax rates. This is essentially the Keynesian solution to the problem of demand deficiency in the private sector of the economy. Increasing

DOI: 10.4324/9781003350514-7

the rates of *indirect* taxes, however, may lead to inflation since these taxes are typically added to the sale prices of the commodities. It is, therefore, increases in rates of *direct* taxes, mainly income and wealth taxes, that are proposed to be increased. Moreover, it is the rates applicable to the *upper* income and wealth brackets that are sought to be hiked. Increasing tax rates at *all* levels of income would have a negative effect on consumer demand since everybody's purchasing power will be reduced. Since the poor and the middle classes spend relatively high proportions of their incomes on consumption, their consumption and standard of living will go down particularly significantly. Consumption by the rich will be relatively unaffected. They would pay the taxes out of their saving. Hence, *inequality* of consumption and, therefore, that of standard of living will increase. Taxing the rich at higher rates will bring in the needed additional government revenue without either reducing aggregate private consumption or increasing inequality. Note also that the reduction in (after-tax) saving by the rich and the middle classes that this will cause will not be much of a problem at times of demand deficiency since the problem at such times is that private saving is not invested for productive purposes.

Given the orientation of the government policies in India at present towards supply-side economics, however, it is difficult to imagine that the proposal to tax the rich at sufficiently high rates would be implemented in India in the near future. Indeed, the only significant modification in the structure of income taxes in India in recent years has been a *cut* in the rate of *corporate* income tax. With effect from 2017–18, the tax rate applicable for domestic companies was reduced to 25 per cent (from the rate of 30 per cent prevailing earlier). This was made subject to an upper limit of Rs. 50 crore on the annual turnover of the company. The upper limit, however, has been pushed up from time to time. Currently (in 2022–23), it is Rs. 400 crore. Even the rate of 30 per cent for *other* companies is low in comparison to the rates prevailing in many other countries of the world. So far, however, this has failed to induce the increase in investment that was hoped for. On the contrary, indirectly this has been counterproductive since this has increased the post-tax profits of the corporate houses. Since new investment is not an attractive proposition at the moment, the companies have spent this windfall income by increasing dividend payments. (It is this that explains, at least partly, why company shares have become so attractive and has led to a booming share market in an otherwise-depressed economic scenario.) Since the distribution of ownership of company shares is highly unequal, this has actually increased the *overall* inequality of the distribution of personal income in India. In one of the previous chapters (Chapter 4) we have seen how inequality has played a causal role behind the problem of persistent economic deceleration in India.

7.3 Printing currency: modern monetary theory

7.3.1 Limitless issue of fiat money

The discussion in the previous section forces us to look at *other* possible ways of raising revenue for financing the required increase in government expenditure. We shall start by discussing, in this section, a proposal that was originally put forward by a number of heretic thinkers and social activists and that has now attracted the attention of academic economists. The theoretical principles underlying the proposal constitute what has been called the modern monetary theory (MMT). In our present context, the proposal is simply to raise the required money by *printing currency* (or, equivalently, by letting the government *borrow from the public* on the basis of its ability to print currency to repay the debt). As a way of dealing with economic slowdowns, the proposal has a very direct popular appeal since putting money in people's hands is the most obvious way of increasing their purchasing power. Printing new currency for the purpose, therefore, has been not only a popular demand in India but also one that has received support from a significant section of the business classes. The CII, for instance, proposed soon after the onset of Covid that the government put into circulation new currency worth at least Rs. 3 lakh crore. We, therefore, discuss the pros and cons of the proposal in detail and show that it is not a sound policy *by itself* from the viewpoint of economic theory. It can, however, be used *in conjunction with* other policies.

Contrary to what its name may indicate, MMT actually has a long history. The earliest clear statement of the theory was in the 1905 book *The State Theory of Money* by the German economist Georg Friedrich Knapp. Later development of the theory drew inspiration from the wrings of Lerner (1947) and others. The name "modern monetary theory" came into fashion in the 1980s. More recently, advocates of MMT have sought to build a full-fledged macroeconomic theory of their own. We do not need to delve into all aspects of the theory here. We shall highlight only those parts that are relevant to the subject matter of the chapter. The more curious reader may look at the comprehensive discussion in Mitchell et al. (2019).

MMT differs from most of the mainstream macroeconomic theories in its view about how money arose in the first place. While most other theories consider the evolution of money into its present form to have been driven mainly by the obvious difficulties of a system of direct barter or exchange between commodities, MMT notes there are many historical instances of money being used by the rulers as an instrument of control. Even in pre-modern times money used for this purpose took the form of *fiat money*. Fiat money is essentially the type of money that we see in the world today. It has no intrinsic value as a commodity. Its general acceptability in an economy is derived *exclusively* from the fact that the government of the country declares the particular currency as the official currency of the country, retains the sole authority of issuing the currency and accepts *tax payments* only in that currency. In the early days of the development of MMT, this view of money was called *chartalism*, the word being derived from the Latin word *charta* meaning a *token* or a *ticket.*

7.3.2 *Change of orientation: limitless government expenditure*

There is an interesting twist in the evolution of MMT from the viewpoint of political economy. Knapp's original version of MMT had a "right-wing" orientation. It supported the view that there should be "minimal government." The government did not need to incur any expenditure to fight unemployment. Taxes also were, therefore, unnecessary. Whenever there is a problem of inadequate demand in the free market, all that the government needed to do was to issue fiat money and hand it out to people. People would use the money to increase their purchases of goods and services. This will solve the demand problem of the *private sector*. There was no need for a *public sector*.

Today, however, MMT is popularly perceived to be a "leftist" theory. It is easy to see why that is the case if we look at the policy regime in the USA in the Ronald Reagan era. Those were the heydays of supply-side economics and neo-liberalism. The government refused to tax the rich on the plea that that would harm investment and growth. The resulting lack of government revenue was then used as the excuse to turn down many popular public expenditure proposals such as those for universal health care and free college education. It was around this time that the modern version of MMT was being formulated. This version emphasised that boosting the growth rate of the economy cannot be the only objective of economic policy. It is also important to pay attention to the problems of poverty and inequality. Proponents of the new version of MMT took the old version and gave it almost exactly the opposite political orientation. By claiming that the government had *limitless powers to finance its expenditure* and that neither taxation nor public borrowing was necessary for the purpose, MMT was now trying to demolish the Reaganite excuses for refusing to fund the various welfare programmes. No wonder, MMT is now perceived by its supporters as a "progressive" theory. The title of the book by Kelton (2020) is also a pointer in this direction. Be that as it may, in the newer MMT the stress is on currency printing as a method of financing deficits in *government budgets*.

In its *most recent* formulation MMT has undergone yet another change of emphasis. This particular change, however, is a relatively minor one. The theory is now often stated in terms of *debt-financing of government expenditure* rather than in those of currency printing. It is emphasised that there is actually no difference between these two methods of deficit financing. It is precisely because the government has limitless powers to issue currency that it also has limitless ability to borrow from the public. There can never arise a problem of repayment of public debt because fiat money can always be issued if the situation so demands. Although the two versions are logically equivalent, in AEs the debt-financing interpretation may be the more realistic of the two in view of the dwindling importance of cash transactions in such economies. In the Indian context, however, we shall concentrate mostly on the "currency printing" version of MMT. We shall, however, also remark briefly on the version that prescribes debt-financing of government expenditure.

7.3.3 The salient points

Before attempting a critical evaluation of MMT, let us quickly state the salient points of the theory. The main point is that any sovereign government has the power to issue (and to enforce the use of) fiat money, provided that it does not need to peg the value of its currency to that of something else (such as gold) on which it has no control. Under the Gold Standard, to issue new currency the government (or the central bank) has to back the new issue by adequate gold reserves (because currency would have to be interchangeable with gold at a fixed rate). This would restrict its power to issue new currency. Gold and other metallic standards are, however, now things of the past. In a modern economy the power of a sovereign government to issue currency is practically limitless. In the time of Georg Knapp, of course, most of the countries of the world (including his own country, Germany) were still on the Gold Standard. Knapp was *proposing* a switchover to the system of fiat money. At that time the proposal was quite unconventional.

Since it is money that buys goods and services in the market, it follows that under the system of fiat money, a sovereign government has limitless command over the goods and services produced in the economy. The only limitation comes from the availability of *real* productive resources. It goes without saying that when these resources are *fully employed*, further money creation will lead to *inflation* caused by *excess demand*. Subject to this limit, the government can finance *any* level of its expenditure simply on the basis of *seigniorage* which is the government's profit from printing currency, that is the difference between the face value of the currency notes and their production cost. Unlike an individual, a government does not have any *financial* constraint. It only has to worry about *real* constraints on the productive capacity of the economy as and when they become binding.

7.3.4 The possibility of inflation

There have been criticisms and defences of MMT. The main criticism is that MMT-inspired currency printing may cause *inflation*. There is a possibility that, lured by this painless way of solving the demand deficiency problem, the government may overdo things and there may be an excess supply of money. To bolster their position the critics point out that in the economic history of recent centuries there have been many instances of governments doing essentially what MMT recommends. The result, however, has frequently been *hyperinflation*, that is inflation at very high rates. A classic example is that of Germany in the years following the First World War, the time of the so-called Weimar Republic. Germany was defeated in the War. It was required to make huge repatriation payments to the victorious side. It was, however, unable to raise the necessary resources. Badly damaged by the war, the economy did not have the required productive capacity. More importantly, the people were unable to pay the necessary taxes. The government resorted to printing currency to cover its expenditure. Soon, inflation raised its head. Too much money was chasing too few goods. The inflation rate spiked in the year 1923 when the prices of almost all goods doubled every four days. For quite some time, the inflation rate remained at a high level. Several other European countries (for instance, Austria, Hungary and Poland) also experienced hyperinflation at different points of time in the first half of the twentieth century. It has been pointed out that all of them were printing large amounts of currency to finance government budget deficits. Similar cases have also been observed in other parts of the world and in more recent times. The experiences of Argentina, Brazil, Venezuela and Zimbabwe have been cited in this connection.

High rates of inflation are known to have negative effects on the standards of living of the majority of the population of a country. Wages and salaries rise at much slower rates than commodity prices. As a result, *real* wages fall. Poverty and hunger become widespread. Moreover, inequality also increases sharply at such times. Since prices increase by leaps and bounds, so do profits. All these, in turn, create social tension and political instability. Many economists have pointed to the economic conditions of Weimar Germany as one of the main causes behind the rise of Hitler and Nazism. Acemoglu et al. (2019, p. 656), for instance, notes that hyperinflation "set the stage for the ascent of the Nazi party." In a similar vein, Robbins (1937, p. 4) described Hitler as the "foster child of the inflation."

It is mainly because of the risk of inflation that MMT has found very few supporters even among Keynesian economists. Keynesians usually are enthusiastic supporters of government expenditure as a remedy for demand deficiency in the private sector of the economy. However, on the question of how to *finance* government expenditure they seem to have parted ways with MMT. Among present-day Keynesians, Paul Krugman is a prominent critic of MMT.

Supporters of MMT have tried to defend their proposal against this criticism. Some of them have argued that that the cases of hyperinflation that are usually cited in this connection must be due to some specificities in the economic features of these particular countries because, as per their observations, there is, in general, very little correlation between the quantity of money that is created and the rate of inflation in the economy. To quote from the book on MMT (mentioned earlier) by Mitchell et al. (2019, p. 263), "no simple proportionate relationship exists between rises in money supply and rises in the general price level."

This particular defence of MMT, however, does not seem to be very convincing. The question here is not so much whether there is an exact proportional relationship between the two (i.e. whether the latter rises in the *same* proportion as the former). Rather, it is whether there is a *significant* positive correlation. It turns out that the answer is "yes." For the USA, analysis of decadal data since 1870 yield a statistical correlation of 0.79. Thus, in the USA, over time the two have moved in tandem. Comparison *between* countries at a given point of time also yield a similar result (i.e. inter-country differences in rates of inflation are, to a significant extent, explainable by differences in the increases in money supply) (see, for instance, Mankiw (2019, pp. 109–110).

There is, however, a stronger defence of MMT against the criticism centred on the possibility of inflation. As long as there is a problem of *demand deficiency* in the market, *by definition* there cannot be inflation caused by excess demand. It is only when the real productive resources of the economy are fully employed that *further* rounds of note printing will lead to a situation of excess demand and will bring about inflation. Advocates of MMT, however, are of the opinion that full employment of productive resources is only a theoretical possibility. In practice, an economy rarely witnesses full employment in the literal sense. Usually, they operate with spare productive capacity and often with high rates of unemployment. In other words, almost always there will be scope for real output and employment to increase in response to an increase in money supply. If and when full employment is eventually achieved, additional currency printing can be stopped.

This defence of MMT is unexceptionable *unless there are other constraints at work*. To identify these "other" constraints, we can use here some terminology that is used in the more conventional economic theories. Following Mankiw, we may distinguish between the *natural* level of output and the *optimal* level. The natural level is the level where the economy operates "on the average" (i.e. most of the time) and towards which the economy gravitates in the long run. The optimal level, on the other hand, is the level of output at which social welfare is maximised. From the society's point of view it is obviously non-optimal to leave productive resources unutilised. Therefore, at the optimal level of output there will be full employment.

An important reason why the natural level is usually *below* the optimal level is the existence of *market imperfection* or *concentration of market power*. If markets were *perfectly competitive*, for every commodity there would be many producers as well as many consumers and there will be *free entry* (i.e. anybody wishing to produce a commodity will be able to do so). No single producer (or no small group of producers) will have the power to dictate what the market price of any commodity would be because each producer's supply will be a negligible part of the aggregate supply of the commodity. Similarly, no single consumer (or no small group of consumers) will have the ability to set prices. Prices will be the determined by the interaction of aggregate demand and aggregate supply. Price of every commodity will equal the *marginal cost of production* (i.e. the additional cost that has to be incurred if output is to be increased by one unit). In the long run, price will also equal the *average cost of production* (i.e. total cost of production divided by the number of units produced) so that no producer will earn *excessive* profits. (*Normal* profit is included in the cost of production.) If existing producers earn excessively high profits, this will attract new entrants into the market and increased competition will push up the prices of inputs so that excess profits will soon vanish.

What we see in reality, however, is that, in many cases, while there are many consumers (so that each consumer's demand is a negligible part of aggregate demand), *supply* is controlled by a small group of large producers. They have the power to set prices. Supporters of MMT as well as those of some of the relatively conventional types of economic theory (such as the so-called "New Keynesian" Theory) contend that this phenomenon of market imperfection or concentration of market power in the hands of a small number of producers is quite pervasive. In *most* markets, producers have *market power*. They set prices by applying high mark-ups on their average cost of production, thus earning what is called *supernormal profits*.

It is not difficult to see that in this scenario inflation takes place when output *exceeds* its natural level (even though it remains *below* its optimal level). It is as if producers then perceive output to be "unnaturally" high and use their market power to achieve what they consider to be a "correction." They *increase* their profit mark-up over costs. The resulting increase in the price level will mean a fall in output if the aggregate demand curve is downward-sloping. As Mankiw remarks, "After all, price setters do not aim to maximise social welfare. They aim to maximise private welfare and they do so by hitting their target mark-ups of prices over marginal costs." Note, however, that output is now below the optimal (and, therefore, the full employment) level. Thus, inflation can arise even *before* full employment is reached. Starting from *any* situation of inadequate demand and unemployment, if the government goes on printing currency and increasing government expenditure, output will increase and prices will remain stable only as long as output is below its natural level. There will come a point after which it will exceed this level and there will be inflation.

The point is often stated in terms of the *rates of growth* of output rather in those of the *levels* of output. The average of the rates of growth of output in the past several years is then the *natural rate of growth*. Producers start increasing prices when the actual growth rate exceeds the natural growth rate.

7.3.5 Two sources of the risk of inflation in the Indian context

Persistent deceleration coupled with concentration of market power

So far we have talked about MMT in a general setting. There are *two* different sources of the risk of inflation arising from currency printing and related policies *in the Indian context*. The *first* source consists of important features of the contemporary economic scene of India. One feature that we have already discussed in detail before is the *persistent* nature of the economic deceleration in India. In Chapter 3, we saw that the growth rate of the Indian economy has been falling *for the past several years*. Another feature of the economy is the high degree of economic inequality, a point discussed in Chapter 4. In that chapter, however, we focused entirely on the inequality of the distribution of income. In the present context, we also point towards the related matter of *concentration of market power*. While estimates of such concentration in the Indian economy as a whole are hard to come by, some estimates of *industrial* concentration are available. For instance, Sedai (2016) reports that the *manufacturing* sector in India became more skewed in terms of the distribution of market shares over the period 1999–2013. Saraswati (2019) finds that in a number of subsectors of the manufacturing sector both the Herfindahl–Hirschman index of concentration and the degree of market imperfection measured by the excess of price over marginal cost were higher in the period 2014–17 than during 2009–14 although in some other subsectors there was a slight fall in these measures of concentration. It is also noted that by conventional standards the absolute value of the overall degree of market imperfection in the industrial sector in India has remained high over several decades.

By a simple extension of our discussion in the preceding Section 7.3.4, it is now easy to see that inflation is a real possibility in an economy characterised by these features. If the economy in question is one that has been in *persistent deceleration* over a period of several years in the past, the *average of the past several years' growth rates* will be a relatively low figure. In other words, an extended period of deceleration in the growth rate will *reduce* an economy's *natural* rate of growth. As soon as there is a turnaround in the rate of growth (brought about by currency printing and the consequent the increase in demand), there is a real danger that producers will interpret this as a case of the current growth rate exceeding the natural growth rate of the economy and *use their market power* to increase prices.

Lack of monetary sovereignty in developing countries

The *second* source of the risk of inflation applies more generally to *monetary* policies and to all *developing* economies. It seems that MMT, implicitly, seems to take the viewpoint of the US economy. Recall the assumption that the government enjoys "monetary sovereignty," that is that it can issue any amount of the domestic currency without bothering about the effect on the value of the currency in terms of some extraneous object. Note, now, that the extraneous object need not be gold. It may be *another country's currency*. While Gold Standard is now a thing of the past, the matter of the value of the currency of one country in terms of that of another (i.e. the matter of the *foreign exchange rate*) remains. Every country needs to import goods and services from abroad and to pay for them by earning foreign exchange through exports. If the foreign exchange rates rise (i.e. if domestic currency becomes cheaper in terms of foreign currencies), prices of imported goods in the home market will rise. This will create an inflationary pressure. Note that this will happen even if the *quantities* of the imports remain unchanged.

From this standpoint, the USA is in a very fortunate position. Its currency, the dollar, is the dominant currency of the world. In the global market, the price of almost everything is quoted in terms of the US dollar, no matter which country is exporting or importing it. Therefore, all countries of the world try to maintain adequate dollar reserves. The US dollar, therefore, is almost always in high demand in the world economy. If there is a recession in the USA the government (via the Fed) can print dollar notes (as per the prescription of MMT). It does not need to worry about a decline in the value of dollar. It is true that, like the value of any other thing, the value of the dollar also is determined by the interaction of the forces of demand and supply. If it was any *other* currency, there would be the possibility that the increased supply of dollar would reduce its value. The high demand for dollars in the global economy, however, ensures that, despite the increased supply of dollars by the USA, the value of dollar does *not* decline. The USA can, therefore, print currency without worrying about inflation brought about by a decline in the value of its domestic currency.

For *other* countries, however, it is a different story. The increased supply of domestic currency would lead to a fall in the dollar value of the currency, leading to inflation. It is now widely recognised that, in all of the cases of hyper-inflation that we have mentioned before, this was one of the main ways in which the inflationary pressures arose. Note that this particular problem is specific to policies of *monetary* expansion as distinguished from other types of expansionary policies.

In *developing* countries, there is also likely to be an *indirect* (or second-round) effect working in the same direction. These countries depend on imports to a much greater extent than the advanced ones. This is particularly true of imported goods that are used as *inputs* in the production process. These include not only capital goods like machines and technologically sophisticated goods (such as computer chips) but also vital raw materials among which oil is the perhaps the most important (so far as the non-oil-producing countries are concerned). Moreover, there are developing countries that are dependent on imports even for their supply of *consumer goods*. If domestic demand and, therefore, production are be boosted by printing currency, demand for all of these imported goods will increase. This will increase the demand for dollars in the country. Since these countries cannot issue dollars, the forces of demand for and supply of dollars will lead to a *further* round of a fall in the value of the domestic currency in terms of the dollar, adding to the inflationary pressure.

To be sure, the indirect effect operating through increased demand in the domestic market will be there if demand is the domestic economy is sought to be boosted by *any* means, monetary or fiscal. It may seem, therefore, that this second round effect is not a problem specific to monetary policies such as currency printing. The fact remains, however, that the magnitude of this indirect inflationary effect is likely to be larger in the case of monetary expansion. The reason is that while the problem posed by the need to import vital inputs may have to be faced in all cases, printing currency or increasing money supply in other ways would *exacerbate* the problem by increasing the *supply* of *domestic* currency at the same time. It is as if the upward pressure on the value of dollar (in terms of domestic currency) will, in this case, come from two sides rather than from one. Inflationary pressure in the domestic economy, therefore, will be likely to be stronger.

Note that this second source of inflation has nothing to do with the difference between the actual and natural growth rates of output. In other words, if the government of a developing country goes on printing currency, there may be inflation not only before the full employment or the socially optimal level of output is attained (as we have seen earlier) but also before even the *natural* level of output (which is itself usually *lower* than the full employment level) is reached. This possibility does not seem to have been noted by the exponents of MMT because, as remarked earlier, the discussion of MMT is almost always set against the background of the US economy.

7.3.6 Limitless debt-financing of government expenditure: is inequality an additional issue?

Consider now the currently more fashionable debt-financing version of MMT. MMT emphasises that unlimited debt-financing of government expenditure can be resorted to since repaying the debt would never be a problem. If worse comes to worst, the government can always print currency. Thus, unlimited public borrowing is essentially equivalent to unlimited currency printing.

If that is the case, then debt-financing is likely to create *inflationary pressures* in the economy for exactly the same reasons as those that we have discussed before in the context of the currency printing proposal. We refrain from repeating the arguments here.

It has, however, been alleged by some critics of MMT that debt-financing has an *additional* drawback. It tends to *accentuate* the already existing *inequality* in the distribution of income and wealth in the economy. This is because, under this method of deficit financing, the government essentially uses the excess saving in the private sector to finance its expenditure. Now, most of the private saving is done by the relatively well-to-do. In India, for instance, about half of the population is in no position to do any saving at all. For another significant part of the population the saving rate is positive but quite small. Hence, at any point in time, most of the accumulated savings in the economy are in the hands of the affluent. In an economy in slowdown, most of it is unutilised. When the government sells bond to the public, most of it is purchased by this section of the population. It is as if the government, on their behalf, finds a way of profitably investing their unutilised money. This adds to their wealth and, therefore, increases inequality of wealth in the economy even further. In this connection, the critics quote Keynes who is reported to have remarked that debt-financing of government expenditure puts extra wealth in the hands of those who are already wealthy. The additional wealth is a "booty" that lands into the "lap" of the capitalists. An increase in the inequality of wealth, in turn, also increases inequality of current income. On this ground, tax-financing of government expenditure would be better than debt-financing.

This particular criticism of debt-financing of government expenditure is, in our opinion, a little off the mark. It considers public borrowing in isolation from the government expenditure that it is supposed to finance. The supporters of MMT did not advocate public borrowing for financing the regular day-to-day expenses of administration. As we have remarked before, in the current version of MMT, the idea is to use the money to finance welfare schemes and the creation of social capital. These types of government expenditure are clearly inequality-*reducing*.

While we are on this point, we also wish to digress for a moment and comment on Keynes' views on the matter. There seems to be some confusion in the literature over this issue. Part of the confusion is due to the cryptic nature of some of Keynes' remarks in his most well-known work *General Theory of Employment, Interest and Money*. In my opinion, a clearer picture can be obtained if the book is read side by side with Keynes's policy writings of the 1940s when he was working with the British treasury. The official policy documents that reflected Keynes' thoughts are the 1942–45 *Treasury Memoranda* (see Moggridge, 1979, pp. 203–419). Keynes considered demand deficiency to be a *long-run* problem of capitalism and his preferred solution also had a long run orientation. He recommended public *investment* spending by decentralised public entities. In the General Theory also, he had commented on the need for "socialisation" of investment. In the Treasury Memoranda, he developed the idea more fully, emphasising the need for accommodative monetary policy to support such investment programmes. Many experts on Keynes's economic thinking now stress that the commonly held perception that Keynes was merely recommending "consumption manipulation" through fiscal stimulus as the solution to a short-run problem of demand deficiency in the private sector is an incorrect or, at least, an incomplete, representation of Keynes's position (see Meltzer, 1981). More recent contributions include Backhouse and Bateman (2008) and Dawyer (2011)

Be that as it may, it seems that an increase in inequality is unlikely to be a special problem of debt-financing of public expenditure (as opposed to financing by printing currency). It is inflation that is the main concern in both cases. Needless to say, however, at times of inflation the inequality of income distribution in the economy tends to rise since profit incomes rise faster than other types of incomes. But that is a derivative of the main issue and not an independent concern.

7.3.7 Policy conclusions from MMT

In this subsection, we look at what policy conclusions can be drawn from the earlier discussion. To begin with, it should be noted that it is the *limitless* currency printing (or borrowing) for *indefinite* periods of the type suggested by MMT that one should be sceptical about. The criticism is not directed at *limited* and *temporary* use of these interventions. On the contrary, it is obvious that in the *very* short run, that is in the *immediate* future, these are the *only* type of policy interventions that can bring much-needed relief to people at the lower ends of the income scale.

Beyond the immediate future, however, there would be need to be more cautious. As we have sought to explain earlier, inflationary pressures may start to appear not only when the productive resources of the economy are fully employed but also much before that stage is reached.

To be fair to MMT, it should be noted here that the supporters of MMT have a rejoinder on this issue. In the context of the US economy, they have argued that the blame for the inflationary pressure cannot be laid on MMT. It is the market power of the corporate houses that plays the crucial role in creating inflation whenever the growth rate exceeds its natural level. But that is inflation caused by supply-side factors and has nothing to do with either of the two issues that are MMT's main concerns (namely the demand deficiency problem in the aggregate economy on the one hand and the needs of the poorer sections of the society on the other). It is the responsibility of the government to tax away the supernormal profits generated by the hikes in their profit mark-ups. This will dissuade the corporates from exerting their market power. While the tax revenue so generated can be used for supporting an even greater amount of public expenditure, that will not be its *main* purpose because currency printing (or borrowing) can go on unabated. In a similar vein, advocates of MMT can also argue that the existence of the other source of inflation, namely the lack of monetary sovereignty, is, again, something for which MMT cannot be blamed.

Policy formulation, however, is not just a matter of apportioning blames. It is a question of what can be done to improve the state of affairs. We have touched upon the MMT recommendation of *supplementing* currency printing with taxes on supernormal profits. Keynesians have raised the obvious counterquestion. If taxes enter the picture after all, then what was wrong with the traditional Keynesian medicine for demand deficiency that we discussed in Section 7.2? Increase government expenditure and tax the rich to finance it. There would be no need to incur any budget deficit at all in the process. If and when full employment is reached, further increases in government expenditure would be unnecessary. Until then, there would be no inflationary pressure from the demand side. As in MMT, *taxes* of the right type will also take care of inflation arising from hikes in the profit markups of large producers.

We wish to emphasise, however, that, apart from taxes, there are two types of inflation-control measures corresponding to the two sources of inflationary pressures discussed before. So far as the issue of *corporate market power* in the domestic economy is concerned, *economic reforms* can play a vital role. Much depends, however, on what we *mean* by reforms. A reform programme was initiated in India in the 1990s and subsequent governments have pursued it zealously. Initially, the emphasis was on dismantling the so-called "Licence-Permit Raj" of the 1950s and the next few decades. This part of the programme was more or less completed by the 2000s. But this was the relatively easy part of the programme, the "low-hanging fruit." Responding to the critics' contention that the *principal* objective of economic reforms is, or, at least, should be, to make the economy more *competitive*, the government set up the Competition Commission of India in 2009. However, while this was a step in the right direction, not much progress towards the desired objective is discernible. We have already mentioned some relevant empirical findings in this regard and we refrain from repeating them here. Reforms of the type that would promote competition by reducing the concentration of economic power in the private sector of the economy come out as a main policy recommendation in the present context.

It is also possible to deal with the *other* source of inflationary pressure resulting from MMT-type policies, namely the effective lack of monetary sovereignty of the developing countries. Start by recalling how, *within* a country, money solves the difficulties of a system of direct barter and also provides a convenient store of value. The important thing is that everybody must accept the same thing (whether it is a precious metal or paper money backed by reserves of such metal or just fiat currency) as money. It is immaterial whether this general acceptability is imposed by some ruler or is the result of a broad social agreement arrived at through a long historical process. In the context of international trade, in much the same way, there arises the need for something that *all countries* would agree to accept for the purpose of paying for imports or receiving payments for exports and that all countries can also use as a store of internationally acceptable value. It is plain common sense, therefore, that what is needed is a *global currency* and that, just as monetary policy at the country level is directed by a central bank (on behalf of the government), there should be a central bank for the global economy for administering the global currency from the perspective of inter-country trade. Again, such a global financial system can be either set up on the basis of some kind of agreement or imposed from above by some country (or countries) on the others.

It was Keynes, again, who, in the 1940s, first thought of a global bank set up on the basis of *mutual agreement*. He called it a *Clearing Union* and proposed a global currency called *bancor*. For details of the Keynes plan, see Horsefield (1969, pp. 3–36). The idea was debated on, but *rejected*, at the Bretton Woods conference of 1944. What was put in place, instead, was essentially the idea of using the US dollar as some kind of a global currency. It may be noted, however, that there was also some criticism of the Keynes plan from the side of leftist economists who were of the opinion that Keynes should have proposed even more radical reforms of the international financial system. For a discussion, see, for instance, Faudot (2021).

To be fair, it should be noted that efforts were made to provide an economic justification of the system that was put in place. It was emphasised that the dollar had long been the most stable currency in the world. What was done was essentially a restoration of the Gold Standard (which the USA had forsaken in the 1930s in order to deal with the Great Depression). The value of gold in terms of the US dollar was, again, proposed to be kept fixed. The values of all *other* currencies were to be kept fixed in terms of the US dollar. Essentially, therefore, all countries signing the Bretton Woods agreement would be, either directly or indirectly, under the monetary discipline of the Gold Standard. While it is true that no country would have monetary sovereignty in the sense of being able to pursue an independent money supply policy, this would be true of *all* countries including the USA. So, actually, there would be no discrimination in favour of the USA. Moreover, two institutions, the IMF and the International Bank for Reconstruction and Development (IBRD), were proposed to be set up. The IMF was to help the member countries in financing transitory balance of payments deficits. Devaluation was to be permitted in the exceptional case of a "fundamental balance of payments disequilibrium." IBRD (which later came more often to be called the World Bank), on the other hand, was to be concerned with the needs of reconstruction of the economies ravaged by the War and, more generally, with the development needs of the member countries. The USA also offered to be the major donor to the capital requirements of these two institutions.

We are not entering here into a discussion of whether the claim of equal treatment of all countries in the Bretton Woods agreement was valid or, more broadly, whether a return to the Gold Standard was the most advisable thing to do at that time. (Keynes, for one, disagreed.) What is more relevant in our present context is that the justification of the system in terms of the fixed nature of gold value of the US dollar gradually became irrelevant over time until it disappeared completely in 1971 when the USA itself formally went off the Gold Standard. Thus, the part of the Bretton Woods framework that was related to the Gold Standard was now gone. But the system of using the dollar as essentially the global currency has survived to this day, depriving all member-countries of the IMF–World Bank system *other than* the USA of the type of monetary sovereignty that the USA retains. As noted before, this has affected the developing countries particularly badly because of their dependence on imports of inputs.

Our *second* policy recommendation), therefore, is that all countries be granted monetary sovereignty. This does not have to result in a chaos in the international payments system. What is needed is a reconstruction of the system along the lines proposed by Keynes. Needless to say, the details of the Keynesian plan may have to be considerably modified in response to some of the major issues that were not in the forefront in Keynes's time but now are. Perhaps the most important of these is the need to finance investments that would address the problem of preserving the environment and the ecological balance (which, again, is a problem calling for an *international* approach rather than a nation-state based one.)

7.3.8 Overall evaluation of MMT

I conclude our long discussion of MMT with a concise statement of the main points. Policies recommended by MMT can be used to give some immediate relief to the needier section of the population in these Covid-ravaged times. Beyond the immediate future, however, it does not seem to be a sensible idea to rely *solely* on unlimited debt-financing of government expenditure (or on unlimited currency printing) for the purpose of bringing the Indian economy out of the present phase of slowdown. There are grounds for believing that these policies would hit the barrier of an unacceptably high rate of inflation (along with a consequent further increase in inequality) even in the short run and much *before* full employment is reached *unless* these are *combined* with other policies. It is such a *combination* that we advocate. Tax policies and the *right kind* of economic reforms can go a long way towards reducing the concentration of economic power within the domestic economy which is the major source of the risk of inflation. However, since lack of monetary sovereignty is another source of this risk, a complete solution of the problem would also call for a restoration of this sovereignty. Obviously, this would involve concerted action in the international arena which seems to be a remote possibility at the moment.

7.4 Public borrowing and government expenditure outside the MMT framework

7.4.1 How it works

We have already said many things about debt-financing of government expenditure in the previous section. It may seem, therefore, that we have already covered this topic. In that discussion, however, public borrowing entered the picture because, as we saw, MMT considers limitless public borrowing and limitless currency printing to be essentially the same things. Obviously, however, that is not the only way of looking at public borrowing. In fact, when the government issues public debt, the *usual* understanding is that the government will be able to repay the debt by using its *other* sources of revenue (such as taxes or profits from PSEs). Printing currency is a last resort that is to be used only if there is no other way of repaying the debt. In this section, we discuss public borrowing as a means of financing government expenditure in this more general framework.

Whenever a government has to borrow money, the usual practice is to borrow from the people of the country or from some institution within the country. This is called *internal borrowing*. It is to be distinguished from *external borrowing*, that is borrowing from governments or peoples of other countries. External borrowing is generally considered to be inadvisable because if, for any reason, there is a problem in repaying the loan on time, the economic security of the country would be compromised. The recent economic crisis in Sri Lanka should be an eye-opener in this respect. One of the mistakes made by the policy planners of that country in the years leading up to the crisis was to depend excessively on *external* loans for the purpose of financing development expenditure. The ratio of external (as opposed to domestic) public debt to GDP rose to unsustainably high levels and it had been obvious for some time that sooner or later Sri Lanka was going to default on its repayment obligations. This happened in April 2022 and the country faced a very severe problem in financing its balance pf payments deficit. This kind of problem does not *usually* arise with internal borrowing. (We shall, however, remark below on an exceptional case.) Yet another type of government borrowing is from such international institutions as the World Bank or the IMF. While, strictly speaking, this is also borrowing from an external source, the debt arising in this way is usually treated as a special category. We shall concentrate here, however, on *internal* borrowing.

One kind of internal borrowing takes place when the government borrows *from the central bank*. However, this particular type of internal borrowing is effectively the same as printing currency. When the central bank lends to the government, it simply credits the requested amount of money to the account that the government maintains in the bank. If, now, the government draws cash from this account (or draws cheques on it) either for the purpose of handing out doles to the people in order to stimulate their demand for privately produced commodities or for that of financing its own additional expenditure, the effect is the same as that of printing currency.

The other (and the more usual) form of internal borrowing that is discussed in this context is *public borrowing*. Here the government borrows from the *public* rather than from the central bank of the country. For this purpose the government sells bonds or securities to the public. The word "public" here, however, refers not only to individuals but also to associations of individuals, companies, institutions, etc. In fact, it is financial institutions such as banks and non-banking financial companies (rather than individuals) that are the major buyers of government securities. There are various types of these securities. Usually the government sells Treasury Bills, a type of short-term government bond, to raise money for covering fiscal deficits and meeting other short-term needs. For long-term needs (such as those related to the financing of large public sector projects), it sells bonds with longer maturity periods. As per the currently prevailing practice, the actual process of sale of these monetary instruments to the public is conducted by the RBI in the form of auctions. A proposal for setting up a separate authority for conducting sales of all types of government securities is, however, reported to be under the consideration of the government.

7.4.2 Public borrowing and printing currency: similarity and differences

MMT, of course, is quite right in pointing out that the government's ability to borrow is limitless precisely because its ability to print currency is limitless. The policy works because the public does not doubt the government's ability to repay the debt. (This is also the reason why *external* borrowing is considered by the public to be a source of risk for the domestic economy: the government cannot issue *foreign* currency.) Yet, public borrowing and printing currency are not exactly the same things. There are at least *two* differences. *First*, while the government can print literally *any* amount of currency, it cannot borrow any amount from the public. While it can *issue* any amount of public debt, the public's ability to *buy* the government bonds is obviously limited by the amount of sparable funds at their disposal. Thus, there *is* a *financial* constraint on the government following from the financial constraints of the individuals although at times of slowdown it does not usually prove to be a *binding* constraint. The MMT view is that the government *never* has a financial constraint. The only constraint that it ever faces is the *real* limitation of the full-employment level of output if and when that level is reached.

Second, public borrowing often needs to be supported by monetary policy action. This is because the increased supply of government bonds may tend to depress their prices. This will tend to increase interest rates in the economy. That will, in turn, have a negative effect on aggregate demand in the economy. (It will also increase the *interest burden* of *new* government loans but, according to MMT, *that* is of no concern since the government can simply go on borrowing. There is no such thing as an unsustainably high level of public debt.) This is why in practice, even under MMT-type policies, public borrowing will have to be followed up by open market purchases of bonds by the central bank. This helps to hold down interest rates in the economy. Thus, contrary to the MMT view, *conventional* monetary policy also does have a role in fighting growth slowdowns.

7.4.3 The inflation question once again

As in the case of printing currency, inflation is a distinct possibility in case public borrowing as well. Borrowing, too, is a relatively painless way of financing budget deficits. Governments, therefore, have a natural tendency to overdo things, that is to borrow (and spend) too much. If that means that the full employment level of output will be quickly reached, that is not a bad thing from the viewpoint of ending economic slowdown triggered from the demand side. It may seem that all that has to be remembered is that when full employment is reached, *further* borrowing for the purpose of financing additional government expenditure should be stopped.

Again as in the case of printing currency, however, things are not as simple as that. The reasons for this are quite similar between the two contexts. Since these have already been discussed earlier in detail in the context of currency printing, there is no need to repeat the whole discussion here. Suffice it to recall that, in an economy that is in a phase of persistent economic deceleration and is also afflicted with a high degree of concentration of market power, increases in government expenditure financed in this way may lead to inflation much *before* full employment is reached. The optimal thing to do would be to combine these types of expansionary policies with reforms aimed at reducing the inequality of economic power both within the country and in the international economic arena.

7.4.4 Sustainability of public debt

There is, however, a somewhat different criticism of debt-financing. It is also indirectly related to the issue of inflation. We have said before that, unlike external debt, internal debt of the government does not usually compromise the economic security of the country. There is, however, an exception. It has been alleged that *too high* a level of public debt is *unsustainable* and may bring about economic problems that can assume crisis proportions. Sustainability here means the government's ability to pay interest on the bonds on the due dates and to repay the principal amount on maturity. Of course, *before* a payment falls due, there is no way of telling whether the government would be able to make the payment. What is apprehended is that if the size of the outstanding public debt is too large, people will *fear* that the government will have a problem paying the interest (or repaying the principal). In that case, they will not only refuse to purchase more government bonds (so that *further* public borrowing will not be possible even if there is still a problem of insufficient demand in the economy) but also sell off the government bonds that are already in their possession. If the government would not buy back the bonds before their maturity dates, these can be sold in the secondary market. For instance, they can be sold to the central bank under its open market operations. The relation with inflation is that if too many people get worried *at the same time* about debt sustainability, there will be a massive unloading of their bond holdings. The money obtained in this way will be sought to be spent on purchases of goods and services. This will create inflationary pressure in the economy, especially in a situation like that of India at the time of Covid because at these times the pandemic creates havoc with the supply lines. The shattered states of production, trading and supply of labour and other inputs will mean that supply will be unable to cope with the sudden rush of demand. The deep plunge of the growth rate will be accompanied by runaway inflation. There is a possibility that the situation will be one of a full-blown crisis reminiscent of Germany of the 1920s.

The question, however, arises as to how much public debt would be considered by the people to be "too much." Obviously, no hard and fast rule can be laid down here. One loose criterion that has been suggested is stated in terms of the ratio of public debt to GDP. If this ratio is greater than one, that is if debt exceeds GDP, then the level of debt is supposed to too high. However, the rationale behind this particular criterion is hard to see.

Most economists now are of the opinion that a better criterion would be the difference between the interest rate on the government bond (i.e. the interest rate at which the government borrows money from the public) and the growth rate of GDP in the economy. If the difference is positive, that is if the interest rate exceeds the growth rate, then public borrowing would face the sustainability problem. On the other hand, as long as it is the growth rate that is the higher of the two rates, there is nothing wrong with continued public borrowing. The idea behind this criterion is based on the fact that the government has to pay interest on public debt and repay the principal out of its *other* incomes, mainly *tax revenue*. Given the *rates* of taxes, the tax *revenue* of the government, roughly speaking, grows at about the same rate as the GDP of the country. Hence, if the growth rate exceeds the interest rate, tax revenue would grow at a rate higher than rate of interest. There will be no problem so far as interest payment obligations of the government are concerned. If tax revenue grows sufficiently fast, the additional tax revenue may also be used for repaying the principal. Besides, in this case new bonds can be issued for the purpose of retiring the old bonds (i.e. for repaying their principal amounts on maturity) *without* increasing the total outstanding public debt. Thus, sustainability of public debt is not an important issue if growth rate of the economy exceeds the interest rate paid on public debt.

Note that there *seems* to be a logical paradox here. For us the question is whether debt-financed government expenditure would be a good way to end the *low-growth* phase of the Indian economy. The answer seems to be that it would be so *only if* the growth rate is *high* enough (in the sense that it exceeds the rate of interest) because otherwise the debt would not be sustainable! The paradox, however, can be resolved by looking at the matter from a dynamic point of view. Even if the growth rate falls short of the interest rate *in the current period*, a debt-financed increase in public expenditure would still be advisable if there is a problem of insufficiency of demand in the current period because the government expenditure will push up the *future* growth rate by boosting aggregate demand in the economy. In other words, while the growth rate may be less than the interest rate on government bonds in the *current* year, the increase in the growth rate in the *subsequent* years would reverse the ranking of the interest and the growth rates.

Economists also point to historical experience of the USA in this regard. Debt-financing of public expenditure, they point out, was the main idea behind the New Deal in the USA in the 1930s although tax rates on the rich were also increased to some extent. The objective of ending the economic crisis was, however, broadly achieved. Dependence on debt-financing increased even further at the time of the Second World War. The debt-GDP ratio at this time exceeded one. Yet, the post-War years witnessed a high-growth phase of the US economy. The debt-GDP ratio gradually declined. The massive increase in public expenditure that made all this possible by solving the demand deficiency problem could not have been financed by taxes alone. At the initial low level of GDP in the early 1930s, tax revenue alone would have been insufficient to support such a huge increase in government expenditure. More recently, the speedy recovery of the US economy from the 2007 financial crisis was also due largely to debt-financed increases in government expenditure although monetary policies such as QE also played a supporting role.

7.4.5 Evaluation of debt-financing of government expenditure

What, then, is our over-all evaluation of debt-financing of government expenditure? In an economy in a phase of low growth rates caused by demand deficiency, government expenditure financed by public borrowing can be a useful way of giving the much-needed boost to aggregate demand. Even if the current growth rate is less than the rate of interest on public debt, the problem of future sustainability is unlikely to raise its head because there will be a positive impact on the growth rate in the future.

This is subject, however, to an important caveat. While debt sustainability is unlikely to be an issue, the risk of *inflation* remains. In the case of USA referred to earlier, inflationary pressures did arise from to time in course of the implementation of the New Deal. The problem, however, did not get out of hand because the government took steps to ensure that large producers in the private sector did not feel encouraged to exert their market power too much. (Recall from our discussion in the previous section that concentration of market power is the main reason why expansionary policies often leads to inflationary pressures in an economy even before full employment is reached.) On the one hand, in the famous Revenue Act of 1935, tax rates on corporate producers and on rich individuals were increased substantially. The marginal tax rate in the highest income slab was raised to as much as 75 per cent. Wealth tax was also introduced for the first time in the USA under this Act. Effective steps against tax evasion were also taken. On the other hand, in the 1940s and the following two decades, many actions were also taken to implement the anti-monopoly laws (called the "anti-trust" acts in the USA) although during the 1930s there was some laxity in this particular respect. The post-war decades witnessed a high growth phase in the US economy. Recall also (from our discussion in Chapter 2) that while monetary policy was also used in the USA in this period, it played only an accommodative role. Moreover, within monetary policy, the stress was on keeping interest rates low rather than on printing currency. The lesson that can be drawn from all this from the Indian perspective is that if inflationary pressures can be kept under control by minimising market imperfections, a policy of government expenditure financed by public borrowing (rather than by limitless currency printing) can be an effective way of ending the phase of economic deceleration that we are now in.

7.5 Sale of public assets

7.5.1 PSEs in India: genesis

Like an individual, a government, too, can sell assets to raise the money needed for current expenditure. Strictly speaking, the assets that we are talking about here are owned by the people rather than by the government. In a democratic set-up, however, it is the government that is the custodian of public assets and can sell these assets if it decides to do so. In India the most important among the public assets that are relatively easily saleable are the PSEs. PSEs are essentially similar to PSUs. The difference is that PSUs are like government departments. Each PSU is usually run as per the provisions of an Acts of Parliament devoted specifically to it. Railways, postal services, etc., are examples of PSUs. PSEs are government-owned but they are more like companies. In particular, they are registered under the Companies Act of 1956. Hence, procedure-wise, PSEs are more easily privatised than PSUs.

A large number of PSEs were set up in India in the first two decades following Independence. Setting up these enterprises was considered to be a right move because the sectors of production in which they operated were of vital importance from the viewpoint of development. These were the sectors of the economy that produced *basic* goods and services such as iron and steel, telecommunication and vaccines and medicines that were in short supply in the country. Some of these enterprises were also said to be of *strategic* importance (meaning that they served the needs of the defence services). The need for setting up the PSEs arose largely from the inadequacy of *private* investment in these lines of production. It was also argued that PSEs would give to the government (and, therefore, to the people at large) controlling power over the "commanding heights" of the economy and would serve to build up the "socialistic structure of society" that the Constitution of India envisaged. Many of the PSEs were *monopolies* in their respective fields of operation. This was not considered to be a problem. It was argued that *public* monopolies must be distinguished from *private* ones. A private sector monopolist would earn supernormal profits by charging a higher price and producing a lower level of output than a competitive producer and would, therefore, be detrimental to social welfare. This problem would not arise for a public monopoly. Even if it earns a supernormal profit, the profit accrues to the government and can be used to finance government expenditure. Moreover, since a PSE is subject to the control of the government, it can be easily instructed to desist from deliberately restricting output to low levels.

7.5.2 Decline of the public sector in India

Over time, however, many, if not most, of the PSEs turned out to be chronically loss-making enterprises. Part of the blame can be laid on the rise of neo-liberal economic policies in India, starting from the early 1990s. These policies implied a lack of attention on the part of the government to the capital requirements and the need for technological improvement in the PSEs. However, this was not the whole story. As in all other countries, in India, too, it turned out that running business enterprises was not the forte of government officials. Managerial inefficiencies plagued the PSEs from the very beginning. Far too often, the issue of chronic losses were sought to be bypassed by using the excuse that profit-mongering cannot be the objective of PSEs and that they have a social role to play. Moreover, some of the PSEs that dealt directly with individual customers neglected to take good care of them. There were frequent complaints of rude behaviour on the part of the front office workers. The public blamed the "excessive" job security enjoyed by government employees for this problem. For the employees it did not matter in the least whether or not the enterprises did good business. All of these diverse issues combined to create an adverse public opinion about the usefulness of the public sector in India. Long before Covid arrived on the scene, the government had started the process of dismantling many of the PSEs. No wonder, in the post-Covid scenario of sharp economic deceleration, selling-off shares of the PSEs have been considered to be an obvious way of financing government expenditure.

7.5.3 Privatisation

In the context of selling-off of PSEs in India, the two terms, *privatisation* and *disinvestment*, have been used in slightly different senses. Privatisation of a PSE means the sale of at least 51 per cent of its shares to a private party. The party that buys the shares acquires effective control of the enterprise. In case of disinvestment, it is the government that retains at least 51 per cent of the shares and, therefore, retains control. The rest of the shares are sold to a private party.

For various reasons, we do not recommend privatisation of PSEs as a method of financing the budgetary deficit of the government. *First* of all, there is clearly little to be said in favour of privatising the *profit-making* PSEs. Even today there are a good number of them in India. When the privatisation programme was begun in right earnest in India in the 1990s, the government sought to assuage the critics by assuring them that there was no intention to privatise PSEs that *earned profits* at *competitive prices*. In other words, the PSEs that were to be privatised were those that either suffered from chronic losses or earned profits by exercising monopoly power. The PSEs that set prices at competitive levels and yet made profits would not be disturbed. Economists, however, soon pointed out that in India in most cases the PSEs had been set up in industries in which there was no competitive private sector. That, in fact, was the *reason* why they were set up in the first place. There was, therefore, no way of knowing what the *competitive* price of a commodity produced by a PSE was. There was no benchmark with which the actual price charged by a PSE could be compared.

Second, the usual argument that privatisation of PSEs would increase their economic efficiency does not always tally with empirical observations. An analysis of the experience of privatisation in other countries of the world does not yield any unambiguous conclusion in this context. There are various measures of efficiency. Results differ depend upon which particular measure is chosen. One frequently used measure of efficiency is *productivity*. What is clear is that privatisation would increase efficiency in this sense if the PSE in question is a monopoly and the private party that acquires it operates in a *perfectly competitive* environment. If these conditions are not met, there would be no significant efficiency gain. In particular, it is not clear why replacing a public monopoly by a private monopoly should constitute an improvement. An analysis of the British privatisation programme under the governments of Margaret Thatcher and John Major during the 1980s and 1990s did not find any increase in productivity that could be claimed to be due specifically to ownership change (see Florio, 2004). Similar remarks apply to the experiences of many other countries.

Third, even from a theoretical point of view, the efficiency argument for privatisation of PSEs is not very sound. Apparently, it is thought that privatisation would boost the efficiency of these enterprises since private enterprises are managed by professional business managers who have expertise in this type of job. PSEs, on the other hand, are typically managed by bureaucrats who do not have the required skill and experience in running business firms. Even if we accept this argument, it is not clear why PSEs cannot emulate the example of private enterprises in this particular respect. Note that in the private sector all large enterprises are joint stock companies. In such companies there is a clear separation between ownership and control. It is the shareholders who are the owners of a company. They elect the Board of Directors. But the directors employ professional managers for running the company. These managers do not own the company although successful managers are sometimes made members of the Board of Directors. There is no reason why PSEs, too, cannot be managed by professional managers. That the PSEs are owned by the government cannot be an argument for *not* separating management from ownership.

Fourth, when a *loss-making* PSE is privatised, the new owners typically seek to cut costs not only by "downsizing" the enterprise by reducing the size of the labour force but also by reducing the wage rate and other benefits of the workers who are retained on the pay-roll. This leads to a decline in the real standard of living of the workers. This would be a particularly lamentable consequence of privatisation since the private sector has already witnessed a massive problem of loss of livelihoods and now the workers in the PSEs would face the same predicament. Economic history abounds in similar examples. A 2009 study published in the medical journal *The Lancet* reported that about a million people died as a result of economic shocks associated with large-scale privatisation in the former Soviet Union and in the East European countries in the decade of the 1990s. An expert in ancient history has expressed the opinion that "transfer of state assets to private owners" has always been one of the main ways in which economic inequality increases in a human society (see Scheidel, 2017).

Fifth, when a *profit-making* PSE is sought to be privatised, it is important for the government to compare the potential loss of future profits with the immediate cash benefit from the sale of the PSE. The result of the comparison may not be obvious because it will depend not only on how far into the future the government wants to look but also on the rate of *discount* that is to be applied to the future profit earnings. The question of discounting arises because the profit that is foregone would have been obtained in the *future* (if the government did not sell the PSE) while the benefit from sale of the PSE would be obtained immediately. An amount of money (say, Re. 1) to be obtained in the *future* is *not* equivalent to the same amount of money obtained *immediately*. Like all of us, the government, too, would *prefer* the latter to the former. Typically, therefore, an income of Re. 1 one year from now is considered to be equivalent to something *less* than an immediate income of Re. 1. In other words, for the purpose of the comparison we have to apply a *discount* on the *future* earning of Re. 1. Much depends on the *rate of discount* that we apply.

A simplifying assumption that is often made in such comparisons is that the rate of discount is the rate of *interest* prevailing in the economy. There is, of course, no single rate of interest in an actual economy. There are different interest rates on different types of lending and borrowing operations. Ignore this complication for simplicity. Suppose that the rate of interest is 6 per cent per year. Re. 1 this year will then grow to Rs $(1 + 0.06)$ next year. Thus, Re. 1 now is equivalent to Rs. $(1 + 0.06)$ next year. To put it the other way, Rs. $(1 + 0.06)$ obtainable one year from now is equivalent to an immediate income of Re. 1. Hence, by simple arithmetic, Re. 1 obtainable one year from now is equivalent to an immediate income of Rs. $1/(1 + 0.06)$. Similarly, Re. 1 obtainable two years from now would be equivalent to an immediate income of $1/[(1 + 0.06)^2]$ and so on.

Suppose now that the PSE under consideration can be sold for a sum of Rs. Y. Suppose that if it is *not* sold, the government would get from it a time stream of profits for the next 10 years: Rs. x_1 one year from now,

Rs. x_2 two years from now and so on. Since every rupee earned one year from now is worth an immediate income of Re. $1/(1 + 0.06)$, the profit of Rs. x_1 that would have been earned 1 year from now is equivalent to an immediate income of Rs. $x_1/(1 + 0.06)$. Similarly, since every rupee earned two years from now is worth an immediate income of Re. $1/[(1 + 0.06)^2]$, the profit of Rs. x_2 that would have been earned 2 years from now is equivalent to an immediate income of Rs. $x_2/[(1 + 0.06)]^2$, and so on. Hence, the total amount of immediate income (Rs. X, say) that would be equivalent to the future stream of profits of the PSE can be easily obtained as the sum of the 10 terms: $x_1/(1 + 0.06)$, $x_2/[(1 + 0.06)^2]$, $x_3/[(1 + 0.06)^3]$, . . ., $x_{10}/[(1 + 0.06)^{10}]$. Exactly similar calculation would apply if any other rate of discount (in place of 6 per cent) was applied and if profits accrued for any other length of time (rather than 10 years).

The answer to the question whether it would be prudent to sell off the PSE is now simple. The answer is yes if and only if Y is greater than X. It is true that future profits cannot be exactly predicted. However, they can be *approximated*. For instance, if the PSE has been making profits for the past 10 years and is expected to remain profitable in the future, the *average* annual rate of profit of the past 10 years can be assumed to be equal to the profit in each of the next 10 years. No such rational decision-making in the context of privatisation of PSEs, however, seems to have been attempted in India so far.

Finally, there is the question of *timing* of the sale of PSEs. In the present depressed state of the Indian economy, such sales may not bring in much revenue to the coffers of the government, particularly if the prospective private buyers sense the government's weak bargaining position in view of its urgent need for cash and its reluctance to make use of other ways of financing its budget deficit (such as printing currency or public borrowing).

7.5.4 Disinvestment

In the case of disinvestment (where the government retains the majority ownership and, therefore, the control of the PSE), the same type of rational decision-making procedure as discussed earlier is recommended. If the proposal is to sell 10 per cent of the shares of a profit-making PSE, it must be ensured that the price obtained from a private party exceeds the discounted present value of the future stream of incomes that would be foregone by the government (i.e. 10 per cent of x_1 in year 1, 10 per cent of x_2 in year 2, etc.). As in the case of privatisation, disinvestment in *loss-making* PSEs may seem to be more acceptable in principle than that in profit- making ones. Again, however, it should be remembered that if chronic losses are due to managerial inefficiency, a better way to deal with the problem would be to separate the issues of ownership and management and to take the help of skilled professional managers in running the enterprise.

7.6 Leasing-out of public assets

In this section we briefly mention a method of financing government expenditure that has recently started being used in India. It consists of leasing out public assets for a stipulated period of time (rather than selling them outright) to private parties. This has been called *monetisation* of public assets. The assets in this case are usually not PSEs. Rather, they are publicly owned facilities such as airports, railway stations, specified rail routes and railway stations.

Note that from the managerial point of view it is inconvenient to implement a *partial* lease- out of a given facility. Hence, the *full* operational rights have to be handed out to the private party that would take it on lease. This is *privatisation* of the *use rights* on the assets (rather than disinvestment in them) for the specified period. *All* of our remarks on privatisation of PSEs in the preceding section apply here with obvious modifications. Moreover, as some critics have pointed out, monetisation is, in fact, even worse than outright sale. This is because, in case of outright sale, the responsibility of proper *maintenance* of the asset falls on the new owners. If they shirk this responsibility, it is they who have to bear the penalty in the form of reduced productivity of the asset in future. In case of monetisation (i.e. leasing out) the private party would have no incentive to look after the long-run maintenance needs of the asset since they know that they would hand back the facility to the government when the lease expires. For all of these reasons, monetisation of public assets does not seem to have much to recommend itself as a method of financing government expenditure.

7.7 Summary and concluding observations

The upshot of our discussion in this chapter is that increasing the rate of taxes on the upper brackets of income and wealth and using the money so obtained to finance an increase in government expenditure is an appropriate economic policy for an economy that is in a phase of slowdown caused by deficiency of demand in the private sector. It increases aggregate demand in the economy and reduces inequality at the same time. Moreover, it does not create inflationary pressures before the full employment level of output is reached.

Among the *other* policies reviewed in this chapter, printing currency for the purpose of giving cash dole-outs (by whatever name it may be called) has the merit of having an *immediate* impact on the purchasing power of the people at large and reducing the severity of the demand problem faced by the *private sector*. Moreover, if the dole-outs are directed at people at or near the lower end of the income scale, it can give much-needed relief to those who have been affected by the Covid pandemic most severely. This policy, therefore, can (and should) be used in the short run.

The older version of MMT recommended currency printing and cash dole-outs in *any* amount in order to bolster demand for goods produced by the private sector. In its newer version, the theory recommends financing *government expenditure* by public borrowing, again in limitless amounts.

The reason why we have discussed MMT in great detail in this chapter is that unlimited currency printing (or unlimited public borrowing) seems, at first sight, to be the most "obvious" way of solving the problem of demand deficiency in an economy. Far too often one tends to wonder, "If lack of purchasing power at the hands of people is the problem, why doesn't the government simply print money and give it to people?" The reasons why the ground realities of the Indian economy would prevent this "simple" solution from working have to be unravelled carefully. The fact is that, beyond the immediate time horizon, continued use of MMT-type policies can cause inflation to raise its head *even before full employment is reached.* In any economy where producers wield market power, this is likely to happen in the long run. Furthermore, if *the* economy in question is one that has experienced *persistent* economic slowdown in the recent past, this may happen *even in the short run*. Moreover, under the present international financial arrangements the developing countries do not enjoy *monetary sovereignty*. In these countries, currency printing, whether for boosting private sector demand or for financing government expenditure, has the additional disadvantage of generating inflationary pressures by increasing the prices of imported goods. For these reasons, beyond the immediate time horizon, what is recommended is the *combination* of an increase in government expenditure financed by public borrowing with appropriate economic *reforms* and *tax policies* aimed at reducing the concentration of economic power.

There seems, however, to be little economic rationale for using *privatisation* of PSEs or *monetisation* (i.e. leasing out) of publicly owned facilities for the purpose of financing government expenditure. *Limited* disinvestment in PSEs (i.e. selling a *limited* percentage of shares of these enterprises) is a slightly better alternative and can be used at times of dire need if appropriate economic calculations indicate that it will be rational to do so.

Finally, while in this book we are mainly concerned about the problem of demand deficiency in the contemporary Indian economy, it may be noted that, even if, in the longer run, the economy is able to solve the demand problem, the need for *government expenditure* is likely to continue since, as well-known, in a developing economy such as ours, the government has a vital role to play in dealing with the various *supply-side* constraints on the growth of output. Hence, the problem of financing government expenditure is likely to retain its relevance even outside the immediate context of demand deficiency.

References

Acemoglu, D., Labison, D. and List, J.A. (2019): *Economics*, Pearson Education, New York.

Backhouse, R.E. and Bateman, B.W. (2008): "Keynesianism," in S. Durlauf and L.E. Blume (eds.), *The New Palgrave Dictionary of Economics*, 2nd edn., Palgrave Macmillan, London, 7304–7309.

Dawyer, J. (2011): "Keynesian economics and the question of public debt", Bachelor of Economics dissertation, University of Sydney.

Faudot, A. (2021): 'The Keynes plan and the Bretton Woods debates: The early radical criticism by Balogh, Schumacher and Kalecki', *Cambridge Journal of Economics*. 45(4), 751–770.

Florio, M. (2004): *The Great Divestiture: Evaluating the Welfare Impacts of the British Privatization, 1979–1997*, MIT Press, Cambridge, MA.

Horsefield, J.K. (ed.) (1969): *International Monetary Fund 1945–1965: Twenty Years of International Monetary Cooperation* (Vol. III), International Monetary Fund, Washington, DC

Kelton, S. (2020): *The Deficit Myth: Modern Monetary Theory and the Birth of the People's Economy*, John Murray, London.

Lerner, A.P. (1947): 'Money as a creature of the state', *American Economic Review*, 37(2), 312–317.

Mankiw, N.G. (2019): *Macroeconomics*, 10th edn., Worth Publishers, New York.

Meltzer, A.H. (1981): 'Keynes's general theory: A different perspective', *Journal of Economic Literature*, 19(1), 34–64.

Mitchell, W., Watts, M. and Wray, L.R. (2019): *Macroeconomics*, Red Globe Press, London.

Moggridge D.E. (ed.) (1979): *The Collected Writings of John Maynard Keynes: General Theory and after* (Vol. 29), Macmillan, London.

Robbins, L. (1937): "Foreword", in C. Bresciani-Turroni (eds.), *The Economics of Inflation*, Allen and Unwin, London, 4–5.

Saraswati, B. (2019): 'Economic reforms and market competition in India: An assessment', Working Paper No. 216, Institute for Studies in Industrial Development, New Delhi.

Scheidel, W. (2017): *The Great Leveler: Violence and the History of Inequality from the Stone Age to the Twenty-Fist Century*, Princeton University Press, Princeton, NJ.

Sedai, A.K. (2016): 'Competition and concentration: Analog or chronology? A study of Indian manufacturing sector post-New Economic Policy', *Arthashastra*, 5(4), 35–47.

8 Afterword

Headwinds and prognosis

8.1 Plan of the chapter

This concluding chapter begins with a quick summary (in Section 8.2) of the major points made in the preceding chapters. Section 8.3 asks whether economic slowdown is likely to be a lingering problem for the Indian economy in the near future and shows that the currently available forecasts do give rise to such an apprehension. Next, we recall that our policy recommendations have, general, stressed the need to adopt measures to boost aggregate demand although the need to supplement them with sector-specific policies to contain inflationary pressures, if and when such pressures arise, has also been emphasised. Section 8.4 asks how relevant this general orientation of our recommended policies for India would continue to be in the future and finds that aggregate demand does seem likely to remain a central concern. Two important supply-side issues, however, are also discussed in this chapter. One of these, the possible economic impact of the Ukraine War, is the subject matter of Section 8.5. The other, the longer-run problem of global warming, is discussed in Section 8.6. It is shown that the reason for mankind's failure to come to grips with this vitally important issue so far is that the countries are trapped in a problem that the game theorists call the Prisoner's Dilemma. A framework of international cooperation is the only real solution of this problem, although each country can also profitably take some unilateral actions in this regard. Section 8.7 consists of a brief statement concluding the chapter (and the book).

8.2 A quick look-back

We start with a quick backward glance. In this book, we have taken the growth rate of an economy as the summary measure of its economic performance. We began by noting that, judged by this criterion, the performance of the Indian economy in the year 2020–21 was poorer than it had been in any other year in recent times. More worrying is the fact that it was worse than the record of many other countries of the world including several of India's neighbouring countries while the Covid-19 pandemic hit almost all

DOI: 10.4324/9781003350514-8

parts of the world with the same ferocity in the same year. We set out to investigate the reasons behind the apparent mystery and to find what policy actions, if any, can be suggested.

It was found that, again unlike many other economies, the Indian economy was in a phase of economic slowdown or deceleration (i.e. one of falling rate of annual growth of GDP) much before Covid-19 arrived on the scene. The pandemic only brought the long-festering problem to a crisis point. A deeper look revealed that the root of the problem was a deficiency of aggregate demand in the economy. The demand deficiency, in turn, was found to be caused by an increasing trend in the degree of inequality of income and wealth in the economy in the 2010s and a downward trend in export performance in the same years.

Since export possibilities are determined to a large extent by external factors, policies directed at the domestic economy seem to be the main way to go. Historical experience shows that fiscal expansion working in tandem with supporting monetary policies is a more effective solution of a demand problem in the domestic economy than exclusive reliance on monetary policies. We, therefore, highlighted tax and government expenditure policies and discussed the various short- and long-run constraints that can confront the policy planners in this context. The *details* of the warranted policy measures were seen to be contingent upon the way the inflation scenario unfolds in the coming months and years.

While our main concern has been with the problem of slowdown in the Indian economy that has persisted for quite some time, it was also seen that the economic policies have an important role to play in dealing with the Covid pandemic that was the immediate trigger of the economic crisis of 2020–21.

Fiscal expansion invariably raises the question how it would be *financed*. We discussed this matter in detail. We argued that while currency printing for the purpose of putting money in the hands of the people may work as a short-run emergency measure, continued use of it as a method of financing deficits in the government budget is likely to create inflationary pressures. We have shown that if we are to undertake fiscal expansion and to avoid the risk of inflation at the same time, the most realistic course of action would be to *combine* debt-financing of government expenditure with measures aimed at reducing inequality in the distribution of economic power. On the matter of inequality, economic reforms *of the right type* can play a vital role. Ideally, attention should be paid both to the issue of the concentration of *market power within the domestic economy* and to that of the *lack of monetary sovereignty* of the governments (or central banks) developing economies. So far as the latter problem is concerned, what would be called for is a restructuring of the international financial system along the lines suggested by Keynes after the Second World War. Modifications of the "Keynes Plan" would, of course, be necessary in order to address the problems of the contemporary world. Needless to say, however, international finance is, again, a field that is outside the domain of control of any national government. Policies directed at the domestic economy must, therefore, hog the major part of the attention of policy planners in India in the ensuing years.

8.3 Is the slowdown a transient problem?

Since economic slowdown in India is what the book is about, it would be of interest to ask whether the slowdown is merely a transient phenomenon or it is likely to persist in the near future. The *actual* growth rate for the year 2021–22 is now known to have been 8.7 per cent. Against the backdrop of the negative growth rate of the year 2020–21 and the low, albeit positive, growth rate of 3.7 per cent for the year 2019–20, this is certainly good news. However, most observers believe this turnaround in the estimated growth rate to be due largely to the "low base effect," a phenomenon that We discussed in Chapter 3. The crucial question, therefore, is what the *future* trajectory of the growth rate of the Indian economy is likely to be.

While prediction is always risky, it seems pertinent to look at the currently available forecasts regarding the growth rates of the Indian economy in the coming years. The growth rates of the world economy as a whole, of the neighbouring countries of India and of the countries that are important export destinations for Indian products are also of relevance.

RBI's forecast for the growth rate of India in 2022–23 is 7.2 per cent (see www.rbi.org). Since the actual growth rate of the preceding year was 8.7 per cent, it may seem that RBI apprehends a slowdown in 2022–23. However, if the previous year's growth rate is taken to be a result of the low base effect, such an interpretation will not be warranted. What we need to look at are forecasts for the *subsequent* years. RBI. however, does not proffer longer-term forecasts.

The World Bank, the IMF and the Organization for Economic Cooperation and Development (OECD) are among the international organisations that provide growth rate forecasts for a somewhat longer time span for their member-countries (and also for some non-member ones) on a regular basis. Tables 8.1–8.3 show some of the relevant growth rates forecast by the World Bank, the IMF and the OECD, respectively.

Table 8.1 Annual GDP growth rate (per cent) forecasts by the World Bank: India, Bangladesh, Pakistan, the world economy and the AEs

Year	*India*	*Bangladesh*	*Pakistan*	*World*	*Advanced economies*
2022	7.5	6.4	4.3	2.9	2.6
2023	7.1	6.7	4.0	3.0	2.2
2024	6.5	6.9	4.2	3.0	1.9

Source: For India, Bangladesh and Pakistan, the GDP growth rates are on fiscal year basis (World Bank (2022))

Table 8.2 Annual GDP growth rate (per cent) forecasts by the IMF: India, the low-income developing economies, the world economy and the AEs

Year	*India*	*Low-income developing economies*	*World*	*Advanced economies*
2022	7.4	5.0	3.2	2.5
2023	6.1	5.2	2.9	1.4

Source: For India, the growth rates refer to fiscal years IMF (2022)

Table 8.3 Annual GDP growth rate (per cent) forecasts by the OECD: India, the world economy, the G20 and the OECD countries

Year	*India*	*World*	*G20*	*OECD*
2022	6.9	3.0	2.9	2.7
2023	6.2	2.8	2.8	1.6

Source: The forecasts for India refer to fiscal years OECD (2022)

The World Bank predicts that the Indian economy will enter a slowdown phase after 2021–22. In the following three years the growth rate will fall steadily. Moreover, the *rate* of slowdown is projected to increase. While between 2022–23 and 2023–24 the growth rate is expected to decrease from 7.5 per cent to 7.1 per cent, a fall of 0.4 percentage points, between 2023–24 and 2024–25 it is predicted to fall from 7.1 per cent to 6.5 per cent. That would be a fall of 0.6 percentage points. The forecasts for Bangladesh and Pakistan, however, do not indicate the same pattern. The growth rate of Bangladesh, in fact, is forecast to *accelerate* between 2022–23 and 2023–24 as well as between 2023–24 and 2024–25. Pakistan's growth rate is forecast to slowdown between 2022–23 and 2023–24 but is projected to speed up between the following two years. The growth rate of the world economy, on the other hand, is predicted to remain more or less the same. It will increase marginally from 2.9 per cent in 2022 to 3 per cent in 2023 and will remain at that figure in the following year. However, the *AEs* as a group will be slowing down steadily.

The IMF (2022) and the OECD (2022) forecasts, displayed in Tables 8.2 and 8.3, respectively, are confined to a somewhat shorter time horizon of two years. As per the IMF forecasts, the growth slowdown in India is likely to continue over the next two years. Similar is the projected trend for the world economy and for the AEs. While this report does not give growth forecasts for Bangladesh and Pakistan, an *acceleration* in the growth rate of the low-income developing economies as a group is predicted.

OECD (2022), too, forecasts that the slowdown will continue. This report does not provide forecasts for the growth rates of the AEs as a group. The G20 is a group of 20 large economies. Some of the countries in G20 are AEs while the others are developing ones. India belongs to the group. OECD itself is also a somewhat mixed group of 38 member-countries. While most of the members are AEs, there are some developing economies as well. India is not a member of OECD. The growth rates of the G20 and the OECD countries as groups are, however, important indicators of the India's export possibilities in future years.

Despite some differences between themselves over matters of detail, the forecasts mentioned above seem to agree on the big picture. Broadly speaking, while the Indian economy has re-entered the phase of *positive* growth, the trend of economic slowdown is apprehended to continue for the next few years. To add to the worry, the same is the likely to the case with both the global economy as a whole and with the economies of the countries that account for the major part of India's exports. However, not all other countries – not even all other *developing* countries – are forecast to remain in the slowdown mode. The cases of Bangladesh (in Table 8.1) and of the low-income economics as a group (in Table 8.2) have already been noted earlier. The region of Sub-Saharan Africa is also expected to register an acceleration of the growth rate. As per World Bank (2022), growth rates of the countries of this region as a group for the years 2022, 2023 and 2024 are expected to be 3.7 per cent, 3.8 per cent and 4.0 per cent, respectively.

We saw in Chapter 3 that while the Indian economy experienced a growth slowdown in the pre-pandemic years, this was not the common experience of all developing countries. It is now seen that most of the available projections lead one to apprehend that the same may continue to be true of the years immediately following the pandemic. Under the circumstances, a discussion of policies aimed at battling economic slowdown seems likely to be of some abiding interest for India.

8.4 Will demand deficiency continue to be important?

In the preceding chapters we have taken the view that the slowdown of the 2010s was caused essentially by deficiency of aggregate demand in the economy. Excepting in the "Covid year" of 2020–21 when lockdowns imposed aggregate supply constraints, supply-side constraints have usually appeared only in specific sectors of the economy. So far as policies are concerned, therefore, we have emphasised the need to boost aggregate demand and to combine demand management policies with measures to remove sectoral supply bottlenecks and to curb sectoral inflationary pressures as and when there is a need to do so. How likely is this emphasis on the demand side to remain relevant in the coming years? In this section we look at the possible trend in aggregate demand. The next two sections will discuss some supply-side issues.

We have seen in the previous section that most of the available forecasts about the global growth rate as well as the growth rates of the AEs point towards the possibility of a slowdown in these rates of growth. There is, therefore, a possibility that the growth rate of Indian exports will fail to pick up in the near future. We saw in Chapter 4 how a creditable export performance in the decade of the 2000s helped the country avoid a slowdown in GDP growth. It seems unlikely that this particular route of escape from the problem of demand deficiency will be available in the next few years.

So far as the problem of deficient *domestic* demand is concerned, how constraining this factor will prove to be depends mainly on whether or to what extent the government will be willing to adopt the combination of fiscal and monetary expansions that is necessary for the purpose. The last few years' experience does not make one very optimistic in this context. Even in the crisis year of 2020–21, the government depended exclusively on expansionary monetary policy in the face of fairly conclusive evidence (some of which we discussed in detail in Chapter 2) that major demand-side slowdowns cannot be fought with monetary policy alone.

On top of this lies the fact that over a long period of time most of the countries of the world (including India) have been experiencing a decline in *labour's share in GDP*. This has exacerbated the problem of inequality and has created demand problems. Labour's share has been falling for such a long time that a reversal of the trend within the next few years seems unlikely (see IMF (2017) for the global picture). As per ILO (2018), the proportion of labour compensation in India fell from 38.5 per cent in 1981 to 35.4 per cent in 2013. It may be noted that labour compensation includes not only wages and salaries but also the incomes of self-employed workers.

Various factors have been held responsible for this trend. There are interlinkages between these factors. The nature of technological progress in recent decades has played an important role in this connection. In the capital-abundant (and labour-scarce) economies of the West, technological progress has almost always been labour-saving in character. The same, however, also seems to be the trend in India. While, to some extent, this has resulted from a mindless imitation of the West, there have also been economic forces at work. For instance, in recent decades the IT revolution has led to a steep fall in the relative prices of investment goods and provided the employers with the incentive to substitute capital for labour. The process has been self-feeding. While it has led to a fall in demand for human labour, the resulting rise in the unemployment rate has, in turn, led to a decrease in the rate of unionisation and in the bargaining strength of the labour unions (because the workers fear the prospect of being thrown out of employment if they are very strident in their wage demands). On the whole, therefore, the problem of inadequacy of aggregate demand seems likely to continue to constrain the growth rate of GDP in India in the foreseeable future. Demand management policies, therefore, are likely to continue to be relevant.

8.5 The Ukraine War

Among the *supply-side* issues that are engaging the attention of economists at the moment, a major one is the possible economic impact of the war in Ukraine. Russia's invasion of Ukraine in February 2022, caused widespread disturbance to the supplies of a number of commodities that are important inputs in some of the Indian industries. Some of them are also important consumption items. The disturbances have been caused both by Russian military operations in Ukraine and by the retaliatory economic sanctions imposed on Russia by the nations of the West. As a consequence, the *global* supply chains of many important commodities including wheat (which is an important export item of both Russia and Ukraine), and oil and natural gas (of which Russia is a major producer) have been severely affected. In effect, commodity prices in the world markets soared. In particular, the prices of wheat, oil, steel and other metals increased dramatically between February and June 2022.

It is apprehended that the sharp rise in global prices would have a negative effect on growth rates of all countries. For India the effect is expected to operate mainly through *wholesale prices* in the domestic market. It may be noted that while the rate of inflation of the Consumer Price Index (CPI) is the guide to the formulation of monetary policies in India, so far as *producers'* behaviour is concerned, it is the inflation of the Wholesale Price Index (WPI) that is more relevant. WPI is calculated on the basis of the net prices received by the *producers* (i.e. prices that that do not include indirect taxes) rather than on the basis of the prices paid by the consumers. Another difference between WPI and CPI is that industrial goods are given much greater weightage in WPI than in CPI. When the WPI inflation rate accelerates, it is taken to be a sign that *costs of production of industrial commodities* are increasing. This acts as a deterrent on the rate growth of output and affects the growth rate of the economy. At the same time, there is cost-push inflation. What results is stagflation. That the WPI inflation rate in India has accelerated significantly in recent months is well-known. In May 2022, the monthly year-on-year WPI inflation rate was 15.88 per cent, the highest since November 1998.

It should be noted, however, that by the end of February 2022, the negative effects that the Ukraine War was going to have on the growth rate of the global economy as well as that of India were quite obvious. The growth *forecasts* that we have reported in the tables in Section 8.3 were made in June or July 2022. Those figures, therefore, already incorporate the possible impacts of the Ukraine War *in the near future*. The *additional* question that arises now is whether the war would *continue* to have adverse effects on growth rates in the *longer run*.

It is obvious that the answer to the question will depend on *how long* the war is going to drag on. While this is obviously not an economic question, there is an economic angle here. Many observers of political and military affairs are of the opinion that Russia seems to have adopted the strategy of making it a war of attrition (rather than the one of aiming for a quick victory). The economic angle is that this strategic choice on the part of Russia may have been based on the fact that the war has pushed up the global prices of commodities that Russia exports. Russia, thus, gains by prolonging the war. There is, however, also an exactly opposite view regarding the strategy of attrition. As per this view, Russia has not adopted this strategy by choice. Rather, it has been imposed on Russia by the strong resistance put up by Ukraine. It has been said that Ukraine may turn out to be "Russia's Vietnam." Note, however, that the Vietnam War dragged on for years. Thus, paradoxically, these two opposite views point towards the *same* possibility of a long-drawn war in Ukraine. The economic slowdown in all countries of the world may, therefore, linger beyond the immediate future.

It has, however, been rightly pointed out that, for India, the Ukraine War has also brought some windfalls. The most important of these has been the chance to import crude oil from Russia at prices that are considerably lower than the prices charged by other oil exporters. The economic sanctions imposed by the Western nations on Russia include a ban on other countries regarding importing oil and gas from Russia. This has hurt Russia's oil export possibilities and forced it to offer oil at heavily discounted prices to those countries that are willing to defy the ban. India has taken up the opportunity and has increased its oil imports from Russia and has cut down on imports from other countries (such as Iraq). Similarly, the increase in the price of steel in the global market that has been a result of the Ukraine War has been a boon for Indian producers of steel. At the relatively low pre-war price, the Indian steel exporters were at a disadvantage because of their high costs of production. With higher prices, thy are now in a somewhat better competitive position. Again, producers of rice bran oil in India are currently having a heyday in view of the difficulties of importing palm oil and sunflower oil and the resulting increases in their prices in the Indian market. (The major parts of the total amounts of palm and sunflower oils consumed in India are imported from abroad. Indonesia is the main source of supply of palm oil. That country has now (in June 2022) imposed an export ban on that item. A significant part of the supply of sunflower oil used to come from Ukraine. The supply line is now disrupted.)

If the war continues indefinitely, however, these advantages are likely to be outweighed by the disadvantages. In particular, it is difficult to tell how long India can continue to utilise the most important of these advantages (namely the opportunity to import Russian oil at low prices), defying the intense pressure on all countries mounted by the Western nations (especially, the USA) to abstain from trading with Russia. It, therefore, seems that there may be a continuing need to adopt sector-specific supply-side policies in the coming years if inflationary pressures are to be kept in check.

Nevertheless, the fact remains that while the Ukraine War has adversely impacted all countries, it is the growth forecasts for India that seem to have been hit particularly badly. (The situation is reminiscent of the impact of Covid-19 on actual growth rates of countries in the year 2020–21.) As we have seen earlier, the forecasts (which incorporate the possible impacts of the war) indicate that while the Indian economy is predicted to remain in the slowdown mode for the next few years, that is not case for all developing countries. It follows that the domestic factors that may constrain future economic growth in India continue to need to be looked into. The supply-side effects of the Ukraine War have superimposed themselves on the pre-existing domestic issues related to demand deficiency, rather than supplanting them,

8.6 Global warming: a secular constraint

8.6.1 Global warming and environmental catastrophe

In this section we discuss a supply-side problem of a quite different nature, namely the problem of global warming. Two aspects of the issue set it somewhat apart from the rest of the book. First, the constraint on economic growth that we are concerned with here is a *secular* (i.e. very long run) one. In contrast with most of our discussion so far, we shall now be talking about what is going to happen in the coming *decades* rather than in the next few months or years. Secondly, a truly satisfactory solution of the problem will depend more on *international* cooperation than on economic policy planning in any particular country. Yet, since the problem is going to afflict the Indian economy as much as it will impact the economies of all other countries, a book on economic slowdown in India will be incomplete without some discussion of the matter.

In the course of the twenty-first century, our planet is going to experience an increase in average temperature of at least 3 °C over what it was at the start of the Industrial Age unless preventive steps are taken. Warming is a consequence of the *carbon emission* that accompanies the production and consumption of commodities. One part of it is related to the process of production itself (i.e. the transformation of inputs into outputs) which emits greenhouse gases, dust particles, etc. Another part relates to the degradation of nature that takes place in the process of supplying inputs to the production process. In particular, in recent decades there has been widespread deforestation (causing climate change and erratic rainfall patterns) and excessive extraction of natural resources (including groundwater). Yet another part relates to the process of consumption. Emission of greenhouse gases by automobiles is a case in point.

Scientists predict that even before the end of the present century global warming will result in flooding of all coastal cities of the world and desertification of entire countries. This will have obvious catastrophic effects on the global rate of economic growth and push it into negative values. Moreover, much earlier than that, there will be loss of biodiversity, acidification of oceans, loss of soil fertility and increased incidence of zoonotic diseases similar to Covid-19 (a point that we have already touched upon in Chapter 6). In fact, many scientists believe that these processes have already progressed to alarming levels. As a result, as early as within the first half of the twenty-first century the global growth rate as well as the growth rates of most of the countries including India may fall significantly from their present levels.

8.6.2 Prisoner's Dilemma

The environmental catastrophe can be avoided if effective preventive action is taken. This, however, would involve a whole series of radical measures. Replacing fossil fuel with other energy sources that are environment friendly, preventive action against deforestation and development of new agricultural technology that would be less intensive in the use of water and chemical fertilisers are just a few of the measures that need to be adopted. The problem is that all of these would involve substantial costs. Apart from the obvious monetary costs of inventing new technology by research and development which often involves huge amounts of investment, the task of achieving a wide diffusion of radically new production methods in any economy is often seen to involve initial complications that result in a temporary fall in productivity. The flow of benefits takes some time to begin. Altogether, the task of achieving a significant reduction in global warming in the *future* involves substantial costs that have to be undertaken *now*.

Even so, however, the question arises as to why the world economy seems to be unwilling to bear these costs even in the face of the nearly certain environmental catastrophe that would strike the world if it continues to ignore the matter. The costs may be too high to bear for a single country. But why can't it be shared between countries?

One explanation of this apparent paradox can be given if we remember that economic policy decisions of countries are taken by the respective governments. The world economy as a whole is not a single decision-making entity. Under these circumstances, it can be shown that even if each country acts rationally in its own interest, the net result may be non-optimal not only for the world economy as a whole but also, more surprisingly, for *each* country. Actually, this may be interpreted as an instance of what game theorists call the *Prisoner's Dilemma*.

Consider, for instance, a situation where there are just two countries 1 and 2. For simplicity, suppose that, at the existing rate of global warming, each country will enjoy a stream of annual outputs x until the environmental catastrophe strikes. Suppose that each country's total benefit from this stream of annual outputs is X. Suppose, now, that a reasonable degree of reduction in global warming can be achieved (so that the catastrophe can be avoided) by incurring a cost C (in terms of foregone production). Suppose that in this case the total benefit of each country is Y. Since the stream of annual outputs (y, say) will now continue indefinitely, we assume that the total benefit, Y, in this case is greater than X (Y > X). This is likely to be true even if $y < x$. However, as explained earlier, the cost C is likely to be high. Hence, assume that (Y – C) < X. Now, if the whole of cost C is borne by, say, Country 1 (and Country 2 refuses to bear any part of it), then Country 1's benefit will be (Y – C). Country 2's benefit will be Y because it does not bear any part of the cost C but will get the same benefit of the reduction in global warming as Country 1. Similarly, if it is Country 2 that bears all of

Table 8.4 Benefits of two countries for different combinations of their strategic choices regarding sharing the costs of reducing global warming: an example

Country 1's strategy	*Country 2's strategy*	
	NS	S
NS	(X, X)	(Y, Y – C)
S	(Y – C, Y)	[Y – (C/2)], Y – (C/2)]

Note: S = Sharing the costs; NS = Not sharing

the cost C, the benefits of Countries 1 and 2 will be Y and (Y – C), respectively. If the countries agree to share the cost, assume that it will be shared equally so that each country spends C/2 on the environment programme. In this case, each country's benefit will be [Y – (C/2)]. We shall assume that X < [Y – (C/2)]. In other words, we assume that while C is high, C/2 is small enough. Finally, if both countries refuse to bear any part of the cost C, then the present rate of global warming continues and each of the two countries get a benefit of X.

Each country then has a choice between two strategies (i.e. policy decisions): sharing the cost of reducing global warming and not sharing it. We denote the two strategies by S and NS, respectively. We can now write down a table showing the benefits to the two countries for each combination of the strategic choices of the countries. This is what we do in Table 8.4.

For each possible combination of the strategies of the two countries, the table displays the benefits of the countries in the form of a pair of entries in which the first entry is the benefit of Country 1 and the second entry is that of Country 2. For instance, if both countries choose NS, the outcomes are described as (X, X); if 1 chooses NS but 2 chooses S, these are described as (Y, Y – C) since in this case the benefit of 1 is Y but that of 2 is Y – C; and so on.

Now, what happens if each country makes its strategy choice from its own selfish point of view (rather than from the viewpoint of the entire world)? Country 1 does not know which strategy will be chosen by Country 2. However, 1 will notice that *if* 2 chooses NS, then 1's optimal strategy would be NS because with that strategy it would get a benefit of X while if it chooses S, it would get Y – C (and Y – C is less than X). Moreover, *if* 2 chooses S, then also the optimal strategy for 1 is NS because with that strategy it would now get Y while it would get Y – C/2 with the other strategy S. Thus, in this story, Country 1's optimal strategy is NS *irrespective* of what Country 2 does. In the language of game theory NS is Country 1's *dominant strategy*.

In a similar vein it can be seen that NS is also the dominant strategy for Country 2. Actually, Country 2 does not know what Country 1 will do. But 2 will realise that, *whatever* 1 may do, 2's own optimal strategy will always be NS.

Thus, if the two countries choose their strategies in isolation from one another and if each pursues its self-interest, then each of them would choose NS and each gets a benefit of X.

Now comes the punchline of this story. From the table it is obvious that, from the point of view of the world as a whole (X, X) is a *suboptimal* outcome in the sense that a *better* outcome could easily have been ensured. Note that nothing prevents the countries from choosing the strategy S. If both choose S, the outcome would have been [Y – (C/2), Y – (C/2)] and both countries would be better off because X < Y – (C/2). Thus, although each country is apparently acting in its own interest, the outcome is not in the interest of the *group* of the two countries (i.e. the world as a whole). More to the point, *each* country actually ends up hurting its own interest.

The assumption that that there are just two countries can easily be relaxed. It can be shown that the conclusion would be similar in the general case of *n* countries although in that case we cannot display the benefits in the form of a table.

The problem discussed above is a form of Prisoner's Dilemma. Shorn of technicalities, the story of Prisoner's Dilemma goes roughly as follows. Suppose that a police officer has arrested two persons *suspected* of having committed, as a team, two different crimes, a major and a minor one. Suppose that the officer does not have enough evidence to convict the two prisoners for the *major* crime. Hence, conviction for the major crime is possible only if *at least one* of the two prisoners confesses to it. However, there *is* enough evidence of the *minor* crime. Now, the officer keeps the two prisoners in *separate* cells so that they would be unable to communicate with each other. Then, to *each* of the prisoners, the officer says the following. (He also lets *each* prisoner know that the same proposition is being put to the *other* one.)

> If neither of you confesses, then I cannot prove the major charge. In that case I will press the minor charge which carries a *light* sentence. If both of you confess, then, of course, you will be convicted for the major crime but I will plead with the judge that *medium* (rather than heavy) punishment be given to each of you since the offence could not have been proved without your help. If only one of you confesses but the other one does not, then also I can prove the major offence. In this case, however, I will ask for *heavy* punishment as prescribed in the law for the one of you who does not confess. But I will plead with the judge that confessor be set *free*. I will not even press the minor charge against him. Now you decide whether to confess to the major crime or not.

What will the prisoners do? Take any prisoner and call him or her Prisoner 1 while the other one is Prisoner 2. Prisoner 1 has a choice between two strategies: confessing (C) and not confessing (NC). Prisoner 2 faces the same choice. The outcome of the game, of course, depends on the choices of *both* the prisoners. Suppose that L, M and H stand for the light, medium

Table 8.5 Prisoner's Dilemma: punishments of the two prisoners for different combinations of their strategic choices

Prisoner 1's strategy	*Prisoner 2's strategy*	
	C	NC
C	(M, M)	(F, H)
NC	(H, F)	(L, L)

Note: C = Confessing; NC = Not confessing

and heavy sentences, respectively, and F denotes instant freedom. It seems realistic to assume that, for each of the two prisoners, F is the most preferred outcome, H is the least preferred, M is between H and L (i.e. M is preferred to H and L is preferred to M) and L is between M and F) in the order of preference. The different possible outcomes for the prisoners are summarised in Table 8.5.

Following the type of argument that we used before for Table 8.4, it is easily seen that if the two prisoners choose their strategies in isolation from one another and if each pursues his or her self-interest, then each of them would choose C and the outcome of the game is (M. M), that is each gets the medium sentence. However, nothing prevents the prisoners from choosing the strategy NC. If both chose NC, the outcome would have been (L, L). Since both of them consider L to be a better outcome than M, this would have been a *better* outcome for *each* of them and, therefore, also for the group as a whole.

After this apparent paradox is pointed out, however, it is not difficult to spot an *implicit* assumption that is causing it. It is the absence of a *cooperative attitude* among the prisoners towards each other that is the problem (for them). In the story it is the fact that the police officer has ensured that the prisoners are unable to communicate with each other that *seems* to prevent cooperation. Game theorists, however, point out that solitary confinement of the prisoners is not the main issue here. Suppose that the prisoners are allowed to have face-to-face discussions and that they come to the agreement that each prisoner would refuse to confess. If, subsequently, they abide by the agreement and act accordingly, it immediately follows that the resulting outcome would be better (for the prisoners) than the non-cooperative outcome. If the agreement is *binding*, then this would be the case. Otherwise, however, upon concluding the negotiations and returning to their respective cells, each prisoner will have an incentive to renege on the deal because that is what their selfish interests will tell them to do. The Prisoners' Dilemma will apply and the non-cooperative outcome will, again, prevail.

One way of preventing a relapse into self-centred behaviour is to make the agreement to cooperate *legally* binding. In the context of the story of Prisoners' Dilemma, however, that would be an unrealistic scenario. No country in the world has a framework of criminal law that would allow prisoners (held on the suspicion of having committed a crime) to draw up such a contract. The prisoners can hope to get the light sentence only if they *voluntarily* cooperate among themselves.

The same remark applies to our present context of countries facing the environment problem. Since there is no way to *enforce* international cooperation, the only hope of a solution to the problem lies in *voluntary* cooperation.

8.6.3 Cost sharing between countries: equal is not equitable

The discussion in the previous subsection was based on an implicit assumption. We assumed that the countries in our example were similar in all respects. This, however, is obviously not the case in reality. Different countries are at different stages of development. There is a view that since commodity production always involves carbon emission, the real solution of the problem of global warming lies in controlling our greed for more and more material comfort and luxury. It is our insatiable desire for ever-increasing material consumption that has brought about the environment problem. If what we have in mind here is the level of consumption in the *AEs*, there may be some substance in this view. Unlike an advanced economy, however, a developing economy such as India where poverty is still rampant can ill afford to accept even a *temporary* cut in the present level of consumption and production (or, indeed, even a temporary cut in the *growth rate* of production). To put the matter differently, the *effective* cost of reducing carbon emission in India would be greater than that in, say, the USA because, apart from the cost of developing and implementing environment-friendly technology, there would be the additional cost of subsidising the poorer sections of the society in order to prevent a fall in their incomes in the short run.

No wonder, therefore, the developing countries have started demanding that the AEs bear the greater part of cost of reducing global warming. There are, in fact, even stronger arguments in favour of this demand. Particularly relevant here is the fact that it is the AEs of today that have contributed the most towards global warming over the centuries since the Industrial Revolution. As per one estimate, while USA, Canada, UK, the European countries, Russia and Japan together account for a paltry 15 per cent of the present world population, these countries have so far contributed about 80 per cent of the emitted carbon that has accumulated in this planet since the beginning of the industrial age. Even more telling are the *annual* rates of carbon emission *per person*. Between 1950 and 2000 this rate reached very high levels in the Western countries: between 25 and 30 tons in the USA and 15 tons in the European countries (see Piketty, 2022). Although the rate has fallen since then, it is still higher than in other countries. Presently it is 15 tons in the USA and 10 tons in Europe. In China, on the other hand, the rate was less than 5 tons up to 2000. Between 2000 and 2020, it was between 5 and 10 tons. The emission rate per person in India has always been by far lower than that in all of these countries. Currently, it is less than 2 tons per year. It stands to reason that countries which have historically been responsible for the major part of the environmental mess that our planet presently finds itself in should bear the major part of the cost of cleaning-up.

8.6.4 Country-level actions

A policy framework based on international economic cooperation and understanding seems a far cry at the moment. However, it is not the case that absolutely nothing can be done *unilaterally* by a developing economy. There are measures that can be taken at the country level and that will benefit the domestic economy significantly. Preventing deforestation, discouraging the use of plastic and other non-biodegradable materials and adopting environment-friendly technology are among the most important examples of such measures. In India, as in all other countries, a large part of the total annual carbon emission is accounted for by the production of energy. Recent research has shown that by choosing appropriate technologies in the energy sector, it is possible to ensure that the Indian economy is set on a growth path that would keep the total annual carbon emission in the country within sustainable limits (see, for instance, Sengupta, 2020).

The limits of such unilateral actions on the part of the developing countries, however, must also be remembered. As long as the AEs do not take effective steps to limit *their* emission rates, even an annual per capita carbon emission rate of, say, between 5 and 10 tons (which is the present rate in China) in the developing countries would be insufficient for the purpose of keeping the overall process of global warming in check. The problem is *global* in nature. A true solution of the problem, therefore, must also have the same characteristic.

8.7 Prognosis

It needs to be emphasised that while this book has been motivated by the economic slowdown that has characterised the Indian economy in the recent past and that seems likely to linger for some time, this should not be taken to imply that slowdown is the unavoidable fate of the Indian economy. On the contrary, by detailed reasoning, the book has sought to establish that there exists a framework of policies that can get the economy out of the slowdown mode in the near future and set it on a path of growth with equity. What is needed is the social will to implement such policies.

If we look beyond the immediate future, the secular constraint on economic growth posed by the problem of global warming becomes an important issue. We have seen that if this problem is to be effectively tackled, what is needed is a framework of economic policy-making at the global level.

Such a framework is not in place at the moment. However, it may very well emerge in the future. It has been seen in the past that new types of economic policies enter into public discourses when there is an economic crisis of sufficient gravity. For instance, as we have noted in Chapter 2, the very concept of macroeconomic policy which is now a familiar notion was born in the 1930s when the Western world was going through an economic crisis of a scale that it had not experienced before. Something similar may well happen in future in respect of the environment issue. At the moment, mankind may be displaying myopic behaviour and refusing to see the disaster on the horizon. But this may change if there is more severe and tangible damage to the performance of the global economy, forcing all countries to join a collective effort to devise radically new types of international economic policy interventions. As has been rightly observed, "large-scale historical change often involves moments of crisis, tensions and confrontations" (Piketty, 2022). If and when the needed kind of policy framework emerges, a book on policies for combating economic slowdowns will be by far richer in content than the present one.

References

ILO (2018): *India Wage Report*, International Labour Organisation, Geneva.

IMF (2017): *World Economic Outlook*, International Monetary Fund, Washington, DC.

IMF (2022): *World Economic Outlook Update*, International Monetary Fund, Washington, DC.

OECD (2022): *OECD Economic Outlook*, Organisation for Economic Co-operation and Development, Paris.

Piketty, T. (2022): *A Brief History of Equality*, Harvard University Press, Cambridge, MA

Sengupta, R. (2020): *Entropy Law, Sustainability and Third Industrial Revolution*. Oxford University Press, New Delhi.

World Bank (2022): *Global Economic Prospects*, World Bank, Washington, DC. www.rbi.org last accessed on 18 June 2022.

Index

Note: Page numbers in **bold** indicates tables on the corresponding page.

For Product Safety Concerns and Information please contact our EU representative GPSR@taylorandfrancis.com
Taylor & Francis Verlag GmbH, Kaufingerstraße 24, 80331 München, Germany

www.ingramcontent.com/pod-product-compliance
Ingram Content Group UK Ltd.
Pitfield, Milton Keynes, MK11 3LW, UK
UKHW020138200926
475702UK00005B/814

* 9 7 8 1 0 3 2 3 9 1 2 4 3 *